SAGE was founded in 1965 by Sara Miller McCune to support the dissemination of usable knowledge by publishing innovative and high-quality research and teaching content. Today, we publish more than 750 journals, including those of more than 300 learned societies, more than 800 new books per year, and a growing range of library products including archives, data, case studies, reports, conference highlights, and video. SAGE remains majority-owned by our founder, and after Sara's lifetime will become owned by a charitable trust that secures our continued independence.

Los Angeles | London | Washington DC | New Delhi | Singapore | Boston

PATEL, PRASAD AND RAJAJI

Other Volumes in the Series:

PATEL, PRASAD AND RAJAJI
Myth of the Indian Right

Neerja Singh

SAGE Series in Modern Indian History—XVII

Series Editors:
Bipan Chandra
Mridula Mukherjee
Aditya Mukherjee

 www.sagepublications.com
Los Angeles • London • New Delhi • Singapore • Washington DC • Boston

First published in 2015 by

 SAGE Publications India Pvt Ltd
B1/I-1 Mohan Cooperative Industrial Area
Mathura Road, New Delhi 110 044, India
www.sagepub.in

SAGE Publications Inc
2455 Teller Road
Thousand Oaks, California 91320, USA

SAGE Publications Ltd
1 Oliver's Yard, 55 City Road
London EC1Y 1SP, United Kingdom

SAGE Publications Asia-Pacific Pte Ltd
3 Church Street
#10-04 Samsung Hub
Singapore 049483

Published by Vivek Mehra for SAGE Publications India Pvt Ltd, typeset in 10/12 Adobe Garamond Pro by vPrompt eServices Pvt Ltd, and printed at Sai Print-o-Pack, New Delhi.

Library of Congress Cataloging-in-Publication Data

Singh, Neerja.
 Patel, Prasad and Rajaji: myth of the Indian Right / Neerja Singh.
  pages cm.
 Includes bibliographical references and index.
 1. Patel, Vallabhbhai, 1875–1950—Political and social views. 2. Rajagopalachari, C. (Chakravarti), 1878–1972—Political and social views. 3. Prasad, Rajendra, 1884–1963—Political and social views. 4. Gandhi, Mahatma, 1869–1948—Influence. 5. Right and left (Political science)—India—History—20th century 6. Indian National Congress—History. 7. India—Politics and government—1919–1947. 8. India—Politics and government—1947–1949. Democracy—India—History—20th century. I. Title
 DS481.P35S56   320.5092'254—dc23   2015   2015008400

ISBN: 978-93-515-0265-4 (HB)

The SAGE Team: Supriya Das, Alekha Chandra Jena, Neena Ganjoo, Nand Kumar Jha and Rajinder Kaur

To

Professor Bipan Chandra
and
Dr Visalakshi Menon

Thank you for choosing a SAGE product!
If you have any comment, observation or feedback,
I would like to personally hear from you.
Please write to me at **contactceo@sagepub.in**

Vivek Mehra, Managing Director and CEO,
SAGE Publications India Pvt Ltd, New Delhi

Bulk Sales

SAGE India offers special discounts
for purchase of books in bulk.
We also make available special imprints
and excerpts from our books on demand.

For orders and enquiries, write to us at

Marketing Department
SAGE Publications India Pvt Ltd
B1/I-1, Mohan Cooperative Industrial Area
Mathura Road, Post Bag 7
New Delhi 110044, India

E-mail us at **marketing@sagepub.in**

Get to know more about SAGE

Be invited to SAGE events, get on our mailing list.
Write today to **marketing@sagepub.in**

This book is also available as an e-book.

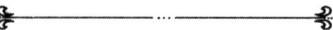

Contents

List of Abbreviations

AICC	All India Congress Committee
AITUC	All India Trade Union Congress
CSP	Congress Socialist Party
CWC	Congress Working Committee
INTUC	Indian National Trade Union Congress
NAI	National Archives of India
NMML	Nehru Memorial Museum and Library
MSA	Maharashtra State Archives
PCC	Provincial Congress Committee
RSS	Rashtriya Swayamsevak Sangh
SPNM	Sardar Patel National Museum
SWJN	Selected Works of Jawaharlal Nehru

Series Editors' Preface

The SAGE Series on Modern Indian History is intended to bring together the growing volume of historical studies that share a very broad common historiographic focus.

Since Independence, research and writing on modern Indian history have given rise to intense debates resulting in the emergence of different schools of thought. Prominent among them are the Cambridge school and the Subaltern school. Some of us at the Jawaharlal Nehru University, along with many colleagues in other parts of the country, have tried to promote teaching and research along somewhat different lines. We have endeavoured to steer clear of colonial stereotypes, nationalist romanticization, sectarian radicalism and rigid and dogmatic approach. We have also discouraged the 'flavour of the month' approach, which tries to ape whatever is currently fashionable.

Of course, a good historian is fully aware of contemporary trends in historical writing and of historical work being done elsewhere, and draws heavily on the comparative approach, i.e., the historical study of other societies, states and nations, and on other disciplines, especially economics, political science, sociology and social anthropology. A historian tries to understand the past and make it relevant to the present and the future. History thus also caters to the changing needs of society and social development. A historian is a creature of his or her times, yet a good historian tries to use every tool available to the historian's craft to avoid a conscious bias to get as near the truth as possible.

The approach we have tried to evolve looks sympathetically, though critically, at the Indian national liberation struggle and other popular movements such as those of labour, peasants, lower castes, tribal peoples and women. It also looks at colonialism as a structure and a system, and analyzes changes in economy, society and culture in the colonial context as also in the context of independent India. It focuses on communalism and casteism as major features of modern Indian development. The volumes in the series will tend to reflect this approach as also its changing and developing features. At the broadest plane, our approach is committed to the enlightenment values of rationalism, humanism, democracy and secularism.

The series we present here consists of well-researched volumes with a wider scope, which deal with a significant historiographic aspect even while devoting meticulous attention to detail. They will have a firm empirical grounding based on an exhaustive and rigorous examination of primary sources (including those available in archives in different parts of India and often abroad), collections of private and institutional papers, newspapers and journals (including those in Indian languages), oral testimony, pamphlet literature, and contemporary literary works. The books in this series, while sharing a broad historiographic approach, will invariably have considerable differences in analytical frameworks.

The many problems that hinder academic pursuit in developing societies—e.g., relatively poor library facilities, forcing scholars to run from library to library and city to city and yet not being able to find many of the necessary books, inadequate institutional support within universities, a paucity of research-funding organizations, a relatively underdeveloped publishing industry, and so on—have plagued historical research and writing as well. All this had made it difficult to initiate and sustain efforts at publishing a series along the lines of the Cambridge history series or the history series of some of the best US and European universities.

But the need is there because, in the absence of such an effort, a vast amount of work on Indian history being done in Delhi and other university centres in India as also in British, US, Russian, Japanese, Australian and European universities which shares a common historiographic approach remains scattered and has no 'voice'. Also, many fine works published by small Indian publishers never reach the libraries and bookshops in India or abroad.

We are acutely aware that one swallow does not make a summer. This series will only mark the beginning of a new attempt at presenting the efforts of scholars to evolve autonomous (but not indigenist) intellectual approaches in modern Indian history.

Bipan Chandra
Mridula Mukherjee
Aditya Mukherjee

Professor Bipan Chandra was the spirit and intellect behind imagining the series and Tejeshwar Singh of SAGE turned it into reality. We lost Tejeshwar in 2007 and now Bipan is no more. He passed away in August 2014. The best tribute we can pay to them is to honour their commitment to the series and take it to newer heights.

Mridula Mukherjee
Aditya Mukherjee

Preface and Acknowledgements

History captures historical facts in a framework defined by space and time but debates and interpretations of historical facts allow it to step into the realm of social sciences. The very process of interpretation makes history relevant to the present and the future. The constant engagement with historical facts and their interpretations enables history to transcend the level of social sciences from the domain of the literature. Debates in history are truly its lifeline. In this work, an attempt has been made to generate questions and debates regarding the genesis of the concept of 'Right' and its various features in modern Indian history.

Chapter 1 deals with the question of the paradigm within which the context and meaning of the term 'Right' are posited. An attempt has been made to examine the degree of relevance or irrelevance of Eurocentric analytical categories in explaining the world view of some major leaders of the Indian National Congress—Sardar Patel, Rajagopalachari and Rajendra Prasad—during 1934–1948. Chapter 2 deals with the position of these leaders on social issues such as the status of women, divorce, caste system, untouchability, child marriage, purdah and religion, in order to contextualize the approach of these leaders. Chapter 3 deals with the approach of these leaders on the communal question, on the issue of secularism, religious–ethnic coexistence and partition. Chapter 4 is an attempt to look into the economic and political vision of these leaders and their relationship with various social classes. In Chapter 5, the ideas of these leaders on the strategic issues during the process of the freedom struggle have been highlighted. This chapter also attempts to examine the inner political dynamics and factionalism existing within the Indian National Congress during the period. Chapter 6 focuses on the strategy adopted and favoured by these leaders towards the states peoples' movements. It discusses the regressive approach of the rulers and the dislike of these leaders for the decadent feudalism practised by the princes and the constraints within which the strategy to sensitize them against colonialism was shaped and sharpened. The Conclusion contains the gist of the politics underlying the usage of the Eurocentric concept of 'Right' and highlights its irrelevance in history writing while defining the nature of the mainstream leadership of the Indian National Congress during 1934–1948.

As this work focuses on the history of ideas, I at times had to overlook the limitations of chronology in order to maintain the continuity of thought, ideas, perceptions and perspectives of the leaders under study.

My debts, both personal and intellectual, are many. The book has grown out of frequent interactions with Professor Bipan Chandra, my teacher and supervisor, who has very assiduously and patiently provided every assistance and guidance to me during the entire course of my study and research. His care and concern has been a constant source of inspiration to me. I am also indebted to my teachers at the Centre for Historical Studies who shaped my understanding of history through their lectures and discussions. In particular, I wish to acknowledge Professor Aditya Mukherjee, Professor Mridula Mukherjee and Professor Bhagwan Josh.

Gyanesh, Salil and Medha helped me with ideas, suggestions and source material. I can never thank them enough. I am deeply obliged to Sucheta, Antony, Ajit Jha, Indivar, Shashi Bhushan, Rakesh Batbyal, Richa Malhotra, Mahalaxmi, Mayank, Archana, Biswajit and Hulas for the keen interest they took in my work.

I am greatly obliged to Visalakshi Menon for meticulously going through the draft and providing editorial insights during the finalization of the book.

I owe special thanks to Professor A.R. Desai and Professor Neera Desai with whom I stayed in Bombay while doing my research work at Bombay Archives. Their affection and loving care made it easy for me to bear with the initial anxiety and apprehensions about the rigours of research. I am most grateful to Shri Ramlal Parikh, Vice-Chancellor, Gujarat Vidyapeeth, Shri Jitendra Desai and Shri Nathu Bhai Naik of the Sardar Patel Memorial Society for granting me special permission to consult the Sardar Vallabhbhai Patel Papers at Sardar Patel National Museum at Shahibag, Ahmedabad. I have also been fortunate in being able to get invaluable anecdotes reflecting on the personality of Sardar Patel from Shri Uma Shankar Joshi, Shri Mool Shankar Bhatt, Smt Tara Bhattacharya and Shri Babu Bhai Patel.

It has been an arduous task to pursue academic research amidst family obligations. The completion of my book is largely due to the support I received from my entire family, in particular from Namit and Mallika.

I am entirely responsible for the content of this book. For any errors of fact or style, the responsibility is solely mine.

1

Crisis of Paradigm: Historicity of the Concept of 'Right'

I do not think it is always correct to take the analogy of other countries and to apply them in their entirety to our own country because conditions differ.

—Rajendra Prasad[1]

There has always been a temptation on the part of social scientists in India to import systemic categories to explain indigenous political, social and economic processes. They often overlook the specific historical context and indigenous characteristics within which these processes were conceived. This is largely a legacy of colonial experience. During the colonial period, many British and European writings on the Indian society and culture were anthropological, sociological and historical in nature. They, however, used conceptual categories which were Eurocentric in cognitive and value terms. They tended to distort history and impute meanings to Indian reality in the abstract so as to perpetuate colonialism. Concepts such as 'nation',[2] 'ethnicity', 'nationalism', 'Right', 'Left' and 'caste' were defined as fragmentary entities, often analogous to the socio-historical equivalents in the European society. The emphasis was on showing how each of these social entities affirmed the principles of segmentation and autonomy rather than being parts of an organic whole.

However, the nationalist historians of the colonial period such as Dadabhai Naoroji, M.G. Ranade, Surendranath Banerjee, Bal Gangadhar Tilak, Gopal Krishna Gokhale and Left and liberal historians, sociologists and political scientists such as R.P. Dutt, Tarachand, G.S. Ghurye, A.R. Desai, Bipan Chandra, B.R. Nanda, Rajni Kothari, Yogendra Singh and others were aware of the bias of colonial ideology and weakness in the use

---

[1] Speech by Rajendra Prasad on 10 December 1947. See Choudhary, *Dr. Rajendra Prasad*, Vol. 7 (Delhi, 1984), 407.

[2] Nation is a constructed conceptual category, and therefore it has a fragmentary character. See Zeldin, *France 1848–1945* (Oxford, 1974); Yogendra Singh, *Social Change in India* (New Delhi, 1993).

of Eurocentric cognitive and value terms and concepts in their studies on Indian society and history. Therefore, there is an ongoing debate among the social scientists on whether the Western paradigm is comprehensive enough to explain Indian historical and social concepts such as 'nation', 'region', 'ethnicity', 'communalism', 'state', 'Right', 'Left', 'caste', 'religion', 'community', 'language', 'culture', etc.

Yet the usage of Eurocentric concepts in studying history is dominant in the writings of historians, either because of the lack of an alternative paradigm or due to ideological commitments as seen in the writings of, particularly, Marxist historians. Whatever may be the impulse for such borrowings, the fact remains that none of the Eurocentric paradigms could comprehensively capture the world view truly representing the Indian historical and social reality. The need of the hour is, therefore, to locate alternative analytical categories akin to the actual Indian historical and social realities. Also, an attempt should be made to see whether it is possible for social scientists to draw categories from the Indian indigenous tradition and philosophy and establish relationships between Indian social sciences based on categories derived from the Indian philosophy, equivalent to the manner in which the Western social sciences are integrated with the Western philosophical traditions. To offer an example, it is obvious that most of the categories of history and social sciences such as nation, state, liberty, rationalism and process of change in the Western discourse are organically linked and derived from the Western traditions of philosophy. To establish equivalent linkages between Indian philosophy and social science, indigenous categorization has been at times attempted by scholars and leaders like Mahatma Gandhi, but it did not emerge as a widely accepted paradigm.

The origin of the terms such as 'Right' and 'Left' is occidental. The frequent usage of the term 'Right' to identify a particular group in the Indian National Congress with a certain ideology along with its limitations emerged in India with the emergence of Left on the Indian political scene during the mid-1920s. The years 1930–1939 were significant in the evolution of the socialist ideology in India. It saw the steady coalescing of the Left-wing point of view within and without the Congress in the form of trade union activities, Kisan Sabha and other mobilizations, and the emergence of the Congress Socialist Party within the Congress. Now, the perspective of the existing leadership of the Congress came to be questioned, criticized and challenged by the newly emergent socialists and the Left in the Congress. They often referred to the existing leadership and their political outlook as 'Right', and 'Rightist'. Moreover, in the usage of the nomenclature 'Right' for the senior leaders of the Congress, the Left also referred to them as 'traditionalists', 'conservatives' and 'reformists', implying that they were quintessentially conformist and non-progressive. The concepts of 'Right' and 'Left' are, however, meaningful in specific contexts of history. The Right in the West, in fact, took shape under specific historical context and under certain constraints of development. It was seen as a post-liberal, post-industrial phenomenon, a reaction to the liberalization of political life, a protest against shrivelling markets, overproduction and apathy towards democracy. Another variant of European Right also practised and propagated the theory of eugenics and anti-Semitism. They rejected multicultural theories of social progress and accepted unidimensional human evolution, dominated by European civilization. They based their belief on the theories of social Darwinism and eugenism.

The 'Right' of the Western kind did not actually emerge in India. The so-called 'Right' in India, on the contrary, rejected social Darwinism and eugenism and accepted the syncretic tradition of human evolution rooted in multiculturalism and Catholicism. This aspect would become clearer in the subsequent discourse. Evidences indicate that the so-called 'Right' in India emerged as a protest against exploitation and domination of foreign rule, social obscurantism, feudalism, communalism, caste, untouchability, illiteracy and suppression of women. The nomenclature of 'Right' was assigned to leaders of this genre who also subscribed to the principles of democratic welfare state, honoured class collaboration, respected private property and stood for the non-violent form of anti-colonial movement. On the ground that they did not accept class struggle, abolition of private property, establishment of socialistic state, the Left scholars termed these liberal, rational, democratic nationalists as 'Right wingers', ignoring the fact that they worked within a specific Indian historical setting, with the primary objective of projecting a united opposition to imperialist forces in the context of national struggle against colonial domination.[3]

Gandhi as well as Sardar Patel, Rajendra Prasad and Rajagopalachari were aware of the problem inherent in the use of the term 'Right', essentially borrowed from the Western historical paradigm, in understanding the political processes during the period. They were apprehensive of the usage of Western analytical tools. Gandhi advised Bose in 1939 to use better and indigenous terms for Patel, Prasad and Rajaji.

[3] See Bipin Chandra, *Nationalism and Colonialism in Modern India* (New Delhi, 1981). Also see Aditya Mukherjee, *Imperialism, Nationalism and the Making of the Indian Capitalist Class 1927–1947* (New Delhi, 2002); Mridula Mukherjee, *Peasants in India's Non-violent Revolution, Practice and Theory* (New Delhi, 2004).

Gandhi wrote to Subhas Chandra Bose: 'I wish you would choose better and indigenous terms to designate the parties of your imagination.'[4]

Prasad too believed that and said: 'I do not think it is always correct to take the analogy of other countries and to apply them in their entirety to our own country because conditions differ.'[5]

Criticizing the attempt of the Left to adopt socialistic ideology, Patel indirectly voiced his apprehension in the use of Western political ideology and concepts to understand India:

> Our youth who, without giving a proper thought to the prevailing attractive sentences of the Western ideology, want directly to adopt them as their own.... But I do have some common knowledge to believe that a certain ideology is not without any defects.... Before our own eyes, the borrowed methodology of socialism has been mis-used in establishing Fascism.[6]

Patel, critical of the proclivity of the youth to accept alluring radical Western theories as sacrosanct, without empathizing with the context and constraints of the country caused by colonial subjugation, said:

> I cannot too strongly deprecate the habit of youth to make a fetish of alluring catchwords and theories mechanically adopted from their readings without regard to the peculiar conditions prevailing in the west. I am neither a scholar nor a theorist, but I know enough of the-ories in general to be able to say that they are not full proof [sic].... Some of the theories that are the subjects of so much controversy here are still under experiment in the west. The technique of social-ism had under our very eyes been exploited in the service of Fascism.[7]

Drawing the attention of the nation towards the fallacies of applying ideological theories whose emergence depended on the specific historicity of space and time, Rajendra Prasad argued that there existed a vivid distinc-tion between the academic revolutionaries who derived inspiration from

---

[4] Gandhi to Subhas Chandra Bose, 16 March 1939, Rajendra Prasad Papers (hereafter R.P. Papers), Nehru Memorial Museum and Library (hereafter NMML).

[5] Speech by Rajendra Prasad on 10 December 1947. See Choudhary, ed., *Dr. Rajendra Prasad*, Vol. 7, 407.

[6] Patel's Speech at Benaras Vidyapith on 1 August 1934. See Chopra, ed., *The Collected Works of Sardar Vallabhbhai Patel*, Vol. 4 (Delhi, 1994), 175.

[7] See *Times of India*, 6 August 1934, Bombay.

the foreign literature and local patriots who depended more on a close and personal study of local conditions. He pleaded his ignorance of abstract theories of revolutions and his inability to draw analogies from the French or Russian revolutions. But a simple farmer that he was, he could identify himself with the poor peasants and the struggling workers in the villages and in the cities. During his extensive Presidential tours throughout the country, he had made a close study of local conditions prevailing in almost all provinces, both rural and urban, when the socialists were engaged in bookish studies on revolution in comfortable cushioned chairs in city libraries.[8]

Prasad, reacting to the textual politics of the Left, appealed to save the country from the disastrous results of a blind application to Indian politics of foreign theories and maxims, as derived from abstract studies of the revolutionary literature of the world. He confessed he did not quite understand or appreciate the true distinction between 'Reformist' and 'Revolutionary'. He accepted that he was not a student of Lenin and had made no study of the Bolshevik policy, but he had a better understanding than any student of politics of the actual conditions of the masses in the country, based not on the Congress or government records but by actually coming in personal contact with all classes of the people during his recent extensive political tours of the country.[9]

THE RIGHT IN HISTORICAL PERSPECTIVE

Usage of the terms 'Right' and 'Left' in history was etymologically a contribution of the French National Assembly in 1792. In the French National Assembly, the progressives sat on the left, the moderates in the centre and the conservatives on the right. The position of the sitting arrangement of the progressives, conservatives and moderates led to the usage of the terms 'Left', 'Right' and 'Centre' basically for broad identification. With the emergence of industrialism, fascism and consumerism in the twentieth century, the use of the term 'Right' came to claim popularity in common parlance.[10]

---

[8] See *Bombay Chronicle*, 28 November 1936.

[9] Ibid.

[10] The concept of 'Right' in the West discussed in this section is to be taken as a backdrop to the understanding of Indian 'Right'. Detailed study of 'Right' in the West is not the focus of study; it is intended to provide a general overview of how the concept emerged and what was its general character and fundamental feature in the Western context.

It is to be noted that scholars cutting across national boundaries, using these Eurocentric concepts, faced similar crises of paradigms while studying political processes within the social and economic matrix of their own societies. The scholars found it difficult to define in terms 'Left' and 'Right' when it came to actual characterization of politics, governance and developmental plans. They also found it difficult to sharply identify the Right or the Left.[11]

Eugen Weber in the Introduction of his edited book *The European Right: A Historical Profile* found the concept of 'Left' and 'Right' quite nebulous. He expressed his difficulty in the categorization, classification and definition of 'Left' and 'Right' because the distribution of a political spectrum remained uncertain. In the political spectrum with both the categories being at each end, it was difficult to place many leaders and political parties such as Kamal Ataturk, Peron, Stalin, Tito, Attlee or Labour Party of England after World War II in a particular direction of the spectrum.[12]

Weber raised fundamental questions faced by social scientists in categorizing such political concepts. According to him, there could be a revolution of the Left and Right, dictatorship of the Left and Right and a planned economy of the Left and Right. He gave examples of Nasser, Kamal Ataturk and Peron to prove his point. According to him, Peron was a Rightist but his power depended on the unions. Similarly Nasser, a Rightist dictator, adopted radical reforms. Both Stalin and Tito accepted dictatorship of the Communist Party. And reactionary demagogues like Hitler depended on popular appeal and universal suffrage. Therefore, according to him, 'The label is cracking. We continue to use it but no longer know, cannot possibly know for sure, quite what it covers, quite what we mean.... Left and Right have become a matter of opinion not of fact, a matter of taste not of definition.'[13]

As Weber observed, the other major epistemological lacuna in the study of the concept of 'Right' was that with the success of communism in the Western world, during the early twentieth century, a great deal of attention was given by the social scientists to the political ideologies and movements of the Left and 'historical materialism', as the basic paradigm for studying historical process and human development in the sphere of ideology, polity, economy, culture and society. It came under the influence of the new

[11] See Hans Rogger and Eugen Weber, ed., *The European Right: A Historical Profile* (London: University of California Press, 1965), 1–8. Also see J.L. Tamlon, *The Origins of Totalitarian Democracy* (London, 1952).

[12] Rogger and Weber, *The EuPropean Right*.

[13] Ibid., 3–4.

world view, the world over. In contrast, the Right was accepted as opposite to the Left, 'identified either with unthinking reaction or with stupid conservation, the latter has appeared largely as a negative force with little interest for the political analysts'.[14] The distinction between the 'Right' and 'Left' became more self-limiting by the generalized use of categories such as 'nationalism', 'socialism, 'revolution', 'nation', 'order' and 'freedom' without much effort to clarify the meaning or accepting the fact that these concepts were historical and culture-specific, although sometimes with apparent similarities.[15]

Writing on the political and social history of France, Theodore Zeldin refers to a similar crisis of paradigm and categories in analysing the historical process of political and social development of French society. Zeldin rejected the Anglo-Saxon model to study and analyse French politics. However, he accepted the fact that France had borrowed ideas and labels from abroad but it had assimilated them thoroughly into its own traditions, so that any resemblance to the original was largely nominal.[16]

Zeldin concludes that the division between Right and Left created an obstacle to clear thought about current problems, and perpetuated historical disagreements long after they had ceased to have significance. It gave a false veneer of simplicity to the issues, obscuring the multiplicity of views and as a result the real options before the French got blurred.

No doubt, the concept of 'Right' over the years had not received as much attention as the 'Left' did, as it appeared largely as a negative force, perpetuating conservative and reactionary forces, limiting progress, liberty and humanism. There were variants of 'Right' but in the 1920s and 1930s, the focus of the political analysts was Fascism and Nazism, viewed as forms of anti-Left activism, opportunistic power politics, based on the cult of race, blood and a messianic leader.

S. Lipset in his book *Political Man* provided the most stimulating definition of the Right. According to him, the Right were those who opposed social and economic reforms and used democratic procedures such as lobbying, pressure group tactics and ballot box to oppose reforms. They employed tactics to threaten the social fabric of democratic politics and encouraged denial of civil liberties.[17]

The Right in Europe was also seen as a single mass party, usually led by a charismatic leader. Its commitment was to a single, positively formulated

[14] Ibid.
[15] For details, see Tamlon, *The Origins of Totalitarian Democracy.*
[16] Zeldin, *France 1948–1945.*
[17] See S.M. Lipset, *Political Man: The Social Bases of Politics* (New York, 1963).

substantive goal, such as industrialization, racial mastering or proletarian unity and it had a concomitant lack of commitment to maintenance of procedural stability. It resorted to large-scale use of organized violence by military and paramilitary forces, uniformed and secret police to bring into line or suppress organizations and associations not geared to the substantive aim of the regime. It also enforced universal participation in public organizations dedicated to the single goal—glorification of nation, race and leadership. This became the universal aim which involved 'the remaking of all making in the image of the state conceived by the 'Rightist', i.e., the totalitarian'.[18]

The Right largely appeared as a negative force, perpetuating conservatism and reactionary forces, delimiting progress, freedom and individualism.[19]

Thus, the concept of *Right* has been understood and interpreted differently, depending upon the specific historical context which varied from one country to another.

According to Lipset, the ideology of the Right appealed to disgruntled, psychologically homeless, personal failures, economically insecure, uneducated, unsophisticated and authoritarian person at every level of society.[20]

As Andre Malraux observes, the Right that emerged in the early twentieth century in the West was primarily a product of 'primitive chaos, socialist failure, underdevelopment of capitalism and democratic decay'.[21] It was identified with anti-democracy, anti-intellectual, anti-people and anti-liberal ideology sponsoring change. But the change was for the establishment of state power, which the Right set out to capture.[22] Since they were anti-people, for them the mass of mankind, to quote from Nietzsche, was 'the sand of humanity, all very equal, very small, very round'.[23] Therefore, for them, humanism was the 'handmaiden' of nationalism and social Darwinism.

The economic crisis, social and cultural pessimism and lack of available means of political expression were often the reasons for the growth and expansion of 'Right' ideology. The Rightward drift of politics in Europe was a result of the anxiety of the displaced persons of early 1919,

[18] Daniel Bell, ed., *The Radical Right: The New American Right Expanded and Updated* (New York, 1964).
[19] Ibid.
[20] Lipset, Political Man.
[21] Andre Malraux, *Man's Hope* (1937).
[22] Bell, *The Radical Right*. Also see Walter Laqueur, *Fascism: Past, Present, Future* (New York, 1997); Eugen Weber in Rogger and Weber (ed.), *The European Right*, 7.
[23] Bell, ibid.

divided into those who were clawing their way upward and those making desperate efforts not to slip down. To them the appeal of class struggle or maintaining 'stable' status quo did not hold any meaning. Slogans of retrieving national honour, restoring national dignity and national glory through national unity appealed to them more. They held: 'Republican, Bonapartist, Legitimist, Orleanist, these are merely forenames. The family name is patriot.'[24]

Like Left, there were variants of Right; for example, in England the Right leaders ranged from Joseph Chamberlain, Milner, Baldwin to Maxse, Lord Beaverbrook and Sir Oswald Mosley, etc. And they became more active during the inter-war period, oscillating between moderate and extreme Right. However, the extreme Right were the members of British Union of Fascists, founded in October 1931 by Sir Oswald Mosley. He was earlier a member of the Labour Party, till March 1931.[25] Similarly, in France, Germany and Italy too, the Right varied from moderate to extreme, but certain features were common to all, i.e., anti-intellectual, anti-liberal, anti-Left and anti-people.[26]

After World War I, the Right, projecting themselves as advocates of change, protectors from Bolshevism and restorers of economic prosperity in central and northwestern Europe, had to struggle against the liberal majority of republicans and some radicals.[27] In eastern Europe, the situation was similar to the revolutionary condition of 1848. The power struggle was waged between representatives of vested interest and new contenders of power in the narrow political space. In eastern Europe, the middle-class conservatism lacked social basis. The influential class was the landowning gentry, and the economy was directed towards serving their conspicuous consumption amidst widespread scarcity. Peasant parties led by the middle class failed to express the aspirations of the peasantry. Within this environment of disillusionment and disenchantment with the existing conditions, national socialist leagues appeared to exploit the mass of wretched small landowners and labourers with their debts and frustrations, their hope for land or more land, their resentment of the new ways of financial or industrial enterprise and of the bureaucratic state. Moderate reforms provided no answer to the problems of these people. Only drastic social, moral and economic changes could improve their lot and eliminate

---

[24] Ibid., 9.

[25] J.R. Jones, 'England', in *The European Right*, ed. Rogger and Weber, 28–69.

[26] Ibid., 65. Also see J. Martin, *The Dialectical Imagination: A History of the Frankfurt School and the Institute of Social Research 1923–1950* (London: Heinemann, 1974), 48–51.

[27] See Rogger and Weber, *The European Right*, 2–28.

the corrupt establishment which was using laissez faire as a license to forage and plunder.[28]

According to Weber, in central and northwestern Europe, the 'power struggle' between the emerging Right and existing liberals emanated in Italy largely from rampant pessimism and disillusionment following unification; in France out of disgust with Republican corruption; in England as in Russia, or in Germany, out of the shortcomings of the state and the debilities of the empire.[29]

Furthermore, Weber argues, the mass society that took over at the end of the nineteenth century, with its democratic structure, egalitarian ideology and parliamentary system, appeared dysfunctional. Its shortcomings stood out; the bargains, compromises and give and take became evidence of corruption. The mass electorate might have been more tolerant had it felt better represented. But petty bourgeoisie on the one hand and the newly significant industrial workers on the other hand did not regard the parliamentary politics as their own. It was seen as the extension of nineteenth century's elitist politics with roots in rationalism and utilitarianism. However, in 1919, parliamentary politics began to appear irrational due to politicians' manoeuvring and manipulations, appeal to emotions and not to mind.[30] The threat of Bolshevism and ineffectiveness of democracy strengthened the hands of the Right. The appeal of the Right in England was that of 'a sane patriotism with the idea of consolidating the orderly elements of society against Bolshevik ideas'.[31]

The conservatives accepted the violence and brutality of the radical Right because to them the Right appeared as the sole defenders against the threat of the Left. The conservatives of Britain and France were worried over the spread of communism. In 1930, Lord Halifax told Hitler that he and other British ministers were aware that the Fuhrer had not only achieved a great deal inside Germany but by destroying communism in Germany he had emerged as a bulwark of Europe against Bolshevism.[32] The non-fascist Right in England and Germany thought that Fascism would do their dirty work for them.[33]

Another major characteristic of the European Right was the propagation of a common dream through reinvention of myths and symbols.

[28] Ibid.
[29] Ibid., 8.
[30] Ibid., 19.
[31] Statement by British Military Attaché, in Berlin in 1931. See ibid., 20.
[32] See Lionel Kochan, *The Struggle for Germany* (Edinburgh, 1963), 11, 103–104.
[33] Ibid., 116.

These were deliberate lies having no basis in truth but employed for ulterior motives. Such needs of the Right made Machiavelli, Pareto, Mosca, Herder, Fitchte, Hegel, Sorel and Nietzsche their new prophets and not Adam Smith or Ricardo. According to Georges Sorel, myths were supra-intellectual whose purpose was to evoke and harness certain dynamic images which would produce an entirely epic state of mind and at the same time bend all the energies of the mind for a great common effort.[34] He further held that myths were energizing, unifying, propagandist devices.[35] In his book *Refletions on Violence* published in 1908, Sorel mentioned that myths were instrumental means and not a reflection of an end.[36]

Myths and dreams were used earlier too by *Jacobins* for the entrenchment of Republican values and society. Similarly utopian reformers such as August Comte and Saint Simon used dreams for perpetuation of universal values such as virtue, humanism, the fatherland.[37]

However, the Right deliberately invented the myth of hurt, pride, and hatred for specific ethnic groups by reviving the memories of bygone rights and bygone greatness, whether true or false. They propagated all kinds of resentments, directing them against evil forces supposed to threaten society either from within or from without. Deeply embedded in the ideology of exclusiveness, the European Right thrived on the notion of intolerance for other ethnic groups in their societies—be it Gypsies, Slavs, Semitic communities or Afro-Asian groups. Sorrel was not alone in his viewpoint; a similar view in support of myths and its usage for ulterior purpose was expressed in the writings of Pareto in Italy. In France Maurice Barres and in Germany Lagarde and Langbehn expressed similar views. In England Rhodes, Kipling, Chamberlain and others used myth to justify 'imperialism' and civilizational superiority of the whites to maintain their hold over the 'weak, barbarian natives'. Thus, they all manipulated myths and dreams for the purpose of establishing, reviving or glorifying a race, a nation and a class, that had a task to perform, the white man's burden to carry or a destiny to fulfil.[38]

---

[34] Ibid.

[35] Ibid.

[36] Ibid. Also see J. Martin, *The Dialectical Imagination*; H. Stuart Hughes, *Consciousness and Society: The Reorientation of European Social Thought 1890–1930* (New York, 1958); Howard Becker and Harry Elmer Barnes, *Social Thought from Lore to Science*, Vol. 2 (New York, 1961), third edition.

[37] See Rogger and Weber, *The European Right*, 22.

[38] Ibid., 22–23.

The larger consensus among the analysts regarding the characteristics of 'Right' are: (a) precedence of loyalty to the nation over every other form of loyalty; (b) hostility towards any extension of democratic rights and towards international socialism; (c) support of militarism and opposition to pacifist movements; (d) glorification of a national mission; (e) appeal to protect national traditions and culture from 'sinister' outside influence; (f) emphasis on duties as opposed to rights, on order as opposed to freedom; (g) stress on the individual family and birthplace as the fundamental bonds of social cohesion; (h) tendency towards the authoritarian regimentation of all human relationships; (i) integration of the national spirit in support of orthodox ideas and (j) tendency to be especially vigilant and suspicious in regard to intellectuals and members of the free professions, on the ground that they are apt to become the disseminators of 'subversive thoughts'.[39]

The concept of 'Right' should, therefore, be viewed in a particular historical context. It appears to vary from one setting to another; in general the elements of pro-people and pro-democracy are conspicuous by their absence or have a negligible presence in Rightist ideology.

In order to locate the contextual meaning of the concept of Right in the Indian situation during the colonial period, it is imperative to analyse the political milieu under which the term Right was used by an ideological faction and the circumstances governing this categorization. A detailed discussion and analysis is attempted in the subsequent section where it has been argued that historical facts do not support the stereotype that our national leaders such as Sardar Patel, Rajgopalachari, Rajendra Prasad, among others were followers of the ideology of the 'Right' and Nehru and Subhas Chandra Bose on the other hand stood for 'Left' ideology. This argument is seriously flawed, both in conceptual formulation and in view of the historical evidence. First, there is fallacy of nomenclature in the very use of the terms 'Right' and 'Left', abstracted as they are from the Western context and applied to the Indian historical realities without contextualization. And, apart from the nuances of style, which could vary, most of the Congress leaders, particularly Patel and Nehru, shared a common vision of a future Indian social and economic reconstruction. Their views on major crucial issues were more convergent in both content and character.

---

[39] See *International Encyclopedia of Social Sciences*, Vol. V (New York, 1968), 334–341; Eugen Weber, *Varieties of Fascism: Doctrines of Revolution in the Twentieth Century* (New York, 1964); Ernst Nolte, *The Three Faces of Fascism: Action Francaise, Italian Fascism, National Socialism* (London, 1965); Emilo Gentile, *The Origins of Fascist Ideology 1918–1925: The First Complete Study of the Origins of Italian Fascism* (New York, 2005).

HOW RIGHT WERE THE 'RIGHT' LEADERS?

The leaders of the Congress, regarded as the lieutenants of Mahatma Gandhi in the anti-imperialist struggle, namely, Patel, Rajaji and Prasad accepted and fought for the basic values enshrined in the Congress ideology, shaped and articulated by the leaders of the national liberation struggle viz. democracy, civil liberty, secularism, *swadeshi*, social reform, pro-poor orientation of development, economic decentralization, anti-colonialism and ethnic coexistence. Social issues such as education of women, their rights and empowerment, removal of untouchability, temple entry, social and religious tolerance, inter-caste and inter-religious marriages, inter-dinning, social upliftment of kisan through education and social reforms incorporated in the constructive programme of Gandhiji, occupied position of significance in the socio-political programme of Rajaji, Patel and Prasad as well.

These leaders envisaged democratic welfare state and society based on social justice and equality, where every man and woman would be ensured equality of opportunity, freedom to develop his or her personality and environment for harmonious coexistence, irrespective of caste, gender, ethnicity, race and religion.[40] This Catholicism was never a defining feature of the European Right. If Rajaji's view in 1937 on democracy was: 'It is a well known and well appreciated fact that self government is not possible unless we trust all our people. On what is the Government based? This is a great moral movement and we may well trust a little more, the village community.'[41]

Patel's vision of India in 1949 was:

In free India there would be no distinction of caste, creed or religion or of classes resulting in the domination of one section over another. There may be rich and poor, happy and unhappy, but there would be no difference in status between one citizen and the other.[42]

For the 'Right' leaders *swaraj* did not mean removal of white sahibs and placing black sahibs, but it meant establishment of *Raj of* farmers and

[40] Patel's Speech at Borsad, August 1936 (date not given). See Patel Papers, File No. 13 (Congress Affairs 1936 to 1942), Sardar Patel National Museum (hereafter SPNM), Ahmedabad.

[41] See Rajaji Papers, 1940, NMML (Microfilm).

[42] Patel's Speech at Delhi, 2 January 1949. See G.M. Nandurkar, ed., *Sardar Patel: In Tune with the Millions-II* (Ahmedabad, 1976), 56.

majoor raj, reviving spinning wheel and village industries and preparation of khadi in every village home to help the starving millions.[43] Democracy, according to them, should be decentralized and it should percolate down to the social and economic sphere, without jeopardizing the nation's security and encourage production and cultural progress of the subjects and the nation as a whole.[44] Patel, Rajaji and Prasad also supported management of corporate life of villages by means of a popularly elected panchayat and attaining economic self-sufficiency in the essentials of life. All the three leaders were supporters of *raj* of farmers, of village industries and agriculture. They felt that a balance should be maintained between agriculture and industry with focus on village industry.[45] But whatever be the instrument of development, according to Rajaji, whether large industries or cottage and village industries or agriculture, the economy should be free and it should establish relationships of cooperation. It is a great decentralized industry which would really serve to maintain the texture of our rural life and not create slums in the towns along with the problems of housing, health and sanitation with which governments are unable to deal satisfactorily.[46]

The three leaders were of the opinion that industrialization was a necessary evil of the modern times but it should support agriculture, as it was the foundation of the Indian economy. The state should own and control key industries and services. According to them, there should be a symbiotic relationship between cottage and large-scale industries.[47] They, therefore, emphasized on promotion of scientific research.

For them, 'This is the age of scientific and industrial research. If we want to achieve our proper place in the community of nations we should carry on our work of research with speed and efficiency.'[48]

Patel, Prasad and Rajaji accepted the critique of colonialism as expounded by the moderate and extremist leadership of the Congress. They also agreed to the earlier Congress leadership's advocacy for modern economic development based on modern industrial science and technology

---

[43] Ibid.

[44] See Chapter 4 of the thesis.

[45] See Chapter 4, Section on Industry and Agriculture.

[46] See Rajaji Papers, 4 November 1942.

[47] Rajaji's Speech on 1 April 1939, in Madras Legislative Assembly. See Madras Legislative Assembly Debate, Vol. XII, 179–181.

[48] Patel's Speech at Ahmedabad, while laying the foundation stone of Ahmedabad Textile Research Association on 30 October 1950. See Nandurkar, *Sardar's Letters Mostly Unknown*, Vol. II, 227.

---

and the development of agriculture. The very fact of India being over-powered by a small nation was stark enough for them not to appreciate the significance of modern industrial economy in a country's growth and strength. Patel well realized this fact. He said:

> If the Indian government is to be seen today on the basis of Gandhian philosophy without army, I am prepared to change the whole thing.... Tomorrow the whole of India will be run from one end to the other if you do not have strong army.[49]

Like the moderate leadership, the so-called 'Right' leaders laid great emphasis on *swadeshi* and self-reliance. The instrument of *swadeshi* and self-reliance were khadi, *charkha* and village industries, later supported by industry.[50] They regarded building of zamindar–peasant and labour–capital relationship on the Gandhian principle of cooperation, compassion, trusteeship and arbitration. They believed that:

> A new way of life, a new culture is what is aimed as this cannot be achieved by coercion but only by a heart change. The doctrine of enlightened selfishness of the nineteenth century utilitarians should be refined into a doctrine of immanent trusteeship.[51]

Patel speaking at Rani Praja Conference in Baroda Estate on 3 March 1935 elucidated the manner in which the relationship between zamindar and peasantry and capitalists and labour should develop:

> Our aim should be that no injustice is done either to the big land-holders or to the sowkars and at the same time to see that no one's fundamental rights are ignored. We may give this much assurance to everybody that however great our difficulties and whatever the injustices perpetuated on us, we do not wish to be unjust to any body or to act in a spirit of vengeance. At the same time we must state firmly that we do not wish to surrender our rights. If anyone still thinks in terms of living like a parasite, I do not propose to tolerate it. Anyone who allows another to live on him is not a man but an animal and we ought to be free from that condition. Our

[49] Patel's Speech, 12 November 1949. See ibid., 215.
[50] See Chapter 4, Section on Industry and Agriculture.
[51] C. Rajagopalachari, *Satyam Eva Jayate* (Madras, 1961), 321–322. Prasad expressed similar views in his book *At the Feet of Mahatma Gandhi* (Bombay, 1955).

welfare does not lie in the hands of the king or on the merchants. Our welfare lies in our hands.[52]

Rejecting the allegations of the left for their being in the hands of zamindars and capitalists, Patel in his speech at Indore on 2 October 1950 stated:

Some people say that I am in the hands of capitalist. I am not in the hands of any one nor can any one dare keep me in his hands. If I feel that I can do without them, I shall even go further than the communists or socialists. I am certainly a friend of rulers and capitalists as I am of Harijan and the poorest of the poor. If I do not entertain friendly feelings towards all of them, I would be unworthy of the responsibility which I carry. There are good or bad men amongst them (capitalists) also. How many of us are prepared to sacrifice for the country? If we ourselves are not prepared to do so, how can people blame them if they are not prepared to give up their profits? If we have capital, we ourselves would not mind being the capitalist. It is only because we do not have it that we make all this bother. I, therefore, ask you not to build your leadership on abuses or enmities but on love and fellowship.

Those who still think that they can revive the old order of things are also doomed to disappointment.... I have behaved with the rulers on the principle of mutual affection and I also wish to deal with the jagirdars similarly. I would not like to spread any poison. I wish to solve this problem amicably, but if any of them feel that they can destroy democracy, by intrigues and by incitement to subversive activities they shall learn a lesson of their lives.[53]

Arguing for the elimination of economic inequality, Rajaji said on 1 April 1936:

The choice before the people is whether they want common management by abolishing the system of individual property or whether they hope to stem the tide of that flood by heavier and heavier taxation on those who are able to bear it and by distributing the

---

[52] Patel's Speech at Rani Praja Conference in Baroda Estate on 3 March 1935. See Chopra, *The Collected Works of Sardar Vallbhbhai Patel*, Vol. V, 43–45.

[53] See Nandurkar, *In Tune with the Millions*, Vol. II, 287–290.

proceeds of that taxation in such common management as will distribute amenities of life to all people. There is no other philosophy behind this proposal or any other similar proposal. It is impossible to stem the tide of communism if I may use an easily available word unless businessmen and capitalist and those who stand for individual property are ready to realize the need and the emergency for imposing upon themselves heavier and heavier taxation, fair but yet heavy taxation, and distributing the proceeds so far as benefits go over the whole of state.[54]

In defining nationalism, Patel, Rajaji and Prasad did not draw from Hindu scriptures and mythologies. They largely repeated the metaphors which Gandhiji used while propounding the ideology of nationalism, explaining the policies, programmes and strategies of the Congress. The nationalism they propagated was in the nature of political nationalism, i.e., nationalism as a product of living in a single territorial boundary and not civilizational nationalism found in the speeches and writings of Tilak,[55] Gandhi[56] and Nehru.[57] Gandhi and Nehru regarded Indian nationalism as a product of composite phenomenon, which emerged over a period of time by intermeshing of several traditions. Tilak gave it a religious tinge by invoking cultural symbols rooted in the religious matrix, for the spread of nationalism.[58] But Patel, Rajaji and Prasad did not invoke cultural symbols for popularizing either nationalist ideology or anti-colonialism. The emphasis of these leaders was on invoking political nationalism and keeping it confined to the moderates' perspective on nationalism. Unlike the extremist leaders, the 'Right' leaders did not revive or initiate any religious festival or fairs for the spread of nationalism. While dealing with the growth of communal tendencies, they criticized communalism by asking people to revive and remember themselves as citizens only: 'If you forget your citizenship and talk of religion, it is a cloak. Therefore when I hear

[54] See Rajaji's Speech in the Assembly, dated 1 April 1936, Madras Legislative Assembly Debate, Vol. VII, 177.

[55] Tilak traced civilizational resonance in the Vedic tradition. See B.G. Tilak, *The Orion or Researches into the Antiquity of the Vedas*, eighth edition (Poona, 1999).

[56] Gandhiji focused on ethical aspect of civilization, i.e., traditions which over a period of time grew to engender human goodness and happiness. See Rajagopalachari, *Gandhiji's Teachings and Philosophy*, 1967.

[57] In *Glimpses of World History*, Nehru traces civilizational roots of multi-layered Indian identity. See Nehru, *Glimpses of World History* (Allahabad, 1934).

[58] See R.P. Dutt, *India Today* (Calcutta, 1979).

some people talking about Hinduism in danger, I feel that they are going a wrong way.'[59] Elaborating on his view on political nationalism, Patel stated that all communities in India would have equal rights as Indian citizens and they would have full protection of the law and government, to live in peace. Speaking further, Patel stated that: 'As in the long run it would be in the interest of all to forget that there is anything like majority or minority in this country and that in India there is only one community—that is one Nation.'[60]

In the tradition of Dadabhai Naoroji, Pherozeshah Mehta, Gopal Krishna Gokhale and also Gandhi and Nehru, Patel, Rajaji and Prasad believed in cultural pluralism, religious tolerance and ethnic and linguistic coexistence. For these leaders, 'religion was a matter between man and his maker and its mixing with politics was seen as a dangerous business.'[61] Being a follower of cultural pluralism, the 'Right' believed that: 'It is the Hindus' duty to help protect Islam by rendering every possible assistance to the Muslims and expressing full faith in the goodness of that community.'[62]

Rajaji, Patel and Prasad placed citizenship above religious, ethnic and caste identities and criticized all kinds of communal beliefs and motives. Rajaji criticized the Hindu communalists for using the concept of *dharma* and *vedanta* as values for differentiating Hindus from other communities. His sharp reaction to such opinions was that *vedanta* and *dharma* had secular ethos rooted not only in the Hindu tradition and culture but also in the composite Indian tradition and culture which was enriched by the intermeshing of *bhakti* and Sufi traditions. *Vedanta*, according to Rajaji, was a living philosophy of life, a part of the mental structure of 'our' people, which they got not from the scriptures but from tradition.[63] Similarly, *dharma* was not to be confused with fanaticism of some followers of Hinduism. *Dharma* was the widespread inner call among people of all

---

[59] Speech of Patel at Eranakulam on 13 May 1949 in Nandurkar, *Sardar Patel: In Tune with the Millions-I*, 100.

[60] Patel's Speech at Hyderabad on 'No Place for Divided Loyalty' on 7 October 1950, in Nandurkar, Sardar's Letters Mostly Unknown, Vol. V, 165.

[61] Patel's Speech at Eranakulam, 13 May 1949 in Nandurkar, *Sardar Patel: In Tune with the Millions*, Vol. I.

[62] Patel's Speech at Bharuch, 1921. See *Sardar Patel Ke Bhashan 1918–1947* (Ahmedabad, 1950), 34.

[63] See C. Rajgopalachari, *Hinduism: Doctrine and Way of Life* (Madras, 1959), 34–36.

classes in India to reduce their wants and to give their possession for the good of others.[64] None of these leaders supported obscurantist cultural traditions and symbols for popularizing nationalism. This was unlike the extremist leaders who opposed reforms like the Age of Consent Bill, supported revival of Ganapati and Shivaji—cultural religious festivals and taking of pledges before Kali and Durga. The 'Right' leaders insisted on propagating the concept of secular citizenship and nationhood under a democratic governance of liberal and egalitarian character.

Thus, like the moderate leaders—Dadabhai Naoroji, Gopal Krishna Gokhale, Surendranath Bannerjee, C.R. Das and Motilal Nehru who favoured British kind of parliamentary system—Patel, Rajaji and Prasad too were supporters of parliamentary democracy. They did not suffer from 'any kind of civilizational delusion of grandeur' by rejecting everything Western as materialistic and crude and accepting everything Eastern as metaphysical and spiritual. Therefore, they generously indulged in social self-introspection, unlike the extremists. The extremist leadership in the name of spiritual superiority protested against social reforms like the Age of Consent Bill. They rejected all social and scientific development in the name of metaphysics and as part of the 'Conqueror's culture'. They accepted caste division, cult of the mother goddess, ritualism and predominance of spiritualism in the political struggle.[65]

On the contrary, the 'Right' leaders rejected such obscurantism and regarded social reform to be a significant plank of the anti-imperialist movement. For the success of the anti-imperialist movement, healthy social foundations were an essential precondition. They wanted Congress to seriously take up social issues such as untouchability, education, dowry, child marriage, widow marriage, purdah, prohibition, rural indebtedness, conversion, ritualism and personal hygiene. These leaders did not, however, want to address any controversial issues which would give rise to social conflict, to the detriment of the anti-imperialist movement.

Speaking against the caste system Patel said:

I do not believe in any caste or community. The whole of India is my village and men of all communities are my friends and relations.

---

[64] Ibid. Also see Rajendra Prasad's statement issued as the Congress President on 10 December 1947 in Choudhary, *Dr. Rajendra Prasad*, Vol. 7, 428–430. Also see Patel's Speech at Eranakulam, 13 May 1949 in Nandurkar, *Sardar Patel: In Tune with the Millions-I*.
[65] See Dutt, *India Today*, 325–328.

All are children of the same God. After a man dies does anyone ask if the corpse is that of a Brahman or a Chamar.[66]

For bringing about healthy, non-violent *swarajya* the 'Right' leadership regarded abolition of untouchability as the most essential humane act. Articulating the feelings of the other two leaders[67] on untouchability Patel said:

I advise you to abolish untouchability which is a curse to the Hindu community of India. You cannot discard your own brother. According to the Hindu philosophy, it is a sin to discard any one who is living. Soul is God and even an untouchable has soul in him. You therefore cannot discard God-soul.[68]

The other most important component of holistic *swarajya* was the upliftment of women. Speaking on the condition of women, Patel on 2 October 1934 said:

The community is trading in darkness on one foot and that too of a male. They are being constantly hammered that they have to shoulder the burden of the house as far as possible. He has not been taught to accept that. In social and national spheres women have some rights and responsibilities. That is why we are lagging behind.... Women in one way are extremely courageous. Men do not endure the miseries to the extent women do. In India misery is destined in women's fate, and she smilingly endures them. She is not aware of her rights. The society fears that if she is educated, she would have knowledge of her rights and will shake off the privations. But that fear is uncalled for. What is good in men is equally good in women also.... The society adopts a partisan attitude between a male and a female. It pardons male but a woman is permanently censured and disgraced, if she commits a blunder ... so long as women are not

---

[66] See Parikh, *Sardar Vallabhbhai Patel*, Vol. 2 (Ahmedabad, 1971), 456.

[67] For more details on the views of these leaders see Chapter 2—Social Vision of the Congress 'Right'.

[68] Patel's Speech at Prantej Taluka Local Board, 23 October 1935 in Chopra, *The Collected Works*, Vol. V, 177.

sufficiently educated and inculcated with national spirit, till then there will be no prosperity.[69]

The 'Right' leaders in their ideology and perception were modern. Their modernity was, however, not dismissive of the utility and efficacy of cultural tradition of the country. They were protagonists of evolutionary change of radical kind. To quote Rajaji:

> My confirmed belief is that women as well as men must be free to marry whomsoever they like.... I am not proposing that boys and girls may run away with each other. I only say that in marriages the choice of the young people should prevail. We can be partners without distinction of caste, friends without distinctions of castes and marriage too need not be bound down by rules of caste.[70]

This revolutionary statement coming from a person like Rajaji who was seen as arch 'Rightist', conservative and reactionary by the Left needs to be taken note of while assessing the so-called 'Rightist' leaders. The statements of all the three leaders highlighted in the preceding discourse disprove the allegations of the Left that they were Right and reaffirm the view of Prasad that most of the so-called 'conservatives are more progressive in their thinking than the so called progressives'.[71]

Thus, the social vision of these leaders was rooted in a realistic understanding of the Indian society. It was not influenced by any fashionable doctrine of an impracticable kind. Since their main aim was to activate the cementing processes of divisiveness in the society for nation building, they appeared to be 'reformist' and pacifist to the Left because they adopted class collaboration as against class conflict, non-violence as against Bolshevic and Maoist radicalism. But the 'Right' leaders understood that to make the social change lasting and harmonious, it had to be gradual and evolutionary. They were of the opinion that social issues should be taken up in such a manner that it would lead to social consolidation rather than weakening the process of nation building.

---

[69] Patel's Speech at Jyoti Sangha, Ahmedabad, 2 October 1934. See ibid., 214. For more details see Chapter 2 on Social Vision of the Congress 'Right'.

[70] See Rajmohan Gandhi, *The Rajaji Story I: A Warrior from the South* (Bombay, 1978), 211.

[71] Prasad to Nehru, dated 24 July 1948. See Choudhary, *Dr. Rajendra Prasad*, Vol. 9, 241.

THE LEFT ON THE 'RIGHT'

R.P. Dutt in his *India Today* respected the limitations within which the moderate leadership of the Congress was functioning in carrying out anti-imperialist struggle against British imperialism. He recognized the fact that as long as the nascent working class was without any organization and the peasantry was still the 'dumb millions', the Indian bourgeois class whose leaders were the moderates, were the most progressive and objectively the revolutionary force in India. They carried on work for social reform, enlightenment, education, modernization, industrialization and economic development, against all that was backward and obscurantist.[72]

In contrast to the moderates, according to R.P. Dutt, Tilak, Bipan Chandra Pal, Aurobindo Ghosh and Lajpat Rai represented the conservative minded Right-wingers. No doubt, they were radical and potentially revolutionary in making a break with the mendicant political strategy of the moderates. However, they did not equip themselves with a modern, social and political outlook, nor did they develop any scientific and political theory regarding general development of the nation and tried to build nationalism on orthodox Hinduism and spiritual superiority of the 'Aryan' civilization. They tried to please the reactionary forces of orthodox Hinduism by opposing social reforms like the Age of Consent Bill, organizing cow protection society, organizing festivals such as Ganapati and Shivaji which were political in content but religious in appearance, and popularizing the cult of Kali and Durga.[73]

R.P. Dutt while analysing the nature of the leadership of the Congress in its various stages of growth and progression, regarded the political phase of Gandhi and his associates as a continuation of the extremist tradition of Hinduistic obscurantism, this was allegedly visible in the Gandhian concept of ahimsa, *Ramrajya and Daridranaryan* which were seen by Dutt as metaphysical and religio-philosophical in nature. According to him, Gandhism brought in an element of petty bourgeois moralizing and reformist pacifism by introducing 'non-violence'.[74] This ideology was accepted by Gandhi's associates because of its practical relevance for the unarmed people's anti-imperialist struggle against a powerfully armed ruling enemy.[75] However, R.P. Dutt who has largely influenced the Left historiography on the

---

[72] See Dutt, *India Today*, 323–343.
[73] Ibid.
[74] Ibid.
[75] Ibid.

national movement till today viewed that the Gandhian paradigm tried to conciliate the interests of the masses with the big bourgeoisie and landed interests, which were inevitably opposed to any kind of class struggle.[76] R.P. Dutt tended to conflate such interests as representing the 'Right' in the Congress.

The Left in the Congress which largely included members of the Congress Socialist Party, Subhas Chandra Bose and Jawaharlal Nehru, regarded Patel, Rajaji and Prasad as 'Right' because they did not believe in Western kind of socialist India. Patel, Rajaji and Prasad were believers in the sanctity of private property and liberal, democratic welfare state. They also believed in economic decentralization from province to village downwards, economy based on symbiotic relationship between village industries and heavy industries, *swadeshi*, social reforms, class collaboration, anti-colonialism, pro-poor orientation of the development, evolutionary transformation, policy of inclusion towards all, ethnic, religious and caste groups and strategy of active non-violence as the revolutionary form of anti-imperialist struggle. They were regarded as 'Right' by the Left groups within the Congress because they believed in the sanctity of private property and rejected class struggle, socialistic economy, dictatorship of the proletariat and progression of society understood through the theoretical perspective of historical materialism.[77]

The perception of the Left about Patel, Rajaji and Prasad as 'Right' actually emerged due to the conceptual rigidity of the Left and their narrow viewing of the ideas and orientation of these leaders. Second, in their ideological framework there was no cognition of class collaboration, non-violence, trusteeship, economic and social regeneration through village industries, khadi and *charkha*. They did not understand that the indigenous variant of 'socialism' based on trusteeship and Panchayati Raj could be equally humane, rational, scientific and secular in ethos as the Western kind, if not more.[78]

The Left used the nomenclature of 'Right' for these leaders but they themselves were not sure and at ease with this naming; therefore, they time and again expressed their misgivings by interchanging the term 'Right' with 'conservatives', 'traditionalists', 'reformists' and 'old guards'. Nor did they provide any scientific definition of what they meant by the term 'Right', on what basis a particular group of leaders was called 'Right', were they

[76] Ibid.
[77] See Chapter 4 for more details.
[78] Ibid.

the same as the Right in Europe, etc? And why then moderates who too did not adopt socialism were seen as liberal democrats and were not called Right, when Patel, Rajaji and Prasad who too were liberal democrats of moderate genre, held the same inclusive world view and secular attitude towards caste, gender and religious minorities and had no keenness to raise religio-philosophical or metaphysical question regarding non-violence and regarded it merely as potent political strategy, were called 'Right'? The 'Right' saw trusteeship as an ideal type, which one could aspire for but which could not be put into immediate practice for practical reasons. They were supporters of a robust economy based on modernized agriculture and industry, and a liberal democratic society based on scientific attitude and rationalism.

Patel in a letter to Nehru in November 1936 accepted that he did not believe in the inevitability of class war. He detested imperialism and admitted that there existed a destructive inequality between the capitalist class and the famishing poor, but the answer was not in the annihilation of one class for the progress of another. Patel reasserted that he being a peasant could not be the friend of capitalists and landlords. He knew where the shoe pinched most; therefore, he subscribed to the doctrine of all wealth and land belonging to all. And the answer lay in more production and purging of capitalism of its hideousness.[79] But his advice to the socialists was that nothing could be done if people were not ready, as it could only be achieved through the power of the people.[80]

The Left within the Congress whether they were socialists such as Narendra Dev, Jayprakash Narayan, Dinkar Mehta, Ashok Mehta, Minoo Masani, Achyut Patwardhan or Left sympathizers such as Nehru and Bose were vague in providing a definition to their usage of the concept of 'Right' for Patel, Rajaji and Prasad.

Dinkar Mehta in his correspondence with Narendra Dev regarding the Tripuri controversy in 1939 accepted the fact that although Congress was a mass organization, Gandhi and his associates' acceptance of indigenous symbols such as Ram Rajya, *charkha*, khadi and bringing them into the folds of national movement succeeded in evoking a response from rural India but gave a non-revolutionary character to the only mass party—the Indian National Congress.[81] Ashok Mehta, too, writing in the Congress

---

[79] See *Times of India*, Bombay, 28 November 1936.

[80] Ibid.

[81] Dinkar Mehta did not define categorically nor did he provide details as to how he defined 'Right'. See Dinkar Mehta to Narendra Dev, 3 March 1939, Patel Papers, Lot I-39-1-3, Ahmedabad.

Socialist in 1934, accepted that there was the Right wing in the Congress without enumerating who were the 'Right' and on what basis he was calling them 'Right'. Yet he accepted that ultimately the Right-Left divide was redundant at that time-point as both accepted the relevance of Gandhian vision which bound them together.[82]

Jayprakash Narayan was more conclusive and definite in providing a framework to the term 'Right' and in naming the leaders whom he considered as Right in his speeches and writings, and correspondences.[83] According to Jayprakash Narayan, Patel, Rajaji and Prasad were the leaders of the 'Right' group in the Congress because they did not accept socialism. They were wrongly accused of being anti-socialist because they were against collective affiliation of peasants and workers to the Congress. The economic policy enshrined in the constructive programme of the Congress supported by these leaders was also said to be reformist and not revolutionary in nature. He argued that Patel, Prasad and Rajaji were ignoring the latent force of the working class and were against the socialists going to the peasants 'not with a spinning wheel, but with the militant force of economic programme'; therefore, it made them 'Rightist' in their political, social and economic thinking.[84]

Further emphasizing the issue, Jayprakash wrote in the *Congress Socialist* that from 1934 onwards the need was to introduce class issue and sharpen class conflict to create mass and class organization. To achieve this, farmer, factory workers and youth were to be mobilized around socialism. The Congress had a base among the farmers but had no support among the labourers and factory workers. The socialist leaders like him and others[85] held the view that the struggle should be such that the farmers, factory workers, labourers and the youth could know that they were fighting for their class interests. The British were the class enemy and through class struggle anti-imperialist movement could be sharpened. Since Patel, Prasad and Rajaji did not agree with this view of the socialists in general and Jayprakash in particular, therefore they were seen as orthodox and 'Rightist' by him and the other socialist leaders.[86]

---

[82] See Patel Papers, ibid.

[83] See Jayprakash Narayan, *Towards Struggle* (Bombay, 1946).

[84] See *Bombay Chronicle*, 19 July 1934.

[85] This view of Jayprakash Narayan got support from almost all socialist leaders, be it Kamaladevi Chattopadhyay or Minoo Masani. See R.P. Papers, NMML.

[86] Ibid., Kamlashankar Pandya agreed with Jayprakash's view on Patel, Rajaji and Prasad. However, he accepted the fact that their knowledge of socialism was more bookish. They gave priority to nationalization of economy, abolition of zamindari without compensation, end of

Besides Jayprakash Narayan and Dinkar Mehta, other socialist leaders such as Yusuf Meherally, M.R. Masani, Kamladevi Chattopadhyaya and Kamlashankar Pandya accepted that Patel, Rajaji and Prasad's rejection of their understanding of socialism had led to their being branded as 'Right'.[87]

Among the Left thinkers, the most sagacious and erudite assessment of who were 'Right' and 'Left' came from Acharya Narendra Dev. He rightly assessed that the main concern of all varieties of political groups in 1939, was to strengthen the united national front against British imperialism and not to raise the issue of 'Right' and 'Left' thus giving rise to disunity in the Congress. Defining the 'Rightists' on 9 March 1939, he said that they were those who were prepared to align with British imperialism, and if anybody could think that a member of the old Working Committee could be called a 'Rightist' in that sense, there could be no hope of freedom for this country. They were not 'Rightist' but anti-imperialists to the core and revolutionaries. The question of 'Rightist' and 'Leftist' could only arise after there was a social revolution.[88]

However, in their draft for the all India Congress Socialist Party Conference, both Narendra Dev and Dinkar Mehta, while emphasizing on how radical and revolutionary the lower rung of the Congress had become, also brought out the dilemma of the socialist and the inefficacy of the Right–Left divide. Narendra Dev admitted that Gandhism was the dominant ideology of the Congress with which the rural masses identified and Congress was the only political mass organization of the country containing diverse elements. Therefore, its programme of complete independence, the Karachi Declaration of Fundamental Rights, the Agrarian resolutions

---

Princely States and of private property. But they were not being realistic to realize the preparedness of rural India. See Bipan Chandra et al., Transcript of interview of Kamlashankar Pandya, History of Freedom Movement Project, Centre for Historical Studies, JNU, New Delhi. Jayprakash Narayan in his later interview recorded as part of Oral History at NMML said:

> We thought that through class struggle, the anti-imperialist movement should be sharpened. However, I think that psychologically we have misled the farmers. The farmers also understood what freedom and Swarajya meant. The British rule must end, this greatly appealed to them. They did not understand 'class interest' etc. that much. We used to talk that they should be made conscious indirectly, should be made anti-imperialist. But they were anti- imperialist; I think so.

See Jayprakash Narayan, Oral History, NMML.

[87] See H.D. Sharma, ed., *Selected Works of Acharya Narendra Dev*, Vol. I (New Delhi, 1998).

[88] Ibid., 148–149.

of the Lucknow and Faizpur Congress, the election manifesto of the Indian National Congress 1937, the Wardha resolution of February 1937 and the Faizpur resolution on war was largely appropriate to the present stage of the anti-imperialist struggle.[89] Yet there was contradiction between the programme of the Congress and its actual realization. For example, on the agrarian question the senior leaders of the Congress did not want any kind of peasant unrest against the zamindars for redressal of their grievances. Similarly, workers of Ahmedabad and Kanpur were frowned upon when they went on strike and their militant activities were suppressed by the Congress Ministry. Students' strikes too were condemned and discouraged. Therefore, the task before the socialists was to form a united national front in the present phase of the struggle because though the Congress Socialist Party and the Left had made considerable advance inside the Congress, they were not in a position to influence the basic policy of the Congress.[90]

He further articulated that without excluding any section of the society, be it capitalist or landlords, as long as they did not put any obstruction in the path of anti-imperialist struggle, the task before the united front would be democratization of the Congress by activising its primary membership and by making the primary Congress Committees the fighting organs of united front struggles in conjunction with the workers, peasants, students and youth organizations. According to the socialists, this development would mean broadening of the base of the Congress by increasing its memberships, by forming primary Congress Committees in thousands, and by making these Congress Committees the centres of the united struggles of all the various sections of the masses comprised in that area.[91] This development would mean the rebuilding of the Congress from bottom upwards so that it could become in a real sense the political expression of the united national struggle for emancipation. Establishing a democratic state, guaranteeing to the people their basic economic demands, civil rights, liberties, unhampered economic, political and cultural development of the people eventually opening up the path of socialism would thus emerge as the concomitant outcome.[92]

However, the socialists, unlike Patel, Rajaji and Prasad, failed to capture the minds of the rural India; and they were thus compelled to be in the Congress and use it as a prop for their political survival. Such understanding by the Left of the so-called 'Right' brought out the superficiality in

[89] Ibid., 285.
[90] Ibid., 287.
[91] Ibid.
[92] Ibid.

their branding of Patel, Rajaji and Prasad as 'Right'. The socialists' need for Congress support for achieving their political goal led leaders like Narendra Dev in 1945 to publicly deny the allegation that Patel was trying to seek liquidation of the Congress Socialist Party.[93]

He also refuted the suggestion that Congress was not a peasant organization. Narendra Dev reaffirmed the fact that the right to organize themselves into unions was recognized by the Congress and incorporated in its resolution of fundamental rights adopted at Karachi in 1931. The Haripura session of the Congress held in 1938 discussed the question of relationships between the Congress and the kisan organizations. It recognized the right of the kisans to organize themselves in peasant unions.[94]

> The truth of the matter is that there is no real antagonism between the two, and, as a matter of fact, they are complementary to each other. Each is strengthened by the support of the other, and there is no reason why they should ever come into conflict with each other.[95]

This was the dilemma of the socialists that they opposed the leadership of the Congress as the leaders appeared reformist and therefore 'Rightist'. But the 'Right' had captured the minds of the rural masses, and they realized this. Also, programmatically the 'Right' did not prevent workers' and peasants' mobilization and in fact, often spearheaded it. Hence, they could not openly and single-mindedly confront them as it could have jeopardized their politics within the very Congress fold.

Bose (and Nehru too during his presidential tenure of the Indian National Congress) regarded the Gandhian leaders as 'Right', 'orthodox', 'conservative' and 'old guards'. Their criterion for branding them as 'Right' was the same as that of the socialists, i.e., for not adopting socialism as the creed of the Congress for political, economic, social and cultural regeneration of the nation. But they too were vague in providing concrete definition to their concept of 'Right'. Political issues such as council entry, acceptance or rejection of federation, Presidential issue of 1939, administrative issues regarding functioning of the Congress, formation of its various committees at central and provincial levels, and the question of membership of the Congress became the reasons for branding the Gandhian leaders as the 'Rightist'.

---

[93] Ibid.
[94] Ibid.
[95] Ibid.

Nehru himself was not confident of usage of the term 'Right' for Patel, Rajaji and Prasad,[96] though in February 1938, while defending the Leftists he said, 'Inevitably there is a right wing of the Congress and a left wing and various middle groups, though this simple classification sometimes misleads. An attempt to drive out the left if successful would be fatal.'[97]

Writing in *The National Herald* over Tripuri crisis on 28 February and 1 March to 6 March 1939, Nehru cogitated over the dissensions in the Congress. The very title of his article 'Where Are We?' is indicative of the state of mind Nehru was in.[98] Despite having sympathy for the Left, Nehru did not approve of the style of functioning of Bose. He found Bose's use of radical slogans with authoritarian functioning distasteful.

Nehru accepted that the Congress had not turned socialist despite his being elected as the president of the Congress and the borrowed language from the Western socialist literature of the organized socialist youth showing intemperance and exuberance was never understood by the rank and file of the Congress. Further arguing, Nehru categorically stated that the old leaders were tried men with prestige and influence among the masses and the experience of having guided the struggle for many years. He further elaborated in his article 'Where Are We?' that the

socialists openly talked of replacing the old leadership.... The socialist group, instead of being the crusaders for a new idea, became to some extent a sect seeking power and creating opposition among those who did not fall in line with them.... They (i.e. the old leaders) were not rightist by any means; politically they were far more left and they were confirmed anti-imperialists.[99]

They disliked the intricate theories connected with socialism and thought that socialism was inevitably connected with violence. Above all, they were irritated by the personal attacks and criticism by the socialists.[100]

---

[96] See Nehru's letter to Bose, 4 February 1939, in J. Nehru, ed., *A Bunch of Old Letters* (Bombay, 1958), 307–312.

[97] *Bombay Chronicle*, 17 February 1938, 7.

[98] See S. Gopal, ed., *Selected Works of Jawaharlal Nehru* (henceforth SWJN), Vol. IX (New Delhi, 1976), 494.

[99] Ibid.

[100] Ibid.

In a letter to Bose, dated 4 February 1939, Nehru wrote:

I do not know who you consider a leftist and who a rightist. The way these words were used by you in your statements during the presidential contest seemed to imply that Gandhiji and those who are considered as his group in the working committee are the Rightist leaders. Their opponents, whoever they might be, are the leftist. That seems to me that many of the so-called leftists are more right than the so-called Rightists. Strong language and a capacity to criticize and attack the old Congress leadership is not a test of leftism in politics.... I think the use of the words left and right has been generally wholly wrong and confusing. If instead of these words we talked about policies it would be far better.[101]

Bose adopted a dismissive attitude in his treatment of the senior leaders of the Congress. He aggressively argued that there existed a reformist, 'pacifist' and compromising Right wing in the Congress, willing to align themselves with the imperialist forces in implementing the federation aspect of the Government Act of India, 1935. They dampened the growing radical, revolutionary support among the Congress's social base who in opposition to the Right-wing leaders was clamouring for relaunching of a new more revolutionary struggle which would lead to direct victory.[102]

In his *Indian Struggle*, the set of goals Bose charted out for independent India was not different from the goals of those whom he regarded as the Rightist. He saw the independent Indian state to be an industrialized nation with strong central government, with National Army, manned by civil administration left behind by the British. The state would guarantee complete religious and cultural freedom for the individual, perfect economic and political equality, removal of poverty and unemployment through industrialization and adoption of scientific agricultural technique. National unity would be enforced through radio, cinema and the press, and Hindustani would be made the national language. Labour would be given living wages, sickness insurance and compensation for accident; similarly, peasants would be given relief from excess taxation and indebtedness. Education would be based on Santiniketan, Gurukul and Gandhi's Basic

---

[101] See Nehru's letter to Bose, dated 4 February 1939, in Nehru, *A Bunch of Old Letters*, 307–312.

[102] See Correspondence of Bose with Gandhi, 25–31 March 1939 in R.P. Papers (microfilm), NMML.

Education model.[103] Lastly, the exploiting princes and zamindars would have to go as they would be anachronistic in the new regime.[104]

Bose defined his perspective of independent India as of a socialistic yet liberal and democratic kind. But in the attempt to achieve that goal he harped on his presumed fundamental differences with the 'Right' leadership of the Congress, while seeking their assistance for the realization of his aims at the same time.

Bose's castigation of the old leadership as 'Right' without enumerating his basic ideological differences, if any, with them, and instead highlighting his differences over policy and programme, did not appeal either to the socialists or to Nehru. Herein lay Bose's weakness in formulating his view on the 'Right'.[105] Socialists like Acharya Narendra Dev complained that,

[I]t is difficult to grasp the theory that underlay the activities of Subhas Chandra Bose. He seems to be living from hand to mouth. He talked of an immediate struggle and does all that lies in his power to make it difficult. He goes about attacking the present leadership of the Congress, declaring that it does not want a struggle, and accuses it of consciously working for a compromise. If one were to believe him, the greater obstacle today is the present leadership of the Congress and not British Imperialism. He openly talks of two Congress and of fighting this leadership with a new Swarajist programme probably in alliance with communal organizations. All that he really appears to be concerned with is the struggle for power within the Congress and the national movement. He has helped to disorganize the forces of struggle in Bengal and is out to spread the rot throughout the country. By making the starting of the struggle difficult, he is helping to create conditions that will embolden our enemies.[106]

Thus, the way Bose articulated and conceptualized his difference with the existing leadership of the Congress and seeing the difference within the framework of 'Right' and 'Left' made the concepts more vague and epiphenomenal. It appeared as if Bose was using the term 'Right' to browbeat the senior leaders of the Congress and capture the Congress. The whole range of personal correspondence between him and Gandhi and his associates

[103] See S. Bose, *Indian Struggle 1920–1942* (Bombay, 1964), 453–459.
[104] Ibid.
[105] See Bose–Bapu Correspondence of March 1939 in R.P. Papers, NMML.
[106] See Narendra Dev, 'The Indian Struggle: Next Phase', 19 March 1940, in Sharma, Selected Works, Vol. I, 219.

during the Tripuri crisis points towards the fact that the ideological debate around 'Right' and 'Left' for him was not so grave as to who was at the 'helm of affairs' of the Congress and whether Congress would launch another struggle immediately or not.[107]

Acharya Narendra Dev too complained at the attitude of Bose towards the Congress in 1939:

> This is our grievance against Shree Subhas Chandra Bose. We had trusted that he would not try to break the integrity of the Congress. The passionate appeal for unity that he made at the outbreak of the war is still ringing in our ears. He opposed in the past the present leadership but never worked against the Congress itself. A great change has come over him since. He seems to be bent upon splitting the Congress now. It is difficult to say how much of his anti-compromise talk is serious. It may, of course, just be a good stick to beat the Congress High Command with. Shree Subhas Chandra Bose has not always stood out against compromise like this. During his presidentship he was for negotiations with the British government over the issue of the war. Today, he asserts that the Constituent Assembly can only be convened after the conquest of power. But he conveniently forgets what he wrote in his organ, the Forward Bloc, on September 9, under the caption 'Lead from Wardha'. He says there that the 'Congress must press the national demand on the Government and insist on its immediate fulfillment.' In the same article he proceeds to observe: 'Let not our leaders who are now deliberating at Wardha ask for a whit less than what is our inherent birthright. If they are called on to negotiate, let them do so honourably.' It is said, however, that such things appeal to the average leftist. He has been fed upon slogans and his political education has been neglected. He is politically immature. He acts, therefore, as an unwise ally.[108]

---

[107] The most significant letter throwing light on the above generalization was Patel's letter to Bose, dated April 1939—'In our minds there was never any question of leftist or rightist. Let it be noted that Subhash Babu knows that the method adopted for his own election last year was precisely the same as that which is being adopted now.' See Patel Papers, File No. Lot I-39-I to 3, Ahmedabad.

In another letter dated 24 April 1939, Patel wrote, 'We may differ in our outlook on matters of public importance, but why should there be anything personal amongst comrades who have no other ambition in life except working for the freedom of motherland.' Ibid.

[108] Equally significant and thought provoking are the letters of Bose to Gandhi dated between 25 March 1939 and 6 April 1939 over how superficial the left and right divide actually was. In his letter dated 25 March 1939 to Gandhi, Bose wrote:

The dilemma of the Left and Bose was that no struggle could have a nationwide character without associating Gandhi and his colleagues with it. To have a powerful mass movement, Gandhi's consent and leadership was essential, as masses and classes could not be drawn towards it solely on the strength of the Leftist call. It, therefore, appeared bizarre to ask the Congress to start the struggle, while trying to relegate Gandhi, Patel, Prasad and Rajaji to the background.[109]

Thus, the evidence suggests that there was no historical context befitting the birth of this branding. It was a political nomenclature dictated by politics rather than history. Both Narendra Dev and Nehru accepted the irrelevance of this 'branding'. They accepted the fact that leaders who were referred to as Rightist were more Left than most of the Left and certainly not Rightist by any means. They were men with prestige and influence among the masses and confirmed anti-imperialists. The Left were seen

---

What is your present conception of the composition of the Working Committee? Must it be a homogeneous body or should it be drawn from different parties or groups within the Congress…In my view there are two main parties or 'blocs' in the Congress. They are probably more or less equally balanced. At the Presidential election we had a majority. At Tripuri it was the other way…. If I am to continue as President despite all the obstacles, handicaps and difficulties how would you like me to function? See R.P. Papers, NMML.

On March 1939, Bose wrote to Gandhi:

If we come to the parting of the ways a bitter civil war will commence and whatever be the upshot of it the Congress will be weakened for some time to come…. It is in your hands to save the Congress…. People who are bitterly opposed for various reasons to Sardar Patel and his group, still have confidence in you…. If struggle takes place in our present circumstances, it cannot be a long drawn one. I am so confident and so optimistic on this point that I feel that if we take courage in both our hands and go ahead we shall have swarajya within eighteen months at the most. I feel so strongly on this point that I am prepared to make any sacrifice in this connection. If you take up the struggle, I shall most gladly help you to the best of my ability.

If you feel that the Congress would be able to fight better with another President, I shall gladly step aside. If you feel that the Congress will be able to fight more effectively with a working committee of your choice, I shall gladly fall in line with your wishes. All that I want is that you and the Congress should in this critical hour stand up and resume the struggle for Swarajya.

Ibid. Also see Narendra Dev, 'The Indian Struggle: Next Phase: 19 March 1940, in Sharma, *Selected Works of Acharya Narendra Deva*, 223–224.

[109] Ibid. Socialists lamented at their situation of helplessness emerging due to their minority status in the Congress. They had to keep convincing the 'Right' of their unquestionable loyalty to the Congress. See Ibid., 124.

as vocal but less disciplined, who believed in the propaganda of extreme rhetoric and methods. Their strength lay in their faith that they were destined to be the torchbearers of a new order. Their weakness was that they indulged in textual politics, were unable to appreciate the realities in the country and expected spectacular change.[110] The 'Right' saw them as active, sincere and determined city men bursting with glorious discontent.[111] However, the steel frame of the Congress was the Gandhian leaders who abhorred the 'scorched earth' politics of the Left.

The 'Right' leaders were engaged in the process of making history; they did not relish the tendency of the Left to make politics out of it in order to overcome their own marginalization in the then political milieu. Realizing the historical significance of the anti-imperialist struggle and the 'irrelevance of the branding of the politics of the time into foreign 'Right' and 'Left' categories, they tried to accommodate all different viewpoints. In 1936, when the 'Right'–'Left' debate seemed to be getting aggressive, Patel said that the Congress was a national organization and 'groups of people have a right to influence it by entering it. Congress does not belong to any individual group or political party; it should welcome new ideas and new parties if they are helpful in leading Congress nearer towards its goal of freedom.'[112] Refuting the politics of the socialists, he said that peasants had no parties; therefore, socialists' work lay among the peasants, as socialism could not be brought about by reading Lenin.[113] And Congress goal had already been defined at the Karachi Congress, so it was not proper now to ask for a change by the socialists. Once they finished their fight then there would be time enough to consider what changes were necessary.[114] Pointing out the irrelevance of the socialists' intemperance when confrontation with imperialism was going on Patel pointed out to the socialists:

> There are always two sides of a shield. We cannot afford to forget law of proportional limitations. When our struggle was in full swing we had as far as practicable, accommodated socialism in our programme during the Congress session at Karachi. You have yourself observed, how much less we could put into practices. And now at this moment, when the entire country has become breathless by making wearisome

[110] Ibid., 148–149. For Nehru's views, see SWJN, Vol. 9.
[111] Ibid.
[112] Patel's Speech dated 2 November 1936, in File No. 13 (Congress Affairs 1936–1942) in Lot I-39-I to 3; Patel Papers, SPNM, Ahmedabad.
[113] Ibid.
[114] Ibid.

efforts for the programme, which has proved to be a dismal failure, you are seeking a hundred percent acceptance of socialism, thinking that the failure of our struggle was due to inherent drawback in our programme! All these clearly show that what you are advocating is far from practicable. I do not believe that there is any wisdom in raising bookish quarrels, lest breaches occur in our already weakened strength and we miss the main points of our struggle against the foreign power.[115]

The Congress 'Right' were all for accommodation in the struggle for independence; they did not view the politics of united India in terms of 'Right' and 'Left'. Patel articulated the Congress 'Right' stance quite categorically. To quote:

We elders have no craze for power as some young people believe. When we were young we carried on struggle in the way we understood and did all possible things we could. You shall now do the remaining work. At a future date when you are prepared, we would also be ready at the same moment to hand over to you the reins of power, and shall bless you that your path may become benevolent. Whenever the Congress determines any programme for implementation, we shall be prepared to render all possible assistance as and when you demand. But there is no justice in your asking us to act as per your whims and create hindrances in our way and want us to concede to the conditions put forth by you. Neither you, nor we, nor Congress shall be benefited by following that path.[116]

---

[115] Patel's Speech at Benaras Vidyapith on 1 August 1934. See Chopra, *The Collected Works*, Vol. IV, 174.
[116] Ibid., 175.

2

Social Vision of the Congress 'Right'

The country is treading in darkness on one foot and that too of a male. They are being constantly hammered that they have to shoulder the burden of the house as far as possible. He has not been taught to accept that. In social and national spheres women have some rights and responsibilities. That is why we are lagging behind. Women in one way are extremely courageous. Men do not endure the miseries to the extent women do. In India misery is destined in women's fate and she smilingly endures them. She is not aware of her rights. The society fears that if she is educated she would have knowledge of her rights and will shake off the privations. But that fear is uncalled for. What is good for man is good for women also. The society adopts a partisan attitude between a male and a female. It pardons a male but a woman is permanently censured and disgraced, if she commits a blunder. So long as women are not sufficiently educated and inculcated with national spirit, till then there will be no prosperity.

—Sardar Patel[1]

One of the reasons for the Congress 'Right' being dubbed as such has been the inadequate understanding or misunderstanding of their social vision and perspective. Their approach to social issues has often been viewed as epiphenomenal or peripheral to their core concern of anti-imperialist struggle. In this chapter an attempt will be made to study their social vision and its place in their overall perspective of the movement.

The Congress 'Right', as would be clear in the subsequent discussion, were deeply concerned with the social ills which were retarding the growth of Indian society and making it decrepit. For the success of the anti-imperialist movement, a healthy social foundation was an essential precondition. The anti-imperialist movement would liven up the dormant political consciousness of the masses, and strong social foundations would make acceptance of anti-imperialist ideology an easy process. They, therefore, wanted the Congress to seriously take up social issues such as child marriage, untouchability, women's rights and education, rural indebtedness, dowry,

---

[1] Patel's Speech at Jyoti Sangh, Ahmedabad, 2 October 1934. See Chopra, *The Collected Works*, Vol. IV, 214.

widowhood, conversion, purdah, cleanliness and personal hygiene in particular and the social degradation caused by the dominance of Brahmanism and ritualism in general.

The Congress 'Right' were believers in the efficacy of tradition. They were modern in their ideology and perception but traditionalist in their treatment of issues. This aspect of their approach was not understood by the 'revolutionaries' who were persuaded greatly by their own narrow confines of ideology.

The understanding of social issues by the Congress 'Right' was quite advanced in perception and ideology. Their approach was indigenous and ingenuous, pragmatic and realistic, progressive and purposive. They talked of tradition not for its preservation as such but for progressive change in the social structure without any sharp and abrupt rupture. This aspect of the 'Right' will become more pronounced in the course of discussion of the social issues in the succeeding pages.[2]

PATEL ON CASTE SYSTEM

Born in a peasant caste which was deeply embedded in the *bhakti* tradition and Swami Narayan cult, Patel was opposed not only to Brahmanical social order but also to ritualized Hinduism and its various rites of passage associated with birth and death. He believed in plain speaking and was forthright and frank in expressing his view, and was highly critical of Brahmanical order and its imposition and perpetuation of the caste system:

> I do not believe in any caste or community. The whole of India is my village and men of all communities are my friends and relations. All are children of the same God. After a man dies does anyone ask if the corpse is that of a Brahman or a Chamar![3]

While referring to the Guruvayur movement, Patel blamed the Brahmins for practising falsehood and deceit in the name of protecting Hindu religion.[4] According to him:

> Hindu religion is at present divided and it now exists only in any outward show, such as applying religious sectarian mark on the

---

[2] Social views of each leader would be discussed separately.
[3] Parikh, *Sardar Vallabhbhai Patel*, Vol. II (Ahemdabad, 1956; reprint, 1971), 456.
[4] Patel to Sri Purushottamdas, 2 May 1935. See Chopra, *The Collected Works*, Vol. IV, 21.

forehead, glimpses of deities and in undertaking religious tours of sacred places of pilgrimage. But the true Hindu religion consists in practicing control of the senses, abstaining from sensual pleasures and in realization of Supreme Being i.e. God.[5]

Patel's vision of free India was:

> In free India there can be no distinction of caste, creed or religion or of classes, resulting in the domination of one section over another. There may be rich and poor, happy and unhappy, but there can be no difference in stature between one citizen and the other.[6]

The strength of Hindu society was, however, seen by Patel in its ability to adjust itself to the changing conditions. Strongly criticizing those who gave the cry of Hinduism being in danger, Patel said:

> Do not be led away that Hinduism is in danger. Hinduism can never be in danger in India. Have we not produced men of religion all over India? What did Shankracharya do? When he died how young he was! But did he raise the cry that Hinduism was in danger? Religion is a matter between man and his maker. If you forget your citizenship and talk of religion it is a cloak. Therefore when I hear some people talking about Hinduism in danger I feel that they are going a wrong way. Do not indulge in scaremongering for selfish ends. Do not employ wrong methods for catching votes or forming the parties. It is a very dangerous game. After all, we too want to serve our own people.[7]

Endowed with a robust sense of peasant pragmatism, Patel abhorred show of any kind of religious duplicity. In his speeches at Dharmshala, Kashindra, Baila and Chaloda in Ahmedabad district on 2 January 1935, he criticized religious hypocrisy and evils of the caste system. He cautioned the rural population that unless they did away with such evils, 'true *swarajya*' would be elusive:

---

[5] Sardar Patel's Speech at Seth Maganlal Chaganlal Hindu Chatralay, Prantij, Gujarat, dated 22 October 1935. See ibid., Vol. V, 180–181.

[6] Patel's Speech at Jodhpur on 25 January 1949. See Nandurkar, *Sardar Patel—In Tune with the Millions-II*, 56.

[7] Patel's Speech at Ernakulam on 13 May 1949. See ibid., 100.

Religion is confined only to the religious signs on the body, glimpses of the deity and outward behaviours. We commit sins for as long as 25 years and go to Ganges in a year for bathing. Are people absolved of sins by taking a bath in the Ganges in a year? I therefore advise you for your own benefit to learn to live like members of the same family in the villages because where there is unity, there is peace and where peace exists eternally it becomes an abode of God.[8]

The Right-wing leaders largely accepted the constructive programme of Gandhi and through it they tried to expand the area of influence of anti-imperialism. Their speeches against ritualism, untouchability and social obscurantism were intended to serve the twin purpose of spreading the Gandhian ideology of *swarajya* and inculcating the spirit of social reform. Patel reminded the farmers that there could not be any caste or religious distinctions amongst them. He said:

Farmers who till the land, whether small zamindars, farmers or agricultural labourers are essentially farmers, regardless of the caste and the religion to which they belong. All are in the same boat; they will sink or swim together. Nature does not recognize any differences on the basis of caste or religion; Nature smiles or frowns on everybody in the same manner. All the farmers find themselves in the same economic trouble.[9]

UNTOUCHABILITY AND CONVERSION

Patel wished every member of scheduled caste to feel that he was superior to the Brahman.[10] Exposing the hollowness of the caste system, he held caste Hindus responsible for the plight of untouchables:

Many superstitions and hypocritical practices are rampant among the farmers and they are all there in the name of religion. We reject our Harijan brothers whose services are needed not only in

[8] Patel's Speech at Ahmedabad on 2 January 1935. See Chopra, *The Collected Works*, Vol. V, 12.

[9] Patel's Presidential Address at the Allahabad Kisan Conference on 28 April 1935. See ibid., 90.

[10] Patel's Speech at New Delhi on 2 January 1949. See Nandurkar, *Sardar Patel: In Tune with the Millions*, Vol. II, 56.

agriculture but also in things nobody else is able to do and we hurt them, all in the name of religion. This is a sin. When a person we call an untouchable embraces another religion he immediately becomes touchable.[11]

Patel exhorted the high castes to treat Harijans as equals and eradicate untouchability from their minds:

I advise you to abolish untouchability which is a curse to the Hindu community of India. You cannot discard your own brother. According to the Hindu philosophy it is a sin to discard anyone who is living. Soul is God and even an untouchable has soul in him. You therefore cannot discard God-Soul.[12]

He believed that along with achieving *swarajya* it was equally essential for the upper caste ego to attain sublimity by shedding their caste arrogance and accepting untouchables in their fold. He castigated upper castes for not giving proper respect to Dr Ambedkar:

Dr Ambedkar studied with you and also took up employment along with you. However you behaved with him in such a manner that he has nurtured nothing but hatred for you. If a Harijan converts himself into Christianity, the orthodox would push him out, but if he remains a Harijan, people treat him as if he were not a human being. Gandhiji undertook fast to prevent division of the Hindu community and forced changes in the Communal Award but no purpose would be served if untouchability is not eradicated from your mind.[13]

Patel was perturbed that untouchability made the position of national leaders like him morally weak in the eyes of the British who exploited the situation to argue that the Indians were incapable of ruling themselves.[14]

---

[11] Patel's Speech at Allahabad on 28 April 1935. See Chopra, *The Collected Works*, Vol. V, 81–91.

[12] Patel's Speech at Prantij Taluka, Local Board on 23 October 1935. See ibid., 175–177.

[13] Patel's Speech at Vadodara on 7 January 1935. See File No. Lot 137–1 to 8, Patel Papers, SPNM.

[14] Patel's Address at Nadiad on 29 December 1934, *Home Political Proceedings*, File No. 28/12/36, National Archives of India (hereafter NAI), New Delhi.

He did not want conversions to be used by the British to show to the outside world how retrogressive, backward and inhuman the Indian society was.[15] He rebuked the high castes: 'If a Dhod becomes a Christian or a Mussalman he can go where he likes. The Sanatan religion has come to such a low degree that a man of other religion came to defend it.'[16] Using social issues as a tool to explain the political situation, Patel used opportunities to create awareness against divisive elements in the society on the one hand and to highlight how it could be exploited by Britishers to enslave India to their interests on the other. Referring to Communal Award and how it was used as a bait to divide the Indians, Patel said:

> The British Empire feels that we have been defeated or are reeling under fear of the authority which has been puffed up with violence.... We have to continue and strengthen the struggle through self purification.... We are not strong enough to protect our own religion. So if our traditional religion may have reached a stage where a foreigner has to search we should perform the shradh ceremony so as to attain emancipation. In the new reforms a plan was put forth to divide the Hindu community into two divisions. The larger division may be amalgamated with such other castes and other co-religionists in such a way as would result in suffocating the so-called high caste Hindus. But I had a companion in Yeravada Jail, who was clad only in loins. He had given a notice to the Government that he would not allow them to interfere in our established religion. If they were trying to segregate the untouchables permanently, he would lay down his life by fasting unto death.[17]

> You may perhaps be aware what the leaders of the Sanatan traditional religion were doing at that moment? Where had they gone? Does the traditional religion belong to the present age? It is current since the time of the Vedas. How many have been converted to Christianity? How many have become Muslims? Who are these traditionalists? They are converting only Hindus into their religious fold. Who are these Missionaries? If you had not treated the

---

[15] Ibid.
[16] Ibid.
[17] Patel's Speech at Allahabad Kisan Conference on 28 April 1935. See Chopra, *The Collected Works*, Vol. V, 89.

untouchables inferior even to dogs, would there have been so many Christians?[18]

Patel empathized with Ambedkar and acknowledged how difficult his task was, but he also requested him not to be too harsh on the high caste Hindus. With reference to the Kavitha episode, where upper castes boycotted Harijans over the issue of permitting Harijan students to study together with the upper caste students in the same school, Patel said: 'Voice of change will seep in slowly as upper castes are "backward and roll in ignorance", but conversion is not the answer.'[19] In his reply to Ambedkar over conversion, he wrote:

> You have stated that untouchability is like a disease in the stomach. It is not going to be cured by applying oil on the stomach; it should be cured by surgery only. You are now prepared to tender advice to the people about conversion. It appears impossible to concur with your surgery on the stomach, you are now telling people to apply knife on the throat and chop off head from the body for getting rid of the stomach disease. Therefore, in spite of having extreme regard and sympathy for you, I am forced to disagree with you. The path you have chosen is quite hazardous. I am fully aware that you are in such adverse circumstances that I would hesitate to criticize you, even if you commit mistakes.[20]

The traditionalist in Patel revolted against conversion, but the reformer in him opposed Brahmanism and its perpetuation of untouchability, and thus, he favoured temple entry and common school for Harijan and upper caste students.

Patel had deep-rooted abhorrence for untouchability. He not only sat amidst the untouchables but also spoke from within their enclosure. With this one significant gesture Patel publicly cemented the wide gulf between 'touchability and untouchability'[21] and left a deep impact on the kisans of Kathiawad.[22]

[18] Patel's Speech at Nadiad on 1 January 1935, 5. See ibid.
[19] Patel to Ambedkar, 8 November 1935. See ibid., 192–194.
[20] Ibid.
[21] Rajmohan Gandhi, *Patel: A Life*, Ahmedabad, 1990, 111–112.
[22] Ibid. Addressing kisans in Bihar, Patel said, 'You kisans who have become willing victims to the tyranny of the zamindar and the Brahmin do not deserve the name of kisans.' See Parikh, *Sardar Vallbhbhai Patel*, Vol. I, 407.

TEMPLE ENTRY

Patel, Prasad and Rajaji were ardent supporters of temple entry programme of the Congress meant for the untouchables. Patel favoured opening of the Somnath temple to Harijans. When Rajaji was facing difficulty in getting the law passed on temple entry during his tenure as premier of Madras Presidency in 1939, Patel stood like a rock behind him and gave full support both moral as well as organizational.[23]

STATUS OF WOMEN

The most significant aspect of Patel's attempt at social reform was the vigorous attack he launched against the servile status of women. He attributed the backwardness of the nation to men, who had not given equal rights and responsibilities to women. Addressing the women members of Jyotisangh at Ahmedabad on 2 October 1934, he said:

> The country is treading in darkness on one foot and that too of a male. They are being constantly hammered that they have to shoulder the burden of the house as far as possible. He has not been taught to accept that. In social and national spheres women have some rights and responsibilities. That is why we are lagging behind. Women in one way are extremely courageous. Men do not endure the miseries to the extent women do. In India misery is destined in women's fate and she smilingly endures them. She is not aware of her rights. The society fears that if she is educated she would have knowledge of her rights and will shake off the privations. But that fear is uncalled for. What is good for man is good for women also. The society adopts a partisan attitude between a male and a female. It pardons a male but a woman is permanently censured and disgraced, if she commits a blunder. So long as women are not sufficiently educated and inculcated with national spirit, till then there will be no prosperity.[24]

The unique mix of tradition and modernity in Patel's thinking can easily be traced. While admiring institutions like Jyotisangh, he said:

---

[23] Ibid.

[24] Patel's Speech at Jyoti Sangh at Ahmedabad on 2 October 1934. See Chopra, *The Collected Works*, Vol. IV, 214.

'We are still entertaining the belief that women have to look after their home and hearth only. Such ignorance can be removed by these types of institutions.'[25] His modernity is quite conspicuous in his advocacy for women's education and branching out of their areas of operation from the confines of homes and hearth while his deep-rooted traditionalism was reflected in his statement like, 'future depends on the chastity of girl students'.[26]

There was a curious amalgamation of traditionalism with modernity in the approaches of all the three 'Right' leaders to various social issues. It would not be appropriate to regard them as socially regressive and conservative leaders. If Patel laid emphasis on the chastity of girl students, he also favoured co-education for the girls:

> Experiments of co-education are rare in schools, but what I have heard and witnessed is that nowhere else I have come across such blind trust and confidence reposed by parents of pupils as is witnessed here in this institution. It is very difficult at least in our country to take care of girl students. It is considered very dangerous, causing constant anxiety, but the fact that they have accepted this challenge is a matter of great pleasure to me.[27]

CHILD MARRIAGE

Sensitive to social issues and concerns, Patel attacked child marriage. Advising the villagers of Gujarat against child marriage, he told them:

> If you do not stop child marriage you will degenerate and the progeny will be very weak. Why should the government frame laws and tell you that there should be no child marriage? You should understand your welfare of what use the progeny of such weaklings will be to the country? Weak persons can never take or retain swarajya.[28]

[25] Ibid.
[26] Patel's Speech at Arya Kanya Mahavidyalaya, Vadodara, 9 January 1935. See ibid., Vol. V, 25.
[27] Patel's Speech at Ahmedabad, 6 January 1935. Ibid., 20–21.
[28] Patel's Speech at Ahmedabad, 2 January 1935. Ibid., 9.

In all his speeches, Patel consistently attacked the prevalence of early marriage among the farmers,

> One social evil, one finds among the farmers, is that they marry their children at an early age. Burdening young children with family responsibilities at such a tender age is akin to murdering them…it is a matter of shame for us that the government had to pass a bill to prohibit child marriages. This is cited as a reason for our being unfit for swarajya.[29]

STATUS OF WIDOWS

Patel was equally perturbed at the status of the widows in the Indian society. Writing to Manibehn about Sukanya, sister of Gandhian Worker Usha Mehta, who had become a widow at an early age, Patel highlighted,

> The one who experiences this sorrow does not wish a rebirth. Now they will shave her head and keep her confined in a dark room for six or twelve months. The society is replete with people who view widows as carrier of curse and bad omen. That is why she has to live in perpetual fear. The relatives would make a claim to whatever property her husband had left behind and this would further bring misery in her life. Nobody else in the world has as difficult a life as the Hindu widow. The social taboos and the society's behaviour towards her tend to be so wicked that even for her to survive becomes impossible. She is educated and today there are institutions, which sympathize with the problems of widows. Therefore she can lead a comfortable life by entering into one of these institutions and by doing some good work for the society.[30]

Patel empathized with the pitiable existence of the widowed women. However, he did not see their redemption in remarriage. He preferred for

---

[29] Patel's Presidential Address at Allahabad Kisan Conference, 28 April 1935. Ibid., 156.
[30] Patel to Manibehn, 27 December 1944. See G.M. Nandurkar, ed., *Sardar Shree ke Vishishta Aur Anokhe Patra* (Ahmedabad, 1981), 386.

them a life-long engagement in a career of social welfare and social service. He wrote:

> In Europe such widows remarry after a year or two after their husband's death. Such instances are on the increase even in our society these days. But their number however is still very small. Who can say as to how much comfort a remarriage brings? In Europe lakhs of such women spend their whole life helping the sick people through training as nurse. In our country there are few girls from the upper sections of the society who will take to this path. Otherwise there could not be a better vocation for a widow than this one.[31]

Thus, while the analysis of the condition of widows in India was objective and rational, the solution Patel suggested remained confined within the matrix of tradition. Therefore, nuances of this kind made Patel appear a 'Rightist' to the westernized intellectuals in the country. His ideas are, however, to be understood in totality of the context, and not in fragments.

Patel stood for liberation of women from the yoke of ignorance, illiteracy and superstition. He wanted women to achieve freedom with a sense of responsibility and participate along with men in the struggle for *swarajya*. 'The brave women of Mansa stood side by side with men and showed marvellous courage, strength of will and purpose. They ungrudgingly suffered all hardships, insult and even physical injury.'[32]

PURDAH

Patel exhorted men not to keep their women in purdah. To him keeping them in purdah was like keeping them away from knowledge and enlightenment. He wanted women to come out from the shackles of illiteracy and acquire knowledge to know what was happening in the world as well as her duties towards her motherland and to provide courage, support and sustenance to the struggle for *swarajya*. He said:

> You must discard the purdah. You must allow women to see the world outside so that they will realize their duties to the motherland. They

[31] Patel's letter to Manibehn, 27 December 1944. Ibid.

[32] Patel's statement to the press in support of activists of Mansa, dated 12 June 1938. See Patel Papers, File No. I-33-4 in Lot 1-33 1 to 4, SPNM.

must be made literate and acquainted with India's affairs. Without it, they will not be able to play their proper role in shaping the destiny of the country; it would be like a cart going on one wheel.[33]

DIVORCE

Patel's strong sense of justice made him protest against any kind of exploitation of women. He even stood for divorce for women, if the situation was not compatible for them. However, he was sensitive enough to visualize the problem divorce might give rise to. Therefore, he reprimanded men to change their ways and atone for their sins if they wanted their wives to be with them. He expressed these views in a letter to Jayantilal Patel dated 3 June 1949:

> You have yourself committed such grave sins that you will have to do Herculean efforts to mitigate their effects. It is futile on your part to seek divorce from your wife. You have absolutely no right to do so as you have done her a great injustice. On the other hand if she herself decides to seek divorce from you, she is fully justified in doing so. So if you wish to undergo penance for your sins, being in the prime of life, you have yet time to alter the course of your life. So instead of craving for the parental property, you must make a resolve to lead a life of purity and service. If you would succeed in this attempt, may be your wife too would like to rejoin you in your changed course of life.[34]

Keeping this aspect of Patel in view it appears that the branding of Patel as a Rightist is more political and ideological than historical.

OTHER SOCIAL EVILS

Patel aimed at healthy, vibrant, and full of life *swarajya* and not pale, diseased, poverty-stricken *swarajya*. Therefore, he often not only inspired the villagers to give up social evils such as untouchability and child marriage, but also encouraged them to go for education, give up drinking, opium eating, keep the village and themselves clean, curtail expenses on marriage

---

[33] Patel's Speech at Udaipur, 4 January 1949. See Nandurkar, *Sardar Patel: In Tune with the Millions-I*, 41.

[34] Patel to Jayantilal M. Patel, 3 June 1949. See Nandurkar, *Sardar's Letters: Mostly Unknown-II*, 265.

and 'Preeti Bhojan' (meal after death).[35] He advised the peasants not to incur debt and fall into the trap of moneylenders. If need be they should borrow from one another. He also advised them to spend on the education, clothing and food for their children. He also advised them to build dispensaries and schools.[36]

Speaking at Prantej Municipality on 22 October 1935, he expressed anguish at the lack of basic medical facilities to take care of delivery cases.

> How much disgusting it is that in such a big town there is not a single maternity home for attending to delivery cases? These are bare necessities of the present times and we have ourselves to solve these problems. We are not weak so as to beg from government for help on each and every occasion. We should understand our own responsibilities.[37]

PROHIBITION

Drinking being common among the tribal and lower castes, Patel saw it as another major social evil in the path of reform of these sections of the society and major obstruction in their participation in the struggle for *swarajya*.

> I tell the Bhils, Gamits and Chodra breathen to be bold. God has bestowed hands, eyes and ears equitably to all. As you are ignorant you are consuming liquor and behaving like beasts. I advise you to abstain from these vices.[38]

Patel was perturbed that evil influence of drinking was leading the farmers into the clutches of moneylenders and sending them further into the

---

[35] Patel speaking at Kavitha, Ahmedabad on 2 January 1935. See Chopra, *The Collected Works*, Vol. V, 9, 44.

[36] Patel speaking at Prantej Municipality on 22 October 1935 said, 'Stop community feasting, stop taking food in dirty environments in connection with marriage ceremonies and in obsequial ceremonies and divert the finances to education so that you will digest whatever education you have received.' Ibid., 178.

[37] Ibid.

[38] Ibid., 28. In his address to the Bhil Sewa Mandal on 17 February 1935, Patel reprimanded *Bhils* and advised them 'to stand on their legs, to store up grain sufficient for their necessities, to spin and weave their own cloth, not to drink, not to spend money on marriage and other ceremonies. They must learn in order to be free from the clutches of the Sahukars.' Ibid., 40.

deep pit of poverty. Broken in spirit and morale they could never become the pillars of strength for the struggle for *swarajya*. Speaking at the Eighth Raniparaj Conference at Baroda, he said:

> We are losing our bread in two ways. One is the consumption of liquor. Those who are addicted to it might as well not earn, because what they produce during the day, they spend it in the evening at the liquor or the toddy shop. A person who is addicted to liquor does not have intelligence. Sometimes we hear complaints that if there is prohibition people will produce their own liquor in their homes. This would be a double sin because, on the one hand, it is an offence against the law, and on the other, a sin against God because by doing this you would be destroying the beautiful body God has given you. If God had intended your body to be receptacle for liquor he might as well have made a cask.[39]

The evil of drinking had permeated so deeply among the lower castes that Patel favoured prohibition and along with other Congress leaders like Prasad and Rajaji made it one of the central social issues to be dealt with firmly by the Congress ministries.

> It is not correct to say that the Congress ministers are more anxious to introduce prohibition than to do anything for the removal of untouchability and uplift of the oppressed and depressed. Both these problems are equally important and all Congress ministries have to give priority to both prohibition and removal of untouchability. I do not agree at all with your views about prohibition. India is not Britain, America or France. Its culture and civilization is entirely different from the Western countries. In their civilization prohibition has no place. In India both Hindus and Muslims consider intoxication as a loathsome vice and drink is forbidden by religion. Half of the untouchability problem will be solved by successful prohibition, as it is largely amongst the so-called untouchables and the oppressed and depressed where this evil has played havoc.[40]

---

[39] Ibid., 45–46.
[40] Patel's letter to T.M. Pillai dated 2 June 1946. See Nandurkar, *Sardar's Letters: Mostly Unknown*, Vol. I, 281.

ASHRAMS FOR POPULARIZING
CONSTRUCTIVE WORK

To carry out the programme of social reform, Patel supervised the establishment of ashrams all over Gujarat, e.g., Bedchchi Ashram where young men were taught to weave. They were told to use *charkha* as it would lead them to freedom from *sahukar* as well as from the British. Harijan Ashram carried out significant work among the untouchables, under the charge of Narharibhai Parikh. He also looked after the education of village boys at Ras. Ashrams such as Satyagraha Ashram, Sabarmati Ashram, Kasturba Seva Ashram, Morali Ashram, Kathiawar Harijan Sevak Sangh, Surat Patidar Ashram, Bhil Sewa Mandal, Poona Mahua Ashram, Navasari Ashram, Kidhwa Ashram, etc., played a significant role in the spread of education of both boys and girls, in educating the people to give up oppressive customs and social evils like untouchability, drinking and *preeti bhoj*.[41]

Speaking at the Harijan Ashram, Ahemdabad, on 3 October 1934, Patel reminded the inmates of the Ashram of what should be the role of the ashram in the struggle for *swarajya*, 'to cultivate strength so that they could overcome severe tests and to inculcate in them national spirit and build up character.'[42]

EDUCATION

Patel laid great emphasis on the spread of education. He viewed it as the only means to remove backwardness, superstition, illiteracy, ritualism and poverty. However, he stressed on *swadeshi* education. 'It is really shameful, if a missionary school is functioning here. They educate our children by fathoming a distance of 5,000 miles and we do not teach our children.'[43]

---

[41] Chopra, *The Collected Works*, Vol. V, 46. Bhil Sewa Mandal was managing four Ashrams, the significant being the Mirakhedi Ashram, 22 schools and one dispensary. Ibid., 40.

[42] Ibid., Vol. IV, 215. In his address at Ahmedabad on 2 October 1934 Patel said, 'I feel that Ashram is as good as my own home. I learnt here lessons of service to the nation as well as of struggle for freedom.' Ibid., 212.

[43] Sardar Patel's Speech at Prantej Municipality on 22 October 1935. Ibid., Vol. V, 179.

According to him, *swadeshi* education should aim at training the children to remain loyal as well as courteous towards parents, their motherland and religion. Their character, courage and heroism should also be built up. In his view,

> The greatest defect of modern education is that children are neither loyal to their motherland nor behave like Indians. Their life is in doldrums. So weak are they rendered, as if they are devoured by white ants and they roam helter skelter in search of jobs. They turn averse to their family, country as well as parents. The chief malady is the foreign power and unstable politics.[44]

KHADI AND *CHARKHA*: TOOLS OF *SWADESHI* AND SELF-RELIANCE

Besides untouchability, prohibition and education, another major focus of Patel's social criticism was of peasants' indebtedness to moneylenders and their indifference towards village industries.[45] Revitalization of the village industries through khadi and *charkha*, in his view, could lead to removal of poverty. He, therefore, advised the peasantry to use *charkha* as it would not only make them self-reliant in their need for cloth, but also restore their self-respect and spirit for freedom, besides providing employment to the lakhs of carpenters and blacksmiths.[46] He denounced excessive mechanization. 'People who are engrossed with the ideas of western civilization may think that only the machine would solve the problem of Indian poverty by a process of mechanization. But it is evident that the machine cannot put all the unemployed to work.'[47] Patel reiterated, 'True socialism lies in the development of the village industries. We do not want to reproduce in our country the chaotic conditions prevalent in the western countries consequent on mass production.'[48]

[44] Ibid., 180.
[45] Ibid., 216.
[46] Patel speaking at Dholka, Ahmedabad on 21 January 1935 said, 'Some 150 years ago we used to prepare our own cloth. Just imagine how many lakhs of charkhas and rentiers must have been working then and how many lakhs of carpenters, blacksmiths must be getting their earnings.' Ibid., 8.
[47] Ibid., 77.
[48] Ibid., 21.

RAJAJI: BRAHMANISM AND CASTE SYSTEM

Rajaji, who was brought up in a conservative Brahmin family, was exposed to nationalism rooted in Hindu scriptures and traditions at an impressionable age at Salem. He later came to believe in Tilak's aggressive politics. But he was a liberal traditionalist who was largely concerned with social problems such as untouchability, inhuman living conditions of lower castes, inequality perpetuated on women, evil social customs like child marriage, ritualism, etc. He adhered to social customs but not uncritically. Throughout his political career he was a rebel with social sensitivity.[49] Like Patel, he believed in evolutionary process of change and therefore favoured introduction of reforms in such a manner which would not cause any major social dissonance, and divert the attention and energy of the people from struggle for *swarajya*.[50]

Although he would sport his Vaishnav *tilak* on his forehead in his early days, he was a product of the liberal education system, which focused on synthesis of Hindu, Islamic and Christian civilizations. He was not only exposed to the study of the classics of his own culture, but he also made extensive and in-depth reading of the Western religious literature.[51] He vehemently spoke and took steps to eradicate untouchability, illiteracy and superstition. He advocated against child marriage, evils of drinking and stood for women's education, divorce and inter-caste marriage.

Rajaji initiated measures against untouchability and attacked and questioned the relevance of the caste system. 'Dear young men, if you wish to

---

[49] Rajmohan Gandhi, *A Warrior from the South: The Rajaji Story I* (Madras: Bharatam, 1978), 227–228.

[50] Ibid.

[51] Rajaji in his Speech at Bombay said:

> When straying from the studies prescribed for me when I was young, I read Bunyan's Pilgrims Progress and chapters in the Old and New Testament of the Bible and later I acquainted myself with the thoughts of Socrates, Marcus Aurelins and Brother Lawrence, the joy and reverence within me swelled towards the Upanishads, the Gita and Mahabharata though no one incited me to it. All spiritual search is one and God blesses it whenever it is done and by whomsoever. If I am today a devout though very imperfect Hindu Vedanti, it is not less due to my contact with some of the sacred books of other people than to the contemplation of what our own great ancestors have left for us. Not by total exclusion of all religion and spiritual thought but by all embracing acquaintance and appreciation of spiritual thought of kinds shall we be safe and shape ourselves properly.

C. Rajagopalachari, *Governor General's Speeches 1948–1950* (New Delhi, 1950), 262.

help the abolition of caste, do so by all means, intermarry. There is legal provision for this open and straightforward attack on caste. There is no other way to abolish it.'[52]

Rajaji not only stood for the removal of the abuses of caste system but also sought to redefine caste. His attempt through social reform was towards integration of the Harijan with the caste Hindus and allocation of new social status to them. These measures he sought to achieve through his programme of temple entry and prohibition.[53]

TEMPLE ENTRY

The anti-untouchability campaign of Rajaji increasingly centred around the issue of temple entry in South India. He carried out the campaign at both the grassroots level by gaining entry for Harijans to significant temples like the Guruvayur temple and at the provincial and national level through legislatures, by trying to get general legislation passed, when he was premier of Madras presidency in 1937.[54] The temple being a dominant centre of power and privilege in South India, the attempt to secure rights for the untouchables to enter into temples was certainly a radical endeavour.

To carry out wide-scale propaganda and publicity for the attempt and to gain public sympathy for the cause, Rajaji fought the case of a Harijan's entry into Tirupati, as early as in 1924 and got him acquitted. While explaining the case, Rajaji wrote to Mahadev Desai,

> I suppose every rule is observed best by the breach of the letter of it when an occasion demands it. The case of a simple, devoted and earnest soul rushing into the temple with coconut and camphor in hand and clothed in bark and sacred marks and returning home and taking him to court where he is punished as having defiled a temple…. That even if the entry could be a civil trespass according to the law, it could not be desecrating under the Penal Code when it was proved that, as far as he was concerned, he went to worship and not to desecrate. The argument was accepted and the man acquitted.[55]

[52] Rajaji's Speech at Madras, 2 January 1948. Ibid., 197–198.

[53] Rajaji said, 'Time will come when the scavenger will be considered the most honourable man in the State as now the mother is considered in the household.' C. Rajagopalachari, *Chats Behind Bars* (Madras, 1931), 34.

[54] Ibid.

[55] Rajaji to Mahadev Desai, 24 December 1925. Rajaji Papers, NMML.

The case got wide publicity and in a letter to Gandhi dated 19 January 1926, he wrote:

The contagion has caught on. Another man charged for temple entry has been let off on the summary ground that a man going to worship could not be said to have insulted religion and this without any appearance or argument—and in Malabar.[56]

PROHIBITION

Linked with the temple entry was the issue of prohibition. Rajagopalachari's involvement on this issue was complete and unrestricted. He launched the attack on the evils of drinking through speeches, bringing out magazines such as *Prohibition* and *Vimochanam* that he edited, and holding anti-drinking *sabhas*.[57] The Gandhi Ashram at Pudupalayam near Tiruchengode became the centre of the prohibition movement throughout India. However, Rajaji faced great odds. In the first place, it was difficult to persuade the government, which was so dependent on excise revenue to accept prohibition. Secondly, provincial Congress Committees too were not showing much enthusiasm for this cause. Rajaji wrote to Nehru:

The great expectations that people all over the world entertain in regard to our Prohibition agitation are however likely to be disappointed if our Congress Committees will not rise to the occasion. In spite of many reminders, many of them do not take any interest. If you can send something special to all the Committees under your signature, there may be some result.[58]

Although Nehru himself was not very enthusiastic about devoting so much energy and time to prohibition, yet he offered his support to Rajaji. In his reply to Rajaji, dated 9 September 1930, he wrote: 'Certainly I shall do what I can to help you in your campaign. I must confess to you however that I do not feel terribly excited about it.'[59] Nehru nevertheless complied

[56] Rajaji to Gandhi, 19 January 1926. Ibid.
[57] C. Rajagopalachari, *Indian Prohibition Manual* (1936).
[58] Rajaji to Nehru, 26 August 1930. Rajaji Papers, NMML.
[59] Nehru to Rajaji, 9 September 1930. Ibid.

and through a circular of 10 September 1930, he instructed the Congress Committees to cooperate:

> I trust you agree with me in thinking that the campaign has not only considerable social and economic value, but also political value and a nationwide agitation will undoubtedly help our cause greatly. Will you kindly circulate your district and town committees and induce them to take part in the campaign?[60]

However, in 1937, with the formation of Congress Ministries, prohibition programme gained strength and despite loss in excise revenue, Rajaji was able to present a balanced budget in the Madras legislature. He got a law enacted, imposing prohibition in the Madras province. The first district to which he made the Madras Prohibition Act, 1937, applicable was his own home district of Salem.

KHADI AND VILLAGE INDUSTRIES: *SWADESHI* AND SELF-RELIANCE

Along with prohibition, Rajaji from his Ashram at Tiruchengode launched extensive movement to publicize and popularize khadi. He regarded it as an ameliorative measure for the chronic problem of poverty and underemployment. In the ashram its manufacture thrived during conditions of famine. When rains failed, the unemployed peasants came to the ashram and did spinning of khadi yarn to earn some income. In more normal times the women would only come in after the harvest period.[61] Rajaji submitted reports on khadi productions in the ashram and sponsored khadi exhibitions. He criticized Congressmen who paid only lip service to khadi popularization campaign.

> Even in our own lifetime we have begun to make mere ceremonial worships of the Mahatma's doctrines. People who do not know how to spin at all compose verses about khadar and the charkha. While this kind of ceremonial has begun during our own lifetime, we may imagine what is going to happen after our lifetime.[62]

---

[60] Ibid.
[61] Rajagopalachari, *Chats Behind Bars*, 40–45.
[62] Ibid., 45.

STATUS OF WOMEN

The other major social disability, according to Rajaji, which hindered the progress of *swarajya*, was the servility and deprivation of Indian women. Like Patel, Rajaji too believed that the constructive energy of women should be employed for the success of *swarajya*. He was dismayed at the colossal neglect of women, their entrapment within evil customs, illiteracy and superstition.[63] He, however, had deep faith in the ameliorative potentials embedded in womanhood. In his speech at Joint Women's Conference, Nagpur, dated 24 August 1948, he said:

> Men have quarrelled and ruined the country. Women alone can save the country by undoing all the wrongs that have been done by men during the last few months. You have no hatred towards one another. If among you, you create a feeling of sisterhood men will automatically become friends. To whatever class or community you may belong keep your hearts pure and not allow hatred to be lodged there.[64]

Rajaji also reposed great faith in the ability of women as peacemakers, in doing social service and in acquiring skills and education. Addressing the Indian Women's Association in Madras, he said:

> What is the disease from which this country is suffering today? It is mutual distrust—there is not so much distrust among women of various communities. Women are best fitted to remove that distrust. May the women of India try to undo what mischief the men have in recent times done to themselves.[65]

Rajaji was a great protagonist for women's education. He was of the opinion that:

> Boys are half as studious as girls. There is a certain extraordinary amount of concentration, which the girls give to what they have taken up. Perhaps girls have a natural advantage over boys, because

---

[63] Rajaji's Speech at Indian Women's Association, Madras, 23 August 1948. Rajagopalachari, *Governor General's Speeches, 1948–1950*, 65–66.

[64] Ibid., 73.

[65] Ibid.

the Goddess of Learning is a woman. Our people who framed our legends and mythology knew these things very well. They knew that learning is best looked after by women folk. The mother looks after the family and brings up, so to say the seed. Men are busy with what has been produced but the mother must conserve the good seed in good conditions.[66]

According to Rajaji, educating women was like establishing universities. He said:

I welcome the growing number of girls in schools and colleges because it means that the schools and colleges are carried bodily into families. We do not need to multiply universities if only our mothers will all be university products. Thereafter, every home is a university. All boys and girls that have to be looked after will be looked after from the earliest stages in the home by a worthy principal, namely the mother of the family.[67]

Regarding the method of education to be provided to the girls, Rajaji said, 'Do not quarrel about the method of education.... Nature is so strong that whatever may be the method, nature will look after herself and girls will grow all right, whether you teach through English, Tamil or even Egyptian.'[68]
Rajaji wanted educated women all over India to acquire courage and self-possession, as it has been acquired by the educated women in Maharashtra. He regarded absence of self-consciousness as a great virtue for educated women. Speaking at the Joint Women's Meeting at Nagpur on 27 August 1948, he said,

In Nagpur, as in other parts of Maharashtra, I see women are as patriotic, courageous and keen about their country as the men. The educated girl in Maharashtra has courage and self-possession ... complete absence of self- consciousness is a great virtue and is very necessary for public work.[69]

[66] Speech of Rajaji at Ethiraj College for Women on 4 August 1948. Ibid., 71.
[67] Speech of Rajaji at the Laxminarayan Institute of Technology on 26 August 1948. Ibid., 52.
[68] Ibid., 72.
[69] Speech of Rajaji at the Joint Women's Meeting at the Convocation Hall at Nagpur, 27 August 1948. Ibid., 73.

Like the socialists and the left in the Congress—Jawaharlal Nehru, Subhas Chandra Bose, Jayprakash Narayan, Achuyat Patwardhan, Acharya Narendra Dev, Minoo Masani and others—the Gandhian leaders believed and spoke for equal rights for women and men. However, their views were influenced by Gandhi and their own innate sensibility and not by any 'isms' of the West. In his Nagpur speech, addressing the 'Joint Women's Meeting on 27 August 1948, Rajaji said:

Equality of rights will come to you like a ripe fruit without your asking for it. Women have served India during the last few years nobly and that is why they have now risen to the extent that they have. Have not women risen to level higher than they were, say in 1920? How did they attain this? During these 25 years women have served and suffered alongside of men, and put in hard work in equal measure with men, so they have automatically risen to the level to which they have now risen.[70]

This perspective of Rajagopalachari was more explicitly expressed in his speech at Ethiraj college, where he reminded the girls: 'Let girls remember that knowledge is not an end in itself. As soon as they get the requisite satisfactory minimum of knowledge they must marry and look after their families.'[71]

However, such views of the Gandhian leaders on what should be the duty of women towards the society were exploited by the Left-oriented leaders in branding them as the Rightist and status-quoist. The 'Right' were in tune with their times and being protagonists of evolutionary change; they foresaw change by women acquiring education and men changing their thinking in a gradual manner, which would be consensual and not conflictual. In this perspective, it was possible for women to carry on with their social as well as familial responsibilities.

Rajaji further stated:

Ultimately, what we have to change is not laws but the culture of the country for the better. Men must learn to respect women and not to treat them as born slaves. Man must be taught to have consideration for his wife. With all due respect to the legislators ... these things

---

[70] Ibid.
[71] Ibid.

are not changed by laws but by culture and education, and we must attend to that.[72]

ON EDUCATION

Rajaji favoured liberal, democratic, scientific and progressive education system which would develop free and faithful intellectual minds.

The stress during youth should be on training, on creating a habit of correct observation, of scientific curiosity and of thinking aright and not on cramming the brain with information. The aim of education is that the pupil should acquire an automatic appreciation of values, moral and other. We do not desire to produce indoctrinated. That is not the democratic ideal. Totalitarians might wish to give a twist when the mind is young in a planned direction but our aim should be to produce a free and faithful intellectual and moral apparatus rather than give pre planned twists.[73]

Rajaji advocated that education should create an environment of cooperation, and assimilation and not an environment of conflict and compulsion. According to him, education should be democratic.

Again, it should be remembered that what is made compulsory automatically induces distaste. If you wish boys and girls to develop a permanent and unreasonable dislike of anything, make that subject a compulsory subject.... The conditions for assimilation should be produced, and there should be no compulsion. Youth should be

---

[72] Ibid., 74. Rajaji said:

> Nothing will save womanhood except having woman teachers everywhere. Fight strongly as you can that women should become teachers of boys also. There is no reason why you should not monopolize that work, because the mother is the most fitted to teach. I do not believe in the notion that in boy's schools men must be the teachers and in girl's schools women. Women should be teachers in all schools ... then culture will change rapidly and education will progress and all rights will come.

Ibid.
[73] Speech of Rajaji at the Annual Convocation of Madras University, Madras, 24 August 1948. Ibid., 88.

helped to choose good things for themselves rather than be forced and drilled.[74]

Rajaji also emphasized that education should be secular but not devoid of tradition and culture. He said:

Students should be taught to love one another, to be kind and helpful to all, to be tender to the lower animals and to observe and think aright. The task of teaching them how to read and write and to count and calculate is important, but it should not make us lose sight of the primary aim of moulding personality in the right way. For this it is necessary to call into aid culture, tradition and religion. But in our country we have to look after in the same school, boys and girls born in different faiths and who belong to families that live diverse ways and follow forms of worship associated with different denominations of religion. It will not do to follow the easy path of evading the challenge by attending solely to physical culture and intellectual education. We have to evolve a suitable technique and method for serving the spiritual needs of children through many religions in the same school. We would thereby cultivate an atmosphere of mutual respect, a fuller understanding and helpful cooperation among all the different communities in our society. Any imposition of a single way of life and form of worship on all children, or neglect of a section of the pupils in this respect or barren secularization will lead to a conflict between school and home life in the pupils concerned which is harmful. On the other hand, if we give due recognition to several prevailing faiths in the educational institutions and organize suitable facilities for boys and girls of all faiths, it may itself serve as a broadening influence of great national value.[75]

The above quotation itself speaks volumes of what a true liberal democrat Rajaji was. A secularist, Rajaji was against imposition of any single way of life and form of worship. He was against ritualism but regarded religion as essential spiritual need to maintain the health of the society. 'We may not throw off religion itself. The skin is not the life but it is necessary for life, I fancy that if we remove religion in India, India will die.'[76]

---

[74] Ibid.
[75] Ibid., 89–90.
[76] Rajagopalachari, 'Social Reform', *Chats Behind Bars* (Madras, 1931).

INTER-CASTE MARRIAGE AND WIDOW REMARRIAGE

On the question of inter-caste marriage, Rajaji shared liberal reformist ideas with Patel and Prasad. He encouraged and arranged not only inter-caste marriage but also supported widow remarriage. As early as in 1910, Rajaji arranged a *Saivaite* and *Vaisnavite* match causing local uproar and opposition, since the bride was also a widow.[77] However, Rajaji had no faith in a 'two *anna*, two minute' court marriage and felt that religious form brought 'strength and durability in the marriage.'[78]

Although regarded as a conservative leader by the Left, Rajaji with his moorings rooted in indigenous education and culture coupled with his subsequent exposures to Western education was much ahead of his time and adopted more revolutionary approach to various social issues than many of the Left leaders of the Congress. Rajaji believed that caste need not govern marriage.

My confirmed belief is that women as well as men must be free to marry whosoever they like.... I am not proposing that boys and girls may run away with each other. I only say that in marriages the choice of the young people should prevail.... We can be partners without distinction of caste, friends without distinction of castes and ... marriage too need not be bound down by rules of caste.[79]

This statement of Rajaji disproved the allegations of the Left and reaffirmed the view of Rajendra Prasad that most of the so-called 'conservatives' were more progressive in their thinking than the so-called 'progressives'. About the *Devadasi* system, Rajaji said: 'I detest the practice of attaching woman servants to temples pledged to celibacy, who have become by accepted practice prostitutes.'[80]

RAJENDRA PRASAD ON THE CASTE SYSTEM

Born into a conservative rural family, Rajendra Prasad too had his initial learning and socialization in the traditional norms and values. At an early

[77] Rajmohan Gandhi, *The Rajaji Story-I.*
[78] Ibid., 191.
[79] Ibid., 211.
[80] Ibid., 227.

age, he was exposed to the Hindu classical literature, epics and religious texts. His exposure to Western education had not replaced his traditional approach to life. Yet he exercised critical and questioning attitude to all customs, traditions and norms practised in the society. He was neither overawed by the deeply entrenched traditions nor was he glamour-struck by westernism. He kept an open mind and liberal attitude to all issues affecting a society. His scale of measurement for the relevance and acceptance of any social practice depended on how humane it was. Therefore, he was highly critical of all practices which could be shackles for humanity, the foremost among them being the caste system, untouchability, superstitions, illiteracy, poverty, subjugation and ill treatment of women, dowry and child marriage.

In his student days, Prasad was influenced by the caste compulsions of his family. During his hostel life in Calcutta, he did not take, 'cooked rice or pulses in the Bengali mess even once.'[81] But once he joined the national struggle for *swarajya*, the influence of Gandhi led him shed his obscurantism. He not only took meal in the common mess but also organized dinners for foreign-returned persons, thus inviting orthodox attacks.

BRAHMANISM AND CASTE SYSTEM

Rajendra Prasad rejected caste, untouchability and religiosity. Writing in his *Autobiography*, he accepted that inter-marriage between sub-castes was accepted and its propriety was not being questioned. Considering the deeprootedness of conservatism and the rigidities prevailing at that time, he emphasized the gradual and evolutionary process of social change in order to ensure long lasting reform.[82]

Prasad had strong views on untouchability. According to him, Harijans were an integral part of the Hindu community and for certain historical reasons and because of certain customs they had come to be treated as untouchables. He looked upon untouchability as a great curse on Hinduism and was determined to eradicate it. Like Patel and Rajaji, he too saw the answer to the question of removal of untouchability not in conversion to Islam or Christianity but in complete abandonment of the practice of untouchability and the social segregation of the untouchables.[83]

---

[81] Rajendra Prasad, *Autobiography* (Bombay, 1957), 157.
[82] Ibid., 55–69.
[83] Ibid., 350.

Rajendra Prasad was an active member of the Harijan Sewak Sangh. He, along with Rajaji, campaigned for Harijan temple entry. Like his other two colleagues, Prasad was of the opinion that one effective way of fighting untouchability was to secure for Harijans entry into temples, which had been barred to them. Harijans should also be allowed access to common wells and other places frequented by caste Hindus. To realize this end, a representative meeting of Hindus was called in Bombay in 1935 under the initiative of Prasad and Rajaji where Hindu leaders took the pledge to make every possible effort to eradicate untouchability.[84] The Bombay conference set a pattern which was emulated in all parts of the country. In Bihar, a similar conference was held at Chhapra.[85]

After the Bombay Conference was over, Prasad accompanied Rajaji to Madras. They tried to get the famous Madurai and Srirangam temples thrown open to Harijans. However, they were unable to succeed but many small temples were open to the Harijans.[86] Significantly, Rajaji and Rajendra Prasad achieved success in Kerala, the biggest stronghold of untouchability; the famous Padmanabhan temple was thrown open to Harijans. In his *Autobiography*, Prasad wrote:

Much remains to be done but when we see that the evil custom is centuries old, the idea entrenched in the innermost recesses of our being and the practice sanctified by and made an almost integral part of religion, the success so far achieved need not be underestimated. With greater effort, the citadel of untouchability can be brought down.[87]

Discarding caste rigidities, he placed human life above everything else in the society.

Human life is sacred and does not become less so because a person holds a different faith or may be even guilty of heinous misdeeds. We must never forget the weak, the helpless and the poor to whatever faith they may belong and that our lives should be dedicated to their service.[88]

[84] Ibid., 352–355.
[85] Ibid., 353.
[86] Ibid., 355.
[87] Ibid.
[88] Choudhary, *Dr. Rajendra Prasad*, Vol. IX, 352–354.

PROHIBITION

Related to untouchability was the programme of prohibition. Rajendra Prasad not only supported the programme but in his letter to Sri Krishna Babu, Prime Minister of Bihar, dated 4 March 1938, he expressed his concern that so far nothing tangible and visible had been done regarding prohibition. He wanted a Bill to be passed by the legislature which would ensure its total implementation; 'even when the ministry goes out, its successors will find it difficult to undo it.'[89] Under his guidance, the Bihar Government was able to introduce complete prohibition in Saran district and intended gradual extension to other districts of the province. He also advised the ministry to provide gainful employment for Pasis (who were initially toddy tappers in Saran and were now rendered jobless with the enforcement of prohibition) either in *gur* (jaggery) making, or as labourers in the construction of railway lines at Chhapra.[90]

KHADI AND VILLAGE INDUSTRIES

Linked with the ideology of prohibition was the concept of khadi and village industries. Prasad believed that for removing poverty, superstition and inculcating a spirit of self-respect, dignity and self-reliance, khadi was the appropriate vehicle. And khadi without the support and expansion of village industries would not be a success story.[91] To spread the message of the spinning wheel, Prasad toured the whole of Bihar. With his support All India Spinners' Association was set up with its headquarter at Madhubani. As early as in 1924, Prasad along with his Congress colleagues organized a khadi exhibition in Patna and invited people from different backgrounds to the exhibition so that they might come to appreciate the benefit that would accrue to the villagers from the village industries and khadi.[92]

---

[89] Prasad to Sri Krishna Babu, 4 March 1938. Ibid., Vol. II, 9–10.
[90] Ibid., Vol. IV, 232.
[91] Letter of Prasad to Dr Raghunandan Prasad, 1 May 1938. Ibid., Vol. II, 45.
[92] Ibid., Vol. II, 61. Also see Rajendra Prasad, *Autobiography*, 138–139. In a letter to J.B. Kripalani dated 8 August 1939 Prasad wrote:

> the Working Committee is of opinion that the activities of the Congress organization relating to Swadeshi shall be restricted to useful articles manufactured in India through cottage and other small industries which are in need of popular education for their support....

See Choudhary, *Dr. Rajendra Prasad*, Vol. IV, 21.

EDUCATION

Prasad appealed for science-based knowledge and opening of more colleges in Metallurgical Engineering, Electrical Engineering, and Agriculture.[93] In his letter to Harinath Misra dated 15 June 1948, he wrote about the kind of universities the nation should establish and the kind of education it should provide. He wrote:

> We need a good genuine university which would fulfil two requirements or at least one. The two requirements in my judgement are that it should be able to produce scholars and scientists who will not only preserve the learning of the past but also increase the bounds of knowledge. The second requirement is that it should be able to serve the people in a practical way by providing them with useful knowledge and by enabling them to take advantage of the latest advances in art and science and apply them practically in their own cases.[94]

Prasad was in favour of implementing the Wardha Educational Reconstruction Scheme. In a letter to Dr Syed Mahmud, dated 9 July 1938, he expressed his views, 'I need hardly to say that as it is an altogether new experiment we should do all we can to give it a fair trail.'[95] The Wardha scheme in the beginning was seen as a seven-year programme, to be implemented in an area where constructive work under the aegis of All India Spinners' Association, All India Village Industries Association and the Harijan Sangh had already progressed to a certain extent. Introducing the Wardha scheme in such an area would help in its easy acceptance since the inhabitants of such an area would have an understanding of the social ideology underlying the scheme and it would be easier for the school to be in contact with the community life in the neighbourhood and to be its centre and source of inspiration.[96] Under the Wardha scheme, free and compulsory basic education was to be provided for seven years. Schools were to impart education through handicrafts and not through printed word, and children would earn and learn through handicrafts which would in return go to meet the expenses of their primary education.[97] However, Prasad

---

[93] Ibid., Vol. IX, 131.
[94] Ibid.
[95] Ibid., Vol. II, 60.
[96] Ibid., 63.
[97] Prasad, *Autobiography*, 467–468.

wrote in his *Autobiography* that the 'earn as you learn' part of the scheme did not generate a consensus opinion. Some members of the Education Inquiry Committee (of which he was Chairman) such as Professor K.T. Shah and Dr Zakir Hussain were of the view that 'the earn as you learn' scheme laid more emphasis on the monetary aspect and less on aesthetic aspect, and children's education would suffer in consequence.[98] Prasad advocated strongly for the spread of education among girls. He felt that girls must get educated and become self-reliant. But he held that women education should also make them realize their primary duty towards their family and household.

> I had been contemplating for some time before my incarceration in August 1942 the necessity of establishing an institution where girls could be educated and given such training that even after finishing their education they could live simply and humbly like the poor people that we ordinarily are in Bihar. I have noticed that as a result of education in modern schools the life becomes artificial and expensive and renders the girls more or less useless for household work.[99]

HINDU CODE BILL

A firm believer in the process of gradual change in the social structure and social relations, Prasad was opposed to the expediency with which the Hindu Code Bill was being introduced. He clarified that he was not opposed to it but recommended to go slow on it. He reasoned that the Hindu law so far operating was centuries old and was entrenched in the innermost recesses of Hindus, and any drastic and sudden change introduced would arouse immense opposition and injure the process of social consolidation in nation building.[100]

In his note to Jawaharlal Nehru dated 24 July 1948, Prasad pointed out that the Constituent Assembly was not the competent body to legislate on personal law of a community. He stated:

> It is true that the progressive elements in the country have supported it but the entire population will be affected by its drastic

---

[98] Ibid., 507.
[99] Rajendra Prasad to Thakkar Bapa, 12 August 1945 in Choudhary, *Dr. Rajendra Prasad*, Vol. VI, 13.
[100] Rajendra Prasad's note dated 30 July 1948, ibid., Vol. IX, 266–267.

provisions which introduce fundamental changes in the personal law of the Hindus as it has been prevalent in the different parts of the country. There is a large section which under the same law is governed in many matters by a customary law. The question is whether the present Constituent Assembly, sitting as the Central Legislature, combining the functions both of the Legislative Assembly and the Council of State, should take up and pass such a controversial measure to which very large sections of the people directly affected are opposed. The Bill has not been circulated for public opinion by the Assembly.... The Assembly too is hardly competent to deal with such a fundamental matter. It was elected for the special purpose of framing the Constitution of India and naturally the electorate had only the framing of the Constitution before it, when it elected its representatives. By a makeshift arrangement the Assembly so elected has been converted into a Legislature, combining in it the functions both of the Legislative Assembly and the Council of State, thus doing away with such safeguard as a second chamber may provide against hurried and hasty legislation. The matter is of fundamental importance to everyone who is governed by the Hindu Law. It substitutes, for the concepts and the reasons underlying that law, new concepts and new ideas which are not only foreign to Hindu Law but may cause disruption in every family. Such a proposal has never been placed before the electorate, which has never had an opportunity to express itself on it. Whatever discussion on the merits of the measure has taken place will on an analysis is found to consist of progressive elements being in favour and the vast bulk of the Hindu mass opposed to it.... No serious or widespread effort appears to have been made to educate and instruct the masses of the people in favour of the proposed measure. Its passage, therefore, will be tantamount to forcing a measure of a most fundamental character introducing basic changes in their personal law, on the Hindus in furtherance of the progressive ideas of a small if not a microscopic minority, and all this is to be done without reference to the electorate and by a Legislature which is competent only for drawing a Constitution but not elected with a view to effecting amendments in the personal law of the largest community in the Country.[101]

---

[101] Ibid.

The path Prasad delineated for social change was to be evolutionary and not revolutionary. He was a firm believer that social change should spring from within since by assimilation and expansion Indians were able to adapt themselves to the changed circumstances. Also the nation had shown immense capacity for elasticity in the past and therefore change would be more effective if it was introduced by slow absorption, assimilation and not by sudden convulsion or revolution. Prasad wrote to Nehru:

I am not impressed by the fact that some people regard the Congress as reactionary or conservative nor do I think that anything and everything which some people regard as reactionary or conservative is necessarily bad and everything that they call progressive is necessarily good. We have to weigh how it will be received by the vast bulk of Hindu public against what foreigners outside India and those who call themselves 'progressive' would say. My feeling is strong on the point that we shall be riding roughshod (over) the cherished sentiments of the vast bulk of our people and that without having any warrant or sanction from them simply because we consider certain things to be right.[102]

He further emphasized:

There is besides, no such urgency about the matter. The Hindus have put up with their personal law for a long time and may well wait till the new Constitution comes into force. It is not a long way off when the electorate may be given a chance by the parties participating in the election to express itself on it.[103]

DOWRY AND EARLY MARRIAGE

Prasad was against both dowry and early marriage. In fact, he held early marriage as responsible for the prevalence of dowry because due to early marriage the boy was dependent on his family to bear the burden of keeping and bringing up his family. He despondently records in his *Autobiography* that the bad custom still persisted in spite of the reformists' efforts. All caste and communal organizations had adopted resolutions against it but instead

[102] Ibid., 267.
[103] Ibid.

of disappearing, this custom was becoming more prevalent. He lamented that the practice had percolated down to even those castes amongst whom the practice did not exist earlier and in those circles where it had been prevalent, it had taken deeper roots.[104] Elaborating on it, he wrote that there was one great difference between the customs of today and those of 50 years ago. Then the parent's approval was enough, but today in addition to the parents, the boy's approval was also required to be sought, leading to two separate demands, thus making the dowry a burden.[105]

CONCLUSION

It appears the treatment of social issues by the Congress 'Right' was very advanced in perception and ideology. Only in methodology, they remained reformist. Responding to social questions within the framework of Gandhian ideology they advocated gradual and evolutionary social transformation. They held that effective social change was possible in the country if it sprang from its own kernel. They viewed that lasting change could be ensured if it was introduced by slow absorption and assimilation and not by sudden convulsion or revolution.

[104] Rajendra Prasad, *Autobiography.*
[105] Ibid.

3

The Congress 'Right' and the Communal Question

Ours is a secular state. We cannot fashion our policies or shape our conduct in the way Pakistan does it. We must see that our secular ideals are actually realized in practice.... Here every Muslim should feel that he is an Indian citizen and has equal rights as an Indian. If we cannot make him feel like this, we shall not be worthy of our heritage and of our country.

—Sardar Patel[1]

The 'Right' understood colonial government's duplicity in encouraging the Muslim League so as to defeat the Congress's ultimate goal of achieving complete freedom for united India and their diabolical political game of keeping Indians divided into various smaller social groups by playing one against the other.[2] At the all-India level, they played Muslim League against Congress to retain their hegemonic control over 'the jewel in the British Crown'.[3] In this chapter, thoughts and views of Patel, Prasad and Rajaji on communal question, their relationship with the Muslim League and Jinnah and their views on secularism and partition will be taken up in three separate sections.

SARDAR PATEL AND THE COMMUNAL QUESTION

Patel believed that the communal question was the creation of the British and unnecessarily it had clouded the main issue of declaration of freedom for India.[4] Indignant at Zetland's branding of Congress as a 'Hindu

---

[1] Patel's Speech at Hyderabad, 7 October 1950. Nandurkar, *Sardar Patel*, 168.

[2] Patel's Speech at Kathiawad, September 1940. In the same speech, Patel said, 'The British Government has begun to show itself in its true colours. It has begun to create division among us.' See Parikh, *Sardar Vallabhbhai Patel*, Vol. II, 434–436.

[3] Ibid.

[4] Ibid., 425.

organization which should reach a settlement with the Muslim League',[5] Patel retorted:

> We asked the Viceroy for the objectives of the War. We did not receive any direct reply but now are being told to go and settle with the Muslims that is with the Muslim League. If we do succeed in coming to an agreement with them we shall probably be told, go and settle with the Indian princes. When that happens no doubt they will say, 'What about the Europeans who have so many interests in the country and who have invested so much money?' Thus they wish to prolong the differences in this country exactly as the monkey did in the story of the two cats who referred their dispute to it.... You (the British) are the real cause of all our quarrels. You introduced communal electorates....[6]

Patel had been consistently and categorically analysing and stating that the quarrel between Hindus and Muslims was the creation of a third party, the British. He asked people to remember how Gandhiji was first to arrive at complete agreement with the Muslims at the Second Round Table Conference. At Allahabad also Congress held Unity Conference and practically all points were settled. But the British statesmen frustrated all these efforts. Morely-Minto reforms were first devised to divide India on religious basis. After that the Muslim demand went on ever increasing. They demanded separate electorates, they were given. Then they demanded special reservation which was also conceded.[7]

Thus, the British intentionally played the game of flaring up communal forces to keep the anti-imperialist forces divided. Patel was angry with the Viceroy and said 'he wanted to show to the world that Britain was prepared to give *swaraj* but it could not be given because "there was no unity in our country"'.[8]

---

[5] Ibid.

[6] Ibid.

[7] Patel's Speech at Berar, while inaugurating the 4th session of the Berar Provincial Congress on 18 January 1940. See Chopra, *The Collected Works*, Vol. VIII, 213.

[8] Ibid. Patel was amused at the concern shown by the British Government, 'The British Government asks what will happen to us if they leave'. Surely this is a strange question as to what will happen to India if they leave? It is as if a watchman were to say to his employer 'what will happen to you if I leave?' The answer will be, 'You go your way. We shall either engage another watchman or learn to keep watch ourselves.' See Parikh, *Sardar Vallbhbhai Patel*, Vol. II, 434–436.

While inaugurating the fourth session of the Berar Provincial Congress on 18 January 1940, Patel rebuked the government for their duplicity. He pointed out that when the Congress ministers resigned in 1939, the colonial government extolled the performance of the ministry. But when the same administration was being accused by the League, the British did not come out in defence of the ministry as now they did not want to displease the Muslims.[9] Thus, according to Patel, there could not be any agreement between the Hindus and the Muslims so long as the third power was there.[10] He denounced British interventions in India's domestic affairs. 'We may fight each other. Some of us may live or die. But that does not prove that the British have any right to rule this country.'[11] He categorically stated that the Congress was always ready to settle the issue with the Muslims on the basis of justice and fairplay, but it would be possible only in the absence of British interference.[12] He clearly discerned the lame excuses given by the British in raising the bogey of 'internal quarrels'.

Government professed that India could not make any constitutional advance because of internal quarrels. These quarrels should be of no concern of the Government. It was easy to create quarrels, difficult to reconcile hostile parties. If he (Patel) were given power to rule over Britain he could produce a war between England, Scotland and Wales.[13]

Thus, for Patel, the British offer of reforms was actually dipped in falsity, which meant merely to placate the Congress and its leaders. The Morely-Minto reform which Patel regarded as the beginning of the British design of balkanization of India,[14] reached its culmination in the subsequent failures of all its missions, be it Cripps Mission, Cabinet Mission or Simla Conference.[15]

Patel was critical of the role of Cripps who had earlier said in the House of Commons, during a debate on India, 'you are not justified in taking

[9] Ibid., 212.

[10] Ibid.

[11] Ibid.

[12] Patel's Speech at Bombay, 29 July 1939. See Patel Papers, File No. Lot I-39-1-3: Patel's Speeches 1935–1945, SPNM.

[13] Patel's Speech, 10 August 1945. Ibid.

[14] See Patel's Speech at Berar on 18 January 1940. Chopra, *The Collected Works*, Vol. VIII, 213.

[15] Ibid.

away the rights of a majority because you assert that you desire to protect the minority,'[16] and now he was willing to accept balkanization of India.[17] Patel called the Cripps mission, 'a bad coin, whose makers had evil designs. It smelt of untruthfulness and betrayal ... no more mischievous scheme had been conceived.'[18]

Patel was perturbed by the encouragement given to Muslims to be intransigent regarding the proposals offered by Cripps.[19] His proposals meant that, 'even if we become independent India will have many partitions and foreign troops will remain in the country.... A Socialist Cripps has today turned into an Imperialist.'[20]

The British were keen to either maintain their permanent hold over India or to divide it if the former failed, and this game plan the 'Right' leaders fully understood.[21] Similarly, Wavell had promised at the beginning of the Simla Conference in June 1945 that no single party would be allowed to torpedo the conference, yet he allowed Jinnah to obstruct the purpose of the conference.[22]

Criticizing Viceroy's action in allowing Jinnah to defeat the purpose of discussion at Simla, Patel pointed out:

Every time the League takes a recalcitrant attitude, they try to placate it. The result is that the League gets stronger and stronger and its attitude of violence gets encouragement. It is a misfortune that the British Government is unable to take a firm stand and call off the bluff.

Complaining further, he said:

You called the League delegation there at a time when there was some realization that violence is a game at which both parties can

---

[16] Sardar Patel's Speech at Ahmedabad in July 1942. See Patel Papers, File No. Lot I-39-1-3, Patel's Speeches, 1935–1945, SPNM.

[17] Ibid.

[18] Patel's Speech in early March 1942 at Bombay. See Parikh, *Sardar Vallbhbhai Patel*, Vol. II, 456.

[19] Ibid.

[20] Sardar Patel's Speech on the midnight of 7 August 1942, seconding the Quit India Resolution. See Patel, *Sardar Patel Ke Bhashan, 1918–1947*, 544.

[21] Letter of Churchill to Linlithgow, 3 November 1937 in Linlithgow Papers, NMML. Churchill had stressed therein, 'I think the main difference between us is that you consider a united All India an end desirable in itself; whereas I regard it as an abstraction which in so far as it becomes real will be fundamentally injurious to British interest.'

[22] See Patel, *Sardar Patel Ke Bhashan*, 544–548.

play and the mild Hindu also when driven to desperation can retaliate as brutally as a fanatic Muslim. Just when the time for settlement was reached Jinnah got the invitation and he was able to convince the Muslims once again that he has been able to get more concessions by creating trouble and violence.

Patel accused Wavell that every action of his 'has been in the direction of encouraging the Muslim and putting pressure on us towards appeasement.'

Patel was informed that the news had come from the White Hall that Mr. Jinnah was not to be antagonized or displeased.[23] He charged the British government that while they were always ready to use the big stick against the Congress, they were afraid to raise even a little finger against the League.[24] Agitated by the recalcitrant attitude of the League and silent encouragement given to its behaviour by the Viceroy and the British Government, Patel sharply reacted to the failure of the Cabinet Mission, too. 'The Viceroy is in full sympathy with the Muslim League and he is not able to fulfil the obligations due to assurances given to us. Mr. Jinnah's game was postponement.'[25]

Finally, over the issue of participation in the interim government, Patel had warned Wavell that Jinnah would only use his position in the Interim Government for purely communal and disruptive purpose and to break up India.[26] Wavell had given assurance to Patel that neither Jinnah nor any other party would be allowed to use Interim Government as a battleground for communal politics. But Wavell failed in reining Jinnah and Patel's words, etched deeply in the history of India's national struggle, proved true. The British were the diabolical players in the game of partitioning India.[27]

He complained to Cripps how brutally any protest movement of the Congress was suppressed, whereas the League's 'Direct Action' which caused rioting, arson and murder was rewarded by Wavell by giving five ministerial berths to the Lea gue members.[28]

[23] Ibid.
[24] Ibid.
[25] Patel's letter to Sir B.L. Mitter, Dewan of Baroda, 2 December 1946. See Nandurkar, *Sardar's Letters*, 258.
[26] Gandhi, *Patel*, 387.
[27] Ibid., 388.
[28] Ibid.

If strong action had been taken or allowed to be taken when Direct Action Day was fixed by the Muslim League … all this colossal loss of life and property and blood curdling events would not have happened. The Viceroy here took the contrary view and every action of his since the Great Calcutta killing has been in the direction of encouraging the Muslim League and putting pressure on us towards appeasement.[29]

Wavell recorded in his diary dated 19 January 1946:

I saw Vallabhbhai Patel for the first time this morning. Not an attractive personality and uncompromising, but more of a man than most of the Indian politicians I have met … Patel at once began with allegations that the British were supporting Mr. Jinnah and the Muslim League, that Jinnah had been allowed to wreck the Simla Conference…. He said that he did not see how there was ever going to be a settlement between Hindus and Muslims while the British were in India, and that the British should clear out and leave Indians to settle matters themselves.[30]

Wavell did not reply to Patel's allegations, but he did record: 'I said he really could not expect us to leave India to chaos and civil war, and that there must be some sort of settlement.'[31] Wavell confessed that he did not raise the issue of Pakistan, 'as the tone of his approach did not favour it',[32] and merely said that, 'it was his business to see that law and order was maintained until some form of Government was settled.'[33] Thus, the diary entry of Wavell reaffirmed Patel's conviction that British game plan was on a bigger scale and more disastrous for the unity of India. They were using law and order issue as a false screen to hide their true intention of balkanization of India by encouraging League and Jinnah.

Patel was vexed not only by the partisan attitude of the British towards the League but he was also weary of their casual attitude while controlling communal riots. In a letter to Cripps, dated 19 October 1946, Patel

[29] Patel to Cripps, 15 December 1946, in Durga Das, ed., *Sardar Patel's Correspondence* (Ahmedabad, 1971–1974), 314.

[30] Gandhi, *Patel: A Life*, 353.

[31] Ibid.

[32] Ibid.

[33] Ibid.

complained to him about the failure of the Governor of Bengal to control riots in Eastern Bengal. He wrote to Cripps:

> The Governor did nothing to prevent the mischief if he had to avoid it.... Would you believe that the Governor of Bengal has all throughout these terrible happenings been enjoying the bracing climate of a hill station known as Darjeeling? I myself received many letters and telegrams from the terror-stricken people of this unfortunate area. Similar warnings were addressed to the Viceroy and the Governor but the Provincial Autonomy served as a screen to prevent governmental action. You would realize how difficult it is for an Indian Home Member to sit in his office quietly day after day when innumerable piteous appeals and complaints are received for some kind of help which would give these unfortunate and helpless victims some protection.[34]

Patel truly understood the implicit and explicit design of both the British and the League to raise and abate communal hatred to justify Partition—the ultimate goal of League and British plan of balkanization of India.[35] 'It is easy to raise communal hatred and to make demands from a foreign power in the hope that the interested power will view the claim with favour because the Congress is fighting for the liquidation of that power.'[36]

PATEL: SECULARISM AND HINDU–MUSLIM RELATIONSHIP

Sardar Patel's secularism rested on the twin pillars of his rural rootedness and faith in the values of the Bhakti movement.[37] Imbued with the peasant ethos of secularism, Patel believed that kisan, who was the sustainer of the society, could never be communal and since he too was a kisan his heart beat in unison with the kisan community, be it Hindu or Muslim. But the attempt was being made by mischief-makers to divide the sustainer of the society into Hindu and Muslim communal factions.[38]

---

[34] Patel to Cripps, 19 October 1946 in Nandurkar, *Sardar Patel's Letters*, Vol. IV, 215.

[35] Patel to Bhimjee, 8 February 1946, ibid., 148.

[36] Ibid.

[37] Parikh, *Sardar Vallbhbhai Patel*, Vol. I.

[38] Patel's Speech at Berar while inaugurating the 4th session of the Berar Provincial Congress Conference, 18 January 1940. See Chopra, *The Collected Works*, Vol. VI, 211.

Patel viewed religion as an individual's private affair. 'Religion is a matter between man and his maker and its mixing with politics would be a dangerous business.'[39]

A true follower of Gandhi and a firm believer in the basic values of the Congress as laid down by the moderate leadership, i.e., democracy, civil liberties, economic development, social reform, secularism and pro-poor orientation, Patel was fully committed to establishing a free secular India.

In this country where we have a secular state, where different communities with different religions and different sects, have been residing for centuries and who we wish should reside in future, we have a responsibility to see that the gulf between the communities is not widened and nothing which is preventable or which can be prevented without violating the principles of justice and fair-play is done.[40]

Patel knew that the politics played by the British colonialists had made the Hindu–Muslim relationship a sensitive issue, as early as in 1921. In 1921, Mopla killings had vitiated the unity achieved during the Khilafat Movement. Therefore, Patel warned the nation saying:

Hindu–Muslim unity is yet like a tender plant. We have to nurture it extremely carefully over a long period; for our hearts are not yet as clean as they should be. We have got into the habit of suspecting each other, and efforts will be made to break this unity. But a golden opportunity lies in cementing such unity for ever through the Khilafat.[41]

However, Patel stressed the fact that the initiative for confidence-building among the Muslims was the responsibility of the majority community. He emphasized, 'It is the Hindu's duty to help protect Islam by rendering every possible assistance to the Muslims and expressing full faith in the goodness of that community.'[42]

Throughout the Khilafat movement during 1920–1921, Patel stood like a rock along with Gandhi in promoting harmony and unity among both the communities. He was perturbed by the attempts to politicize

---

[39] Patel's Speech at Travancore dated 13 May 1949 in Nandurkar, *Sardar Patel*, 100.

[40] Patel's address to the Constituent Assembly on 19 November 1947. See ibid., Vol. I, 189.

[41] Patel's Speech at Bharuch, 1921. See *Sardar Patel Ke Bhashan, 1918–1947*, 34.

[42] Ibid.

the relationship between both the communities. In 1920, he warned the Hindus saying, 'The Hindus cannot remain unmoved when the Muslims are in such agony. If the Hindus desire the Muslims' friendship, they must share their sorrow.'[43]

In Patel's definition, secularism did not mean rejection of one's religious and cultural identities. According to him secularism meant freedom for Muslims, Hindus, Sikhs and Christians to express their religious and cultural identity, yet share each others sorrows and happiness.[44] 'While protecting our religion, we have to follow the path whereby we can protect all creeds and religion.'[45]

The character of independent India envisaged by Patel was thus of a free secular India.

> Ours is a secular state. We cannot fashion our policies or shape our conduct in the way Pakistan does it. We must see that our secular ideals are actually realized in practice.... Here every Muslim should feel that he is an Indian citizen and has equal rights as an Indian. If we cannot make him feel like this, we shall not be worthy of our heritage and of our country.[46]

The League's politics of separatism, however, prompted Patel to demand loyalty to the country from the minority community, whose citizenship they had not renounced. Such tone of his speeches came under scathing attack, but a rational secularist that he was, Patel's attitude was to take the bull by its horn and not to shy away from the stark reality, however unpalatable it might be. Therefore, in his address to both Hindus and Muslims of Kathiawad, he had defined the parameters of relationship within which these communities would have to function.

> In the past, Muslims of Kathiawad contributed to the League propaganda of 'two nation' theory and took part in League politics. But I have forgotten the past which is dead and gone if only they will treat it as such, but if they still feel an attachment to the 'two nation' theory and look to an outside power they have no place in Kathiawad. It was to put an end to this dual loyalty that we agreed

[43] Ibid., 16.
[44] Patel's Speech on 'What Freedom Means', 17 December 1947 at Jaipur in Nandurkar, *Sardar Patel*, Vol. I, 10.
[45] Patel's Speech at Hyderabad, 7 October 1950. Ibid., 168.
[46] Ibid., 166–169.

to create Pakistan so that those who preferred to abide in that faith can find a place where they can pursue it. In India there is no place for such persons. If they stay in India it can only be as loyal citizens; otherwise they have to be treated as foreigners with all the attendant disabilities. They should live in India like brothers and in harmony with non-Muslims. To Hindus I would say that they should follow Mahatma Gandhi in his creed of Non-violence. The recent disturbances have disgraced India in the eyes of the world and it is for them to win back their lost reputation by correct behaviour and noble conduct.[47]

Patel derived a sense of great pride from the fact of united action of Hindus and Muslims in the fight against the colonial power. In his Amritsar speech on 30 September 1947, he said, 'How at Lahore Hindus, Sikhs and Muslims took the pledge of complete Independence! In the blood-bath of Jallianwala Bagh was mingled the blood of Hindus, Sikhs and Muslims.'[48] But in the changed political environment his heart, 'bleeds to think that things have now come to such a pass that no Muslim can go about in Amritsar and no Hindu or Sikh can ever think of living in Lahore.'[49]

It was, therefore, not in the schema of things for a secular Patel to accept the formation of Pakistan on communal lines. 'My opinion about Pakistan is not based on any communal grounds and I am quite aware of the fact that millions of Muslims, Christians, Sikhs and others agree with me in my view.'[50]

Patel was equally intolerant of communalism of majority community.

If you forget your citizenship and talk of religion, it is a cloak. Therefore when I hear some people talking about Hinduism in danger, I feel that they are going a wrong way. Do not indulge in scare-mongering for selfish ends. Do not employ wrong methods for catching votes or forming parties. It is a very dangerous game.[51]

Patel had no resentment against Muslims as a community. What he abhorred or detested was Muslims' separatist politics.[52] Rejecting the idea

---

[47] Patel's Speech at Rajkot, 13 November 1947. Ibid., 149.

[48] Sardar's Speech at Amritsar on 30 September 1947. Ibid., 133.

[49] Ibid., 133.

[50] Patel to S.A. Bhimjee, 8 February 1946 in Nandurkar, *Sardar's Letters*, Vol. IV, 178.

[51] Speech of Patel at Ernakulam on 13 May 1949 in Nandurkar, *Sardar Patel*.

[52] Patel's Speech at Rajkot on 13 November 1947 in Nandurkar, *Sardar Patel*, 49.

of reservation of seats for the minorities, he appealed to the protagonists of communal reservations:

> For a community to think that its interests are different from that of the country in which it lives is a great mistake.... I do not want to harm the poor common masses of Muslims who have suffered much; whatever may be your claim or credit for having a separate state and a separate homeland.... Please do not forget what the Muslims have suffered—the poor Muslims. Leave them in peace to enjoy the fruits of their hard labour and sweat.[53]

He advised the separatists to keep the welfare of the Muslims in mind while demanding Pakistan. 'They believed that if they had Pakistan they would ensure full protection to Muslims. But have they ever thought of Muslims living in India? Have they ever sympathized with them?'[54] 'If anybody has played false to the interests of Indian Muslims, if anybody has damaged their cause irreparably, if anybody has exploited the feelings and sentiments of Indian Muslims, it is those who wanted this country's partition.'[55]

Therefore, Patel derived great solace from the fact that despite the spread of communal poison and rabid attack of League on him, 'over three fourths of the country's Muslims are following their normal avocation and showing no signs of. They are living peacefully in their ancestral homes or on lands in complete protection of their lives and property.'[56]

Public opinion and how history would appraise him did not deter Patel in speaking out his mind and stating the facts. His thinking was not influenced by any ideology other than nationalism. While criticizing the League, he did not spare the Congress workers in not bringing Muslims into Congress fold and thus aggravating insecurities among the Muslims. He accused the Congress of not working among the Muslim communities either in rural or in urban areas.

> Congressmen have not worked in rural areas and in the cities, they work only amongst non-Muslims. The results of elections in UP,

---

[53] As Chairman of Minorities Committee of the Constituent Assembly Patel's Speech in the Parliament, 26 May 1949. See Nandurkar, *Sardar Patel*, 155–156.

[54] Patel's Speech in the Constituent Assembly, 19 November 1947. See Nandurkar, *Sardar Patel*, 192.

[55] Patel's Speech at Hyderabad on 7 October 1950, Nandurkar, *Sardar Patel*, 166.

[56] Patel's reply to Liaqat Ali, prime minister of Pakistan, who criticized his speech delivered on 11 October 1947 at Amritsar, ibid., 145.

Bihar and other Provinces have shown that there is a good field for work amongst Muslims all over and if Congressmen will work honestly for communal unity, there is excellent opportunity for unity all over India.[57]

Patel's secularism was also the result of statecraft management and integrative development of Indian society. Since India had suffered a great deal from the wounds inflicted on it by partition and mass exodus, Patel's anxiety was to build a united secular India on a harmonious and reciprocal relationship between all the segments of the Indian society especially between Hindus and Muslims. To achieve this end, Patel did not hesitate in calling a spade a spade. 'I do not hesitate in saying what I feel whether it displeases Hindus, Muslims or anybody else. I admit that I do so in blunt language—but to learn the proper language I shall have to spend my next birth also with Gandhiji.'[58]

In consonance with the above viewpoint, Patel warned the recalcitrant members of both the communities saying:

In this country where we have a secular state, where different communities with different religions and different sects have been residing for centuries and who we wish should reside in future, we have a responsibility to see that the gulf between the communities is not widened and nothing which is preventable or which can be prevented without violating the principles of justice and fair-play is done.[59]

Patel had the same message for all the communalists. He warned the Rashtriya Swayamsevak Sangh (RSS):

Change your plans, give up secrecy, respect the Constitution of India, show your loyalty to the Flag and make us believe that we can trust your words. Whether they are friends or foes and even if they are our own dear children we are not going to allow them to play with fire so that the house may be set on fire.[60]

---

[57] Patel's letter to Industrialist Shanti Prasad Jain, 26 March 1946, in Nandurkar, *Sardar's Letters*, Vol. IV, 66–67.

[58] Patel's Speech at Jaipur addressing the Subject Committee of the Congress dated 17 December 1948 in Nandurkar, *Sardar Patel*, 142.

[59] Patel addressing the Constituent Assembly on 19 November 1947. Ibid., 189.

[60] Patel's Speech at Madras, 23 February 1949. Ibid., 6.

Patel's assessment of RSS as an organization was quite realistic and
he missed no occasion to highlight its communal nature and culture. In
response to M.S. Golwarkar's lamentation on the ban imposed on RSS,
Patel in his reply dated 11 September 1948 clearly stated:

> There can be no doubt that the R.S.S. did service to the Hindu soci-
> ety. In the areas where there was the need for help and organization,
> the young men of the R.S.S. protected women and children and
> strove much for their sake. No person of understanding could have
> a word of objection regarding that. But the objectionable part arose
> when they, burning with revenge, began attacking Mussalmans.
> Organizing the Hindus and helping them is one thing but going in
> for revenge for its sufferings on innocent and helpless men, women
> and children is quite another thing…. All their speeches were full
> of communal poison. It was not necessary to spread poison in
> order to enthuse the Hindus and organize for their protection. As
> a final result of that poison, the country had to suffer the sacrifice
> of the invaluable life of Gandhji. Even an iota of the sympathy
> of the Government or of the people no more remained for the
> R.S.S. In fact, opposition grew. Opposition turned more severe,
> when the R.S.S. men expressed joy and distributed sweets after
> Gandhji's death. Under these conditions it became inevitable for the
> Government to take action against the R.S.S.[61]

Patel was also apprehensive of the manner in which the RSS had been
working. He complained:

> [T]here was something secret about the R.S.S. It had no constitution
> of its own. Its provincial heads, the Sangh Chalaks, were all Mahratta
> Brahmins. The R.S.S. had an army of its own. One could understand
> the existence of an army outside India, but the raising of an army,
> whatever name it might be given, within the boundaries of India,
> would not be permitted. Such an army was a potential danger to the
> State and, therefore, had to be put down. The members of the R.S.S.
> claimed to be the defenders of Hinduism, but they must know that
> Hinduism would not be saved by rowdyism.'[62]

[61] See Patel's letter to M.S. Golwarkar, dated 11 September 1948, in Home Political
Proceedings, Government of India, NAI.
[62] See *Hindustan Times*, 20 December 1948.

On another occasion, he commented, 'Some say that the R.S.S. members are going to offer Satyagraha. They can never do so. Those whose minds are full of poison can never succeed in launching Satyagraha.'[63]

Further elaborating on the role of the RSS, Akalis and Muslims, Patel stated that the communal threat had principally come from the RSS and the Akali Dal.

Insofar as the RSS may seek to bring about a regeneration of the Hindu community by peaceful and legitimate activities, there can be and need be no quarrel with its activities. It is only when it seeks to achieve this object by spreading poison and hatred against other communities who are entitled under the law to equal protection from the established government and when it seeks to achieve its object by resort to unlawful or violent means then it pits itself against the forces of law and order.[64]

Further, he warned the Akalis,

> I fully appreciate their apprehensions and the disquiet with which they have to approach their position which has been so badly dislocated by the partition and its aftermath.... It was, therefore, most painful to me that a section of that community was misled into putting their faith in a futile and harmful extremist policy of which master Tara Singh was the exponent. We dealt with him and that section of the community with patience and forbearance and it was only when they took to overt acts of defiance of the law and became a serious threat to peace and security of the capital city that we had to take action.[65]

In Patel's view, both the RSS and the Hindu Mahasabha celebrated the assassination of Mahatma Gandhi, but it was the fanatical wing of the latter under the leadership of Savarkar that was directly responsible for carrying it out. In his letter to Jawaharlal Nehru dated 27 February 1948 he wrote,

> It (findings of investigation) also clearly emerges from these statements that the R.S.S. was not involved in it at all. It was a fanatical wing of the Hindu Mahasabha directly under Savarkar that hatched the conspiracy and saw it through. It also appears that the conspiracy

---

[63] See *Hindustan Times*, 6 December 1948.
[64] Patel's Speech in the Parliament on 17 March 1949 in Nandurkar, *Sardar Patel*, 117.
[65] Ibid., 118.

was limited to some ten men.... I have come to the conclusion that the conspiracy of Bapu's assassination was not so wide as is generally assumed, but was restricted to a handful of men who have been his enemies for a very considerable time—the antipathy can be traced right to the time when Bapu went for his talks with Jinnah, when Godse went on a fast and some others of the conspirators went to Wardha to prevent him (Bapu) from going. Of course, his assassination was welcomed by those of the R.S.S. and the Mahasabha who were strongly opposed to his way of thinking and to his policy. But beyond this, I do not think it is possible, on the evidence which has come before us, to implicate any other members of the R.S.S. or the Hindu Mahasabha. The R.S.S. have undoubtedly other sins and crimes to answer for, but not for this one.[66]

In relation to Muslim communalists, Patel was equally forthright and blunt.

Except for sporadic activities of their old organizations, such as the Muslim League and Muslim National Guards ... they have on the whole kept the peace of the country and have settled down somewhat disillusioned but more or less willingly to their new loyalties. I can assure them that so long as they behave as loyal citizen of this country they shall have every protection to their life, property and religion which this Government can extend to them.[67]

The India of Patel's dreams was to be a nation founded on diversities and differences within an overarching umbrella of consensus. He specified, 'In return for all this the state does not expect from the Muslims anything more than what it demands from other communities, namely a complete and unquestioned loyalty to their state.'[68]

A rational secularist, Patel was ruthless in taking administrative measures to curb the disruptive and destructive activities of the RSS, Hindu Mahasabha and the Muslim communalists. Addressing the Bombay Municipal Corporation on 16 January 1948, he lashed out at Hindu Mahasabha:

[66] See Patel's letter to Jawaharlal Nehru, dated 27 February 1948 in Home Political Proceedings, NAI.
[67] See Nandurkar, *Sardar Patel*, 118.
[68] Ibid.

We have just now heard people shouting that Muslims be removed from India. Those who do so have gone mad with anger. A lunatic is something better than a person who is mad with rage. One can be treated and perhaps cured, but the other loses complete control of himself…. Shouts like these cause me worry and agony…. If we cannot act as trustees for the entire population irrespective of religion, caste or creed we do not deserve to be where we are. The guilty have to be punished and wrong doers have to be censured. Those who indulge in such shoutings must therefore realize what the consequence of breaking the law would be.[69]

Similarly, for those Muslims who still harboured divisive tendencies Patel's advice was: 'Muslim should feel as secure as the rest of the population. For this, however, Muslims will have also to change their outlook. They must forget the lesson which has been taught to them of the two nation theory.'[70]

So as a friend of Muslims, I want to say a word and it is the duty of a good friend to speak frankly. It is your duty now to sail in the same boat and sink or swim together. I want to tell you very frankly that you cannot ride on two horses. Select one horse whichever you like best.[71]

In Patel's view, India's history 'tells us that we have bartered away our freedom because narrower objectives and selfish ambitions secured ascendancy over larger aims and national aspiration.'[72] And he saw repeat of this in the divisive politics of the League and this caused certain apprehensions in Patel's mind about the course of the country's integration. Activities like the Conference of Mussalman-e-Hind in December 1947 in Lucknow did not allay Patel's distrust of the minority in the vitiated atmosphere of communal poison. Statements like Hindus and Sikhs should know that Muslims might be finished in India but they should know that they also in that case would not survive, coming from the Conference of Mussalman-e-Hind which was also attended by Azad and about 70,000 Muslims gave rise to doubts about minorities' loyalty in the mind of Patel.[73] In response

---

[69] V. Shankar, *My Reminiscences of Sardar Patel*, Vol. I (Delhi, 1974), 146–147.

[70] Ibid., 148.

[71] Patel's Speech at Lucknow on 6 January 1948 in Nandurkar, *Sardar Patel*, 193.

[72] Addressing the students of Allahabad University, Patel's Speech dated 27 November 1948. Ibid., 285.

[73] Speech of Dr Syed Mahmud from Bihar, a Nationalist Congress Muslim. See *Statesman*, 28 December 1947, NMML.

to such provocative statements, Patel gave his controversial and fiery speech at Lucknow, demanding from Muslims not only to be loyal citizens but also exhibit their loyalty towards India.

I am a true friend of Muslims although I am dubbed as their greatest enemy. I believe in plain speaking. I do not know how to mince matters. I want to tell them frankly that mere declarations of loyalty to the Indian Union will not help them at this critical juncture. They must give practicable proofs of their declarations. To Indian Muslims, I want to ask only one question. In the recent All India Muslim Conference why did they not open their mouth on the Kashmir issue? Why did you not condemn the action of Pakistan? These things create doubts in the minds of people.[74]

The ever-increasing number of Hindu and Sikh refugees from West Punjab and the condition in which they arrived grieved Patel. His public statements became more harsh on the League. His efficient handling of administrative machinery in taking immediate drastic action against any violation of law and order, however, helped in maintaining peace. He warned the administration, 'Any act of showing partisanship in favour of one or the other community will be attended with the most serious consequences to the perpetrators and no slackness of duty will be tolerated.'[75] Patel's appeal to the Sikhs of East Punjab to allow safe passage to trains carrying refugees to Pakistan had an immediate impact.[76] But Patel did not find a similar response from the 'other side'. He complained that Mr Liaqat Ali 'has also repeated the oft-heard assurances to the minority communities of Pakistan.... The value of these assurances is writ large on thousands of murders, abductions, forced marriages, burnt houses and maimed children and the treatment of non-Muslim men, women and children leaving Pakistan in utter distress when they are being subjected to most harassing and humiliating experiences.'[77]

Being at the helm of affairs in 1947, Patel was daily exposed to the plight of the refugees coming from West Punjab and the ambivalence of

---

[74] Patel's Speech of 6 January 1948 at Lucknow, in response to views expressed at All India Muslim Conference—Mussalman-e-Hind held in December 1948. See Nandurkar, *Sardar Patel*, 193.

[75] Ibid., 169.

[76] Patel 's appeal to the Sikhs of East Punjab at Amritsar on 30 November 1947. Ibid., 133–135.

[77] Patel's reply to his criticism by Mr Liaqat Ali Khan, 11 October 1947. Ibid., 144.

Pakistan towards communal violence. Testimony to Patel's claim was the fact that 'in India over three fourths of the country, Muslims are following their normal avocation and showing no signs of leaving. They are living peacefully in their ancestral homes or on lands in complete protection of their lives and property vouchsafed to them by their Government.'[78]

Patel categorically spelt out the terms of coexistence for both the majority and the minority communities. He made it clear that he would not accept submission of majority to the dictates of the minority since he believed in peaceful coexistence of all communities. 'A minority that could force the partition of the country is not a minority at all … the future of any minority is to trust the majority. If the majority misbehaves it will be a misfortune to this country.'[79]

However, Patel without mincing words told the minorities, 'we can not expect to have peace with the minority, which is aggressive and which is bent upon coercing the majority and to compel it to accept its own terms.'[80] Throughout his political career he maintained that

> Having fought against communal reservations and having accepted a non-communal approach to all political matters recently, we cannot but object to and refuse to accept any communal reservations which are in the nature of a concession to a militant minority. I can allow for generous and liberal concessions to the minority in order to give it confidence and security but it goes entirely against my grain to concede a vicious weightage almost at the point of a pistol and under pressure from a militant organization.[81]

According to Patel, 'No community should think that its interests were different from that of the country in which it lived.'[82] As Chairman of the Advisory Committee on Minorities, his advice for the minorities was that they should think of themselves as citizens of secular India and that the rights and interests of both the communities rested on mutual goodwill, trust and cordiality.[83] He elaborated that, 'even if separate electorate is accepted the minorities will fail to join the mainstream and accordingly

---

[78] Ibid., 145.
[79] Patel's Speech in the Parliament, 26 May 1949 on 'India is One Community', in Nandurkar, *Sardar Patel*, 156.
[80] Sardar Patel to Rajendra Prasad, 15 October 1938 in R.P. Papers, NMML.
[81] Patel to Jawaharlal Nehru, 4 June 1948, in Nandurkar, *Sardar's Letters*, Vol. V, 109.
[82] Ibid., 155.
[83] Ibid., 153–155.

will have marginal share in the Government and remain perpetually in minority.'[84] Patel emphasized that the supremacy of nationhood had to be realized by one and all.

> I do wish to say to Muslims that they are equals, that they have equal rights as Indian Citizens and that they are entitled to live in peace and in complete protection of the law and Government. At the same time every Indian citizen whether he is a Hindu or a Muslim, will have to behave as an Indian and act as an Indian and the sooner they realize this the better ... in the long run it would be in the interest of all to forget that there is anything like majority or minority in this country and that in India there is only one community—that is one Nation.[85]

PATEL ON PARTITION

Patel remained a true follower of Gandhi throughout his political career, but he had his own understanding of political realism. This aspect was most apparent in his dealing with the League and Partition question. Favouring practical solution over emotional or ideological one in resolving the communal problem, Patel was under no illusion about the political design of Jinnah who by 1946 ruled over majority of Muslim minds.[86] To a suggestion for showing generosity to the League made by Sir Norman Smith, Chief of Government Intelligence, as it would dissolve the psychological mistrust, Patel retorted, 'If you think that generosity will placate the Muslim Oliver Twist then you do not understand either the Muslim mind or the situation.'[87]

[84] Patel speaking at Hyderabad on 'No Place For Divided Loyalty', 7 October 1950, ibid., 165.

[85] Ibid., 153.

[86] In a letter to Shri Nalinaksha Sanyal on 21 April 1946 Patel wrote:

> Undoubtedly joint electorates would reverse the process of the spread of communal hatred and distrust. But a settlement presupposes willingness on the part of both the parties. The League people will do nothing or will be able to do nothing against the will of its leaders whose declared policy is to follow all the tactics of the German Fuhrer.

See Nandurkar, *Sardar's Letters*, Vol. IV, 182. Also see Patel's Speech in Delhi, 11 August 1947, ibid., Vol. I, 3–5.

[87] See Norman Smith's account, January 1945 in *Transfer of Power*, Vol. IX, NMML, 544.

A political realist he had read the mind of Jinnah and knew that no amount of generosity could now turn the direction of League from its separatist politics.

It appears that the League has stiffened rather than relaxed its attitude to Pakistan. Their mood is hardly one of compromise or conciliation. It is not a question of give and take on both sides but the demand for 'give' on one side and 'take' on the other. Conciliation and compromise can only be achieved when the desire is mutual but if there is only one way traffic only either surrender or firm stand can bring about the close of this sorry episode.... This process can not go on indefinitely and we must cry a halt sometime. That moment has now come and if there could be no further agreement to a united India owing to League's intransigence, there is no alternative but to divide.[88]

Realizing that if solution to separatism was not arrived at soon, the country would sink deep into the whirlpool of communal anarchy taking away with it the nobility and halo of truth, non-violence and *satyagrah* of the anti-colonial movement. Patel was by 1944 resigned to the inevitability of partition.

Nobody likes the division of India and my heart is heavy. But the choice is between one division and many divisions. We must face facts. We cannot give way to emotionalism and sentimentality. The Working Committee has not acted out of fear. But I am afraid of one thing that all our toil and hard work of these many years might go waste or prove unfruitful. My nine months in office have completely disillusioned me regarding the supposed merits of the Cabinet Mission Plan. Except for a few honourable exceptions Muslim officials from the top down to the chaprasis are working for the League. The communal veto given to the League in the Mission Plan would have blocked India's progress at every stage. Whether or not we like it, de facto Pakistan already exists in Punjab and Bengal. Under the circumstances I would prefer a de jure Pakistan which may make the League more responsible.[89]

---

[88] Patel to Arthur Henderson, 16 April 1944, P.C. India Office White Hall. See Documents collected from India House Library, London, at SPNM (Ahmedabad).

[89] V.P. Menon, *Transfer of Power in India* (Calcutta, 1957), 385.

Patel's simmering difference with Gandhi over his relationship with the League and minority, and his blunt and forthright approach to the problem compelled him to explain in his public speeches why he accepted partition and why he differed from Gandhi:

> [N]ot given to debates or verbal disputes I claim to be nothing more than an obedient soldier of him like the millions who obeyed his call.... There was a time when everyone used to call me his blind follower, but both I and he knew that I followed him because our convictions tallied.... For several years, Gandhiji and I were in perfect agreement. Mostly we agreed instinctively; but when the time for big decision on the question of India's Independence came we differed. I felt that we had to take Independence there and then. We had therefore to agree to Partition. I came to this conclusion after a great deal of heart searching and with a great deal of sorrow. But I felt that if we did not accept Partition, India would be split into many bits and completely ruined.... Gandhiji felt that he could not agree with this conclusion. But he told me that if my heart bore testimony to rightness of my convictions I could go ahead. Our leader whom he nominated as his heir and successor was with me. Gandhiji did not oppose us nor did he consent to what we thought was right and proper. Even today I do not repent for having come to that decision, though it was with a great wrench of the heart that we did so.[90]

In order to settle the issue immediately and to avoid communal mayhem, Patel accepted division of the country, but its acceptance did not mean surrendering to the League's threat of civil war or the policy of appeasement.[91] In fact, Patel found Partition artificial, 'as one cannot divide a sea or river, similarly how can one divide a nation where the Muslims have their roots, their sacred places and their cultural centres are located in India.'[92] Patel's secularism did not allow him to accept Partition as concretization of communal politics, nor was he of the view that any community or group should be coerced into joining in the formation of a nation against its will as it would tantamount to committing violence and going against the Congress's principles of democracy and self determination.

---

[90] Patel's address to the students of Benaras Hindu University, 25 November 1948, in Nandurkar, *Sardar Patel*, 277.

[91] Ibid., 278.

[92] Patel's address to the citizens of Delhi, 11 August 1947. Ibid., 5.

The Congress position has always been that it will not coerce any group or area which does not want to remain. At the same time it will not be coerced by any group or community. Therefore if the Muslim League insists it wants separation then Congress will not compel them to remain by force.[93]

The design of the League to carve out a niche for itself appeared to Patel as an attempt to subvert the anti-colonial movement. The League was encouraged by the 'third party', whose aim lay in digging the grave of the anti-colonial movement and reducing it into ashes in the conflagration of communalism.[94] 'We know that just as in securing Pakistan outside elements were with them, they were with them also in the nefarious designs they harboured.'[95]

In the separatist design of the League, Patel saw all that the Congress had achieved in its anti-colonial struggle so far being crumbled down, and the goal for which the earlier leaders of national movement and leaders of his time had sacrificed their selves being threatened due to factious and communal politics of the League. His heart bled with sadness while visualizing the result of separatist politics of the League. And he had been reduced to a state of despondency and helplessness by the League's politics. Till then he had held in command all significant nationalist movements, be it Kheda, Bardoli, Non-cooperation or Quit India Movement of 1942. He lashed out at League, Jinnah and the like-minded separatist Muslims with equal virulence, as he had harboured the notion of a united India.[96] In his personal note dated 17 November 1945, Patel observed:

[T]here was a little chance of any compromise with the League so long as the leader of the League did not reform his manner. The League would have to come to the Congress if it wanted a settlement with it. The League and its leaders had been the greatest obstacle in the way of India's freedom, but they would not be able to block it for all times.[97]

---

[93] Patel's interview given to the Associated Press of America at New Delhi, 9 May 1946. See Documents Collected from India House Library, at SPNM, Ahmedabad.

[94] Patel's Speech at Bombay on the eve of his 74th Birthday, 30 October 1948, in Nandurkar, *Sardar Patel*, 36–38.

[95] Ibid., 37.

[96] Ibid.

[97] Sardar's personal note, 17 November 1945. See Patel Papers, Lot 1-39-1-3, SPNM, Ahmedabad.

He further elaborated on this point in his Bombay speech of 30 October 1948, while explaining why he accepted Partition:

> When I accepted Partition, in a sense I was unwilling and was full of sorrow. It went against the grains of all my innermost feelings, against all we had aspired, but in another sense we accepted partition willingly and after a full weighment of its consequences. We felt that if we could not remain united we must part. At that time we were quarrelling and fighting bitterly amongst ourselves. The third party was reaping the full benefits out of the dilemma in which we were placed and out of the situation in which we had landed ourselves. We had to pay the price for our liberty. We suffered grievously as a result of Partition. A limb was torn asunder and we bled profusely.[98]

A pragmatic Gandhian, he stood for a united, strong and secular India, resting on the foundations of social justice and welfare. His message for both the injured nations was:

> Let not emotions and prejudices overpower our reason. Let us face the problem as human realists comprehending fully the limitations within which we have to work and taking our stand on trust and confidence when a reasonable atmosphere has been created for these virtues to play their part. I am sure if we approach the present situation in this spirit and if we discharge to the full the obligations which we have incurred under a sense of national honour and prestige, we shall have done our part in a big hearted attempt to heal the wounds and to reverse the process of misunderstandings and bitterness.[99]

RAJAGOPALACHARI AND THE COMMUNAL QUESTION

Rajagopalachari too regarded the communal question as a creation of British imperialism, to divide the anti-imperialist struggle and to maintain their hold over 'the colony'.[100] He knew the designs of the British government and so he spoke from all public platforms that the

---

[98] Patel's Speech at Bombay on the eve of 74th birthday on 30 October 1948 in Nandurkar, *Sardar Patel*, 36–37.

[99] Patel speaking on the Nehru–Liaquat Pact, at Calcutta, 21 April 1950 in ibid., Vol. II, 314.

[100] See *Hindu*, 23 August 1940.

British Government was not going to declare India's status as a free country and it was using the issue of unsettled differences between Hindus
and Muslims as an excuse for not accepting and giving legal effect to any
constitution which Indians, including all minorities would prepare and
in which safeguards for the protection of minorities would be included.[101] He regretted that instead of delegating the responsibility to Indians
to frame a Constitution with essential safeguards for the protection of
minority rights and thus proving their sincerity, they were trying to evade
the main issue by linking it to the settlement of the Hindu–Muslim
dispute.[102]

Rajaji made a radical proposal to show Congress's willingness to settle
minority issue and also to expose the duplicity of British intention:

> Let me make a sporting offer. If H.M.G. will agree to a provisional
> national government being formed at once, I undertake to persuade
> my colleagues in the Congress to agree to the Muslim League being
> invited to nominate a Prime Minister and let him form the national
> government as he would consider best.[103]

But the Secretary of State Leopold Amery refused to discuss it. He told
the House of Commons that, 'no new approach to the Indian question
would be considered.'[104] This attitude of the British confirmed Rajaji's
opinion that the Muslim issue was more of a pretext for the continuance
of the Raj.

Rajaji, in a sharp and incisive manner, articulated the intention of the
British to retain the empire. Although an admirer of British democracy, he
did not forget nor did he allow the Indians to forget that the British were
imperialist first. 'The British are a democratically governed people. But
they are an imperialist people—They do not want any other people to rule
over them but the Secretary of State is to govern India.'[105]

Further emphasizing his viewpoint, he said,

> I have got great affection for Englishmen. They like me and I like
> them. But I object to their sitting on my back any longer …

[101] Ibid.
[102] Ibid.
[103] See *Hindu*, 6 September 1940.
[104] See *Hindu*, 17 September 40.
[105] Rajaji speaking in Madras Legislative Assembly on 25 October 1939. See Gandhi, *The Rajaji Story: 1937–1972* (Bombay, 1984), 50–51.

whenever the people of India demand freedom, they are told that there is a quarrel between Hindus and Muslims and that consequently they are not fit for self-government. It seems as though the British should rule wherever there is a mixed population by some chance.[106]

The erudite man of the Congress, Rajaji's reaction to issues was not guided by emotions but by reason. He admired good qualities both in an individual and in a nation. Yet he did not allow his admiration to overshadow their flaws. He admired the British for their tenacity and progressiveness, yet he did not spare them for their dishonesty towards India in denying her Independence on the pretext of instability due to communal divide. 'When South Africa demanded full freedom, to the accompaniment of gun powder music, the English did not tell them that they should solve all their minority and untouchability questions before they could justly ask for a free constitution.'[107]

Concern for India's freedom was in the very being of Rajaji. Therefore, despite the fact that British would try their utmost to delay the process of granting freedom to India, Rajaji was prepared to support the British in their war effort and try for a 'national government,' with their support and the support of the Muslim League, if the British acknowledged complete Independence of India as the only solution to the problem.[108]

But with so many stakes in the colony how could Britain let go of its golden goose so easily despite articulating phrases like 'concept of natural laws propounded during the Enlightenment' as enshrined in the British constitution. Exasperated at the attitude of the British, Rajaji reacted strongly to the evasive attitude of the British.

I am a reasonable man, a practical-minded fellow, a conservative, a lover of peace and one who dislikes to gamble on poor people's lives. But I cannot give in to Britain's arrogance or be victimized by her trickeries. I have gone to the point that Honour can take us to and I cannot surrender any further and am prepared for the worst thereafter. I have seen enough of these people. I see no greatness of conduct in their present attitude towards India, I see only a desire to loot and exploit.[109]

[106] Rajaji's Speech at Virudhunagar, 9 March 1942, Rajaji Papers, NMML.
[107] Speech of Rajaji, 20 December 1941, Madras, ibid.
[108] Rajaji to G. Natesan, 18 April 1940, See Natesan Papers, NMML.
[109] Ibid.

Anguished at the attitude of the British, Rajaji questioned the genuineness of the British intention:

> In the statements with which England went to war it was stated that the world should be free … that they are attacking Germany not because England or France was attacked territorially or on the waters, but because they wanted to defend liberty against aggression. Naturally the people of India began to ask themselves: Is this liberty only for Europe, for the small peoples of Europe, or is it also for the large and ancient people who have been in this land for thousands of years and who have been in friendship with Britain?[110]

Rajaji like Patel accepted the truth that communal question could not be resolved as long as the British were there to play mischief, saying, 'I could easily give a grand fight to Jinnah now and perhaps demolish him in his own organization but even Hercules is not a match for two; had the British not been here the thing would have been totally different.'[111]

As early as 1926, Lord Hardinge, the ex-Viceroy, wrote to Sir Harcourt Butler, Governor of Uttar Pradesh (UP), 'Hindu–Muslim riots served as a very useful abject lesson to idealist of the necessity of the British Raj'.[112] This ploy was so effectively used by the British to colour the minds of the League and its leader that for the League the issue of independence became secondary to the issue of defining and achieving a territorial 'enclave' for the minorities.[113] Saddened by this development Rajaji acknowledged the fact:

> We could have had Swaraj in the palm of our hand if the Muslim League had played the game. If it be necessary, we could even have fought afterwards among ourselves. If we had asked for that which belongs to India together we could have got it.[114]

Rajaji in his long speech in the Madras Legislative Assembly in October 1939 attacked the double talk of the British and blamed them for playing

---

[110] Rajaji's Speech in Madras Legislative Assembly, 31 October 1939. See Gandhi, *The Rajaji Story 1937–1972*, 50–51.
[111] See Letter of Rajaji to Sapru, 12 September 1942, ibid.
[112] See Gandhi, *The Rajaji Story-I*, 1970.
[113] Ibid.
[114] See Rajmohan Gandhi, *The Rajaji Story 1937–1972*, 51.

up the fear psychosis of the minority community so that they could never join hands with the Congress and always doubt the intentions of the majority community.

> What the Muslim League says is that the minorities can only be protected by the standing army of a foreign government always being here.... Do I not know Mr. Jinnah? Do I not know the innermost ambition of his heart that India should be free? But what I do say is that knowingly from one wrong step to another, from that wrong step to a still further wrong step they (the members of the League) have come to this conclusion that India cannot have self rule to say, Let England be always here is a terrible conclusion to which this Assembly cannot possibly be a party.[115]

ON THE LEAGUE, JINNAH AND PAKISTAN

Rajaji supported the demand of the League for right to self-determination despite the fact that the League's surrender of its independent position to the British interest was damaging the cause of India's independence.[116] He argued that major concessions would have to be made to the Muslim League to get the cooperation of Jinnah for joint rule with Congress during the war.[117] Rajaji reasoned, 'The threat to India by Japan has precipitated matters—I want a national army for which I want a national front to secure a national government.'[118] He further said:

> Today the battle fronts include bazaars, the houses of civilians, plantations, fields and factories. Is it good in such a situation, that there should be division between government and soldiers on the one hand and ... tremendously popular organizations like the Congress and the Muslim League on the other, over whom such illustrious persons as Mahatma Gandhi and Quaid-e-Azam Jinnah preside? These are not small individuals ... one has become almost as famous as the other....

---

[115] Ibid.
[116] Ibid.
[117] Report of *Indian Express*, 22 October 1939, in Rajaji Papers, NMML.
[118] *Hindu*, 5 May 1942 and 6 May 1942, NMML.

I do not want to surrender to the Japanese. Why should I? I am not carried away by mere hatred. I do not want to be ruled by anybody. I want to defend my country and I want to defend it at once.[119]

Defending his position, Rajaji further said:

There are a few morbid-minded persons who are imagining that I am anxious to become a minister once again, and that is why I am engaged in this propaganda. Even granting the assumption will you lose anything? ... In modern war even ministers would be bombed and these morbid minded people may feel some satisfaction in that.[120]

Rajaji's plea for formation of national government should not be viewed as reversal of his basic position. He always abhorred the League's attempt at balkanization of the country on communal lines. He accused Jinnah in 1940 of trying to take India into the condition of the Balkan states:

Surely he knows in what state the Balkan peninsula is with Germany and Russia waiting for a convenient hour to take them over. A sovereign Muslim state carved out of India was absurd and impracticable and hardly the remedy for the minority problems. Were Hindus and Muslim going to divide the ancestral property the homestead or even the milch-cow?[121]

Rajaji saw Pakistan as a 'diseased and tribal concept' to which 'present day India would never agree.'[122] Moderating his disagreement with the League, Rajaji in his criticism of Jinnah and the League tried to provide an answer to Jinnah's demand for more freedom for the Muslim provinces and also an assurance that they would not be overborne by a Hindu controlled centre. Rajaji felt that this was a 'laudable desire' attainable 'without cutting up India'.[123] But Rajaji clarified that his stand should not be seen as a sign of desperation if the League wanted a division. If the League insisted

---

[119] Rajaji's Speech at Madras on 21 January 1942. See Rajagopalachari, *Defence of India*, Madras, 1942; Rajaji Papers, NMML.

[120] Rajaji's speech in defence of his position against the criticisms leveled against him alleging that he is supporting formation of national government for his personal aggrandisement at Tirunelveli, 10 March 1942, ibid.

[121] See *Hindu*, 4 January 1940 and 23 February 1940, NMML.

[122] Ibid., 26 March 1940.

[123] Ibid.

on 'puncturing the tyre and stopping the progress of the Indian car, Congress would have to fight both the Raj and the League.'[124]

In tune with the Congress ideology, Rajaji's opinion about the League and what Muslim masses desired was:

> I do not believe that the Muslim League represents the Mussalmans, if the former oppose the Constituent Assembly idea. What the Mussalmans may be taken to seek is that the Constituent Assembly should be so constituted as to safeguard their interests and provide for their apprehensions. This is automatically provided for in the Congress formula that the decision of the concerned minority will prevail in regard to their social interests and not to the decisions of the majority.[125]

Rajaji had an uncanny understanding of the mercurial personality of Jinnah and knew that he would not allow the Congress to arrive at any settlement unless the proposals of sharing political space with the Congress after the British departure were accepted in toto by the Congress.[126] Rajaji wrote to Devdas Gandhi on 29 November 1942:

> I could easily give a grand fight to Jinnah now and perhaps demolish him in his own organisation, but even Hercules is not a match for two. Had the British not been here, the thing would have been totally different. We should clench our teeth and choose our opponent.[127]

Rajaji's talk with Jinnah on 9 November 1942 failed over the scheme for a provisional government. In this plan, the Viceroy was free to select his government from whichever of the Congress leaders he believed to have most national following and from as many members of the Muslim League as Jinnah decided. Rajaji still showed optimism. He wrote to Sri Prakasa on 27 December 1942,

> We should not mind what the Viceroy has said or not said but must come to an agreement with Mr. Jinnah unless the Mussalmans in the meanwhile depose Mr. Jinnah, which of course is an unlikely

[124] Ibid.

[125] Ibid.

[126] See A.R.H Copley, *The Political Career of C. Rajagopalachari: 1937–1954* (Madras, 1978), 214–215.

[127] Rajaji to Devdas Gandhi, 29 November 1942. See Rajaji Papers, NMML.

contingency in the near future. If we come to a settlement or at least make a final maximum proposal to him and he refuses to agree and join a common drive against British obstinacy, it will then be time for us to tell the Mussalmans that we should not follow him and take our chance.[128]

Yet an ardent believer in democracy and the democratic way of life, Rajaji opposed the idea of a brute majority oppressing the people and suppressing their sacred rights under the Constitution because of its voting strength in Parliament and state legislature. He acknowledged that Muslims' right to self-determination would induce unity rather than partition.[129] In keeping with his view of right to self-determination for Muslims, Rajaji in his speech at Nagpur University convocation in 1944 rebuked the Hindu extremists and said:

And what is this heresy I am guilty of? I stand for a solution of the Muslim issue.... Let us by all means prefer to let things remain unsolved rather than agree to anything dishonourable or tyrannical; but it is not dishonour or submission to tyranny to allow the majorities in any area to be in more than subordinate charge of those areas, which is the offer we make to Mr. Jinnah and with which he is not satisfied.[130]

RAJAJI AND SECULARISM

A staunch secularist who was rooted in the Hindu Vaishnavite tradition and yet a modern rationalist, Rajaji believed:

It takes all sorts to make this world and the highest virtue of every citizen is to try to conduct himself so that a mode of life may be evolved by which people of differing religious faiths, occupations and attainments who constitute our society may live together in peace and amity. The law of love is a practical code of life as our dear departed leader so strenuously sought to teach us. My confirmed opinion is that in India there is in fact no communal hatred.

[128] Rajmohan Gandhi, *The Rajaji Story 1937–1972*, 1984, 85–86.
[129] Ibid., 85.
[130] Rajaji's Speech at Nagpur, 1940. See *Rajaji's University Address* (Bombay: Hind Kitab, 1949), 39–40.

Greed and fear of defeat in economic competition produce what is
mistaken for communal ill feeling. I am convinced that there is really
no hatred between Hindu and Muslims or between any other communities. There is neither hatred nor conflict of interests. There is
misunderstanding, pride and consequent stupidity. The long drawn
out controversies of the recent past cannot be put aside all at once....
But basically, there is, among widely differing creeds and races, far
greater understanding of the fundamentals of human fellowship in
India than probably anywhere else. This being so my hope is not ill-
founded that India will lead the way in demonstrating harmony in
diversity and furnishing a striking example in human co-operation
in the midst of seeming heterogeneity.[131]

A compassionate leader, whose values were rooted in the philosophy of
Advaitism, Gita and Upanishad, but whose wisdom had acquired depth
with the influence of the old and new testaments of the Bible, Bunyan's
Pilgrim Progress and reading of Quran and thoughts of Socrates and
Marcus Aurelius, he believed:

All spiritual search is one and God blesses it whenever it is done and
by whosoever. If I am today a devout though very imperfect Hindu
Vedantin it is not less due to my contact with some of the sacred
books of other people than to the contemplation of what our own
great ancestors have left for us. Not by total exclusion of all religion
and spiritual thought but by all embracing acquaintance and appreciation of spiritual thought of all kinds shall we be safe and shape
ourselves properly.[132]

Rajaji held that although 'we have inherited the broadest culture and
the most tolerant of all religious creeds, it did not mean that the Gita was
better than any other scriptures.'[133] Rajaji explained that his attempt to
explain the Gita was to reach those Hindus who had less scholarship than
him and who 'like me stand greatly in need of grace.'[134] To Hindus he said,
that they should envy and emulate the average Muslim's trust in God.[135]

---

[131] Rajaji' Speech at the Annual Convocation of the Madras University, 24 August 1948.
See *Rajaji's Speeches*, 84–85.

[132] See Rajaji's Speech at Bombay, 1949, in *Governor-General's Speeches*, 62.

[133] Ibid.

[134] Ibid.

[135] Ibid.

He held, 'The Bible, the Koran and the Gita are like lamps that light our paths in darkness.'[136]

By elaborating on the nature of vedanta and dharma, Rajaji highlighted the secular ethos of India rooted in its tradition and culture.

Vedanta is undoubtedly a living philosophy of life in India, a part of the mental structure of our people. The people of India get it not from a study of books but from tradition. It is in the air so to say of India and Asia.[137]

To the fanatics of Hinduism, Rajaji's explanation of dharma was: 'Dharma is not to be confused with fanaticism of some followers of Hinduism. Dharma is that widespread inner call among people of all classes in India to reduce their wants and to give their possessions for the good of others.'[138]

Following the above line of argument, Rajaji elaborated: 'If the Musalmaan community wants protection the Hindus must give all that is demanded. Not merely must we concede the substance but also adopt the methods which the Mussalmans feel should be adopted.'[139]

Rajaji was perturbed that Hindu–Muslim relationship was not evolving as it should have been and since he was a Hindu and, therefore, belonged to the majority community, he could speak to Hindus with moral authority:

We have earned the positive ill will of thousands of Mussalmans. Why do I reproach only the Hindu folly and not point my finger of complaint at the Mussalman? Because I am not so pure—as I must be before claiming to chastise him, I am a Hindu and have birth right to speak harshly to my Hindu brethren.[140]

He also rebuked those who were questioning the loyalties of the Muslims living in India.

I acknowledge the loyalty of Muslims to India. I realize also that such loyalty requires sacrifice. If anyone doubts this, he has only to place

[136] Ibid., 359.
[137] See Rajagopalachari, *Hinduism, Doctrine and Way of Life* (Madras, 1959), 35.
[138] Ibid., 36.
[139] *Hindu*, 20 April 1931.
[140] See Gandhi, *The Rajaji Story-I*, 138.

himself in the position of a Hindu in Pakistan and imagine that he was offering allegiance to that state and flag.[141]

And he believed that Hindu–Muslim unity could be achieved if 'the Hindus who pretend to greater education and who are superior in numbers are not opposing any demand for special concessions.'[142]

Anxious to respect the sentiments of Muslims, as Premier of Madras during 1937–1939, Rajaji took various steps. For example, a film called *The Drum* was banned in Madras by Rajaji because Muslims in Bombay objected to it. He also banned a book written by a Hindu priest entitled *Hinduism versus Islam*. Rajaji's approach in dealing with the Muslim question was thus refreshingly free from any kind of narrowness.[143] Rajaji suggested in 1941 for the formation of the National Government based on the joint cooperation of the League and the Congress, aimed at strengthening both the national defence in the face of impending Japanese attack and the Hindu–Muslim unity.[144] His views drew criticisms from the wider Congress circles.[145] Enduring bitter attacks from his colleagues and friends, Rajaji stood firmly on his stand and proposed to the British that:

> Let the Viceroy invite League and Congress leaders to join his Council, with the War Cabinet in London retaining the right to prosecute the war from India. And let Jinnah nominate more members than Congress. The question of partition could be decided by the United Nations at the end of the War or in any other agreed way.[146]

Rajaji made the generous offer to Jinnah to ward off the League allegation that Congress-backed Government would prejudice the future of the minorities.[147] Rajaji in a press statement dated 23 August 1942 said on Jinnah's response to his proposal,

---

[141] Rajaji's Speech quoted in *Statesman*, 17 December 1947, NMML.
[142] Ibid.
[143] See Gandhi, *The Rajaji Story-I*, 47.
[144] Ibid., 85.
[145] Gandhi regarded Rajaji's proposal of Hindu–Muslim unity to ward off Japanese intrusion as 'wholly unnatural'. See *Hindu*, 31 May 1942. Nehru blamed Rajaji for splitting the Congress over 'Pakistan'. See Shiva Rao, *India's Freedom Movement* (1972), 192. And Patel criticized Rajaji's attempts by stating that he is behaving in such a mannner because he is suffering from 'mental fever'. See Patel to Manibehn, 23 March1945 in Nandurkar, *Sardar Patel*, 390.
[146] *Hindu*, 13 October 1942 and 23 October 1942.
[147] Ibid.

Mr. Jinnah had a great chance. He could have done something, which would have produced more power than any contemplated second front in Europe. All eyes were on him. There were unmistakable signs that his own people were restive and wished for a change in his attitude and the arrival of a National Government.... Instead of responding to the call of his countrymen, Mr. Jinnah has reiterated the old controversies with the impossible addition that Muslim votes outside the Pakistan areas should decide the fate of those tracts and not the votes of the people of those areas. Mr. Jinnah has failed at a critical hour when a great opportunity presented itself.[148]

However, there was no response from Jinnah, nor were his Congress colleagues prepared to accept his proposals, which appeared to them premature. Psychologically, they were not yet ready to accept partition. Rajaji argued that the ground reality had petrified from partition being a matter of just an opinion among only certain sections of the Muslim community to an unchanging feeling in a mass of people.[149]

Rajaji in the All India Congress Committee (AICC) session in May 1942 at Allahabad advised the Congressmen that it was not the time for inaction but to give to the Muslims what they were asking.[150]

PARTITION AND PAKISTAN

Rajaji felt exasperated at the stubbornness and moribund attitude of many of his Congress colleagues. He had realized that unity of India could not be imposed by force as it would result in civil war.[151] He was the only leader from the Congress who articulated with clarity on partition as early as in February 1943. Rajaji said:

Remaining together might mean treachery, separation could mean peace.... You can of course tie a cat and a dog together, drag them along the road and say what perfect unity! The way to real unity

---

[148] See India, *The Transfer of Power* (HMSO), Vol. II (1970), 772.

[149] Rajaji's Speech at Madras, 17 May 1942, Rajaji Papers, NMML.

[150] Rajaji speaking at the AICC session in May 1942, at Allahabad. See *Hindu*, 3 May 1942, NMML.

[151] See C. Rajagopalachari, *Reconciliation* (Bombay: Hind Kitab, 1945), 22–24.

however was to say, 'Go if you want. Come back if you want. Remain if you want'.[152]

Rajaji viewed separation between Hindus and Muslims as a division, 'between two brothers who do not become enemy in the eyes of the world.'[153] And 'bonds of alliance' could be maintained between India and Pakistan. Therefore, independence had to precede separation.[154] To the League members and Jinnah, Rajaji advised:

It was idle to imagine any material difference arising out of the order in which the two events, withdrawal of British domination and partition take place. Mr. Jinnah does not imagine that the British will leave behind when they retire from the scene an army in India to protect the partition from being unsettled. The power to sustain a separate state must come from within not from without, whether the actual partition is prior to the transfer of responsibility or thereafter.[155]

Therefore, following from the above line of thought, Rajaji put forward his formula of self-determination for the Muslims before Gandhi, who approved of it. But Jinnah rejected it on the ground that it offered a moth eaten Pakistan.[156] Failure of Gandhi–Jinnah talks in 1944 finally made Rajaji realize that 'there can be no agreement with Jinnah under present conditions'.[157] And when the Simla Conference failed, Rajaji's dismay was immense:

I share the universal regret that no agreement was arrived at between the Congress and the League representatives at Simla. The further steps to be immediately taken would be so much easier and more beneficial if founded upon a Congress-League agreement rather than as a result of British Government's decision. But we cannot help accepting the second best sometimes. The pity is that we do not realize that the future can correct any errors that we may commit now and that nothing is permanent in the affairs of nations.

[152] Ibid.
[153] Ibid.
[154] Ibid.
[155] Ibid.
[156] See Gandhi, *The Rajaji Story 1937–1972*, 105.
[157] Ibid.

The powers of a central Government expand or contract according to the laws of nature that govern governments and not according to the contracts of obstinate politicians.[158]

Rajaji criticized Wavell for favouring Jinnah, saying, 'It seems we misunderstood Lord Wavell's purpose in summoning the Conference.... If it was only to get Mr. Jinnah to agree, and failing that, we had to disperse, we could have told Lord Wavell that it would be a waste of energy.'[159]

In summing up the Congress mood in 1940s, Rajaji ruthlessly dissected in a non-partisan manner the failings of both the Congress and its leadership while dealing with the Pakistan issue. He also questioned how Indian nationalism should be defined and what should be the meaning of right to self-determination.

The Congress leadership thoroughly misunderstood its own mind and duties towards the nation; and has managed to create the most difficult situation which mismanagement could ever produce. Its programme has made every wicked element ten times more wicked. And barren mood of negation has seized the intellectuals of India.[160]

Rajaji further elaborated that Satyagraha had degenerated from a vigorous doctrine based on common sense into a sentimentalism, 'a morbid desire to see people suffer without its having any relation to political results'.[161] He argued that 'Independence must be built up of consenting units if it is to rest not on any outside force but on abiding cohesive strength.'[162] Reviewing the position of Congress on Pakistan without mentioning it, Rajaji put forward rational and pragmatic arguments:

Indian nationalism should make up its mind clearly on how far it is prepared to go and draw the line beyond which it would deem it more honorable for the present to remain under British rule than to make any further concession to the Muslim League. In the face of the demand made on behalf of the Muslim areas, it is difficult to see how the principle of self-determination for such areas can be avoided in any plan for a free and independent constitution. Ruling out

---

[158] See *Statesman*, 17 May 1946, NMML.
[159] See Ashok Mehta and Kusum Nai, *The Simla Triangle* (Bombay, 1945), 63.
[160] Rajaji to Sri Prakasa, 27 December 1942. See Rajaji Papers, NMML.
[161] See C. Rajagopalachari, *The Way Out* (Oxford, 1944), 4.
[162] Ibid.

coercion as one must, we cannot but consent to some plan by which the ascertained wish of the people in those areas must ultimately prevail. Even if the six provinces of Madras, Bombay, Bihar, UP, CP and Orissa decide to stay together it will not be an insignificant Union and the law of political gravity must inevitably bring the others into its fold provided the Union has patience and good will.[163]

Finally, as 1947 approached nearer, the proposals of Rajaji of 1942, seen earlier as surrender to communal forces, were now regarded as far-sighted. History proved him right. In his letter to his friend Rama Rao, Rajaji could not restrain himself from deriving 'Puckish' humour from the earlier reaction of his colleagues to his suggestion on Pakistan:

A great incubus is off India's chest: Yet it is what I asked them to do but one need not claim credit for having discovered a necessary evil. The only credit is that I was rash enough to stand up for it. I find a mischievous pleasure in watching and enjoying my colleagues' studied silence on the subject. Vanity all over. But one abiding thing there is love.[164]

Thus, in keeping in tune with the Congress ideology and in congruence with the view of his senior colleagues of the Congress like Patel and Rajendra Prasad, Rajaji's message to the nation was:

In the national structure we are dealing with, communalism has no place. Unless we are very strenuous in our conduct and honest in our minds, we cannot make a glorious Indian whatever may be the science of politics, its application or organisation of the government.[165]

RAJENDRA PRASAD AND THE COMMUNAL QUESTION

On the British Attitude

Patel, Rajaji and Prasad agreed that the communal question was made a red herring by the British to deprive the nation of its legitimate right to *swaraj*.[166] The British economic and financial stake in India was enormous

[163] Ibid.
[164] See Rajaji's letter to Rama Rao, 8 June 1947, Rajaji Papers.
[165] Rajaji's Speech at Nagpur, 26 August 1948. See Rajaji's Speeches, 53–54.
[166] Rajendra Prasad on Viceroy's Statement, 3 November 1939. See R.P. Papers, NMML.

and anything which interfered with this systematic exploitation would have been a blow to the interest of the British people. Rajendra Prasad viewed the issue as an excuse used by the British for postponing the issue of granting of independence to India.

> The British Government is not prepared to promise that it will accept and give legal effect to any constitution, which Indians including all real minorities would prepare and in which safeguards for the protection of minorities will be included. We have made a public demand for such a promise and I cannot understand what objections British Government can have to this on the score of our differences with the minorities. If we are unable to produce a constitution satisfactory to all, the British government will be free from all blame and the responsibility will be entirely of Indians. The minorities which are really for attaining freedom for India can have no reasonable objection as the proposed Constitution will not be produced without the cooperation of all.[167]

Rajendra Prasad accused the British of playing politics and not being truthful about conceding freedom to India, and by making it conditional to the issue of resolving the communal question, the British had made the problem difficult: 'The real difficulty is not communal but political. The British Government is not yet prepared to concede the right of self-determination to India in practice, however much it may proclaim it in theory to the world.'[168]

Along with Patel and Rajaji, Rajendra Prasad accepted the political truth that communalism was raised, reared and aggravated by the British as an instrument to rein in the anti-imperialist movement of the Congress.[169] Otherwise what objection could a democratic nation involved in the War for liberty have in giving India its right to self-determination? Prasad expressed his anguish at the attitude of the British saying:

> This crisis is entirely political and is not related to the Communal issue in India.... Indian freedom must be based on democracy and unity and the full recognition and protection of the rights of all minorities.... It has pained us to find the Communal question being dragged in this

---

[167] Ibid.
[168] Ibid.
[169] Rajendra Prasad, *Autobiography*, 506.

connection. It has clouded the main issue. It has been repeatedly said on behalf of the Congress that it is our earnest desire to settle all points of communal controversy by agreement and we propose to continue our efforts to this end. But I would point that this question does not in any respect come in the way of declaration of Indian freedom as suggested above. Such a declaration applies to the whole of India and not to any particular community and the Constituent Assembly, which will frame India's Consitution, will be formed on the widest possible basis of franchise and by agreement in regard to communal representation. We are all agreed that there must be full protection of minority rights and interests and this protection should be by agreement between the parties concerned. The British government taking or sharing the burden has, in our opinion, made a settlement of the question much more difficult than it should have been.[170]

Rajendra Prasad expressed his unhappiness at the attitude of the British in not being straightforward and forthright on the status of India, if the Congress agreed to cooperate with Britain in its War efforts.

Our regret is that instead of adopting this straight course and throwing the responsibility upon Indians to frame a constitution with necessary and satisfactory safeguards for the protection of minorities and thus showing its own bona fides beyond doubt and cavil, the British Government has befogged the main and moral issue by asking us to settle our differences without telling us at the same time that the result of such settlement will be a free Constitution for the country.[171]

Informing the British about unity in the ultimate goal of all the political parties, of whatever hue, Rajendra Prasad in his note to Viceroy's statement of 18 November 1939 said that the two principal organizations, the Indian National Congress and the All India Muslim League had declared that their aim was independence of India. He further clarified that there was no party or group in India which did not want full powers for India to manage her own affairs by whatever name or expression that freedom might be called or described.[172]

[170] Prasad to Linlithgow, 3 November 1939, R.P. Papers, NMML.
[171] Rajendra Prasad commenting on the statement of Viceroy, 8 October 1939 in Choudhary, *Dr. Rajendra Prasad*, Vol. VIII, 264.
[172] Ibid.

Commenting on the Muslim League's stand Prasad stated:

The resolution of the Muslim League is equally clear that it does not accept the Viceroy's announcement and insists upon the clarification of the same and a consideration de novo of the Indian Constitutional question. How then does any communal difference stand in the way of a clear recognition and declaration of India's status as a free country? Whatever differences there are (they) relate not to India's status but to certain other subsidiary matters which we are prepared to settle among ourselves.... The Congress has been insisting on a 'constructive programme', an essential element of which as Mr. Jinnah recognizes, is communal unity. We propose to do our best to achieve success in this essential programme but the fact that we are still engaged in this most urgent work should not stand in the way of a clear declaration of the kind demanded by us.[173]

Rajendra Prasad was of the opinion that the communal problem was a domestic affair of the Indians to be settled by Indians themselves which they would do to the satisfaction of all, if once the British Government proved its own bona fides by ceasing to interfere in the domestic affairs.[174]

While speaking at a meeting of the All India Congress Committee, held at Wardha from 9 to 10 October 1939, Rajendra Prasad accepted the fact that the differences between the two communities, the Hindus and the Muslims, were insurmountable and were not being underrated. The differences did manifest themselves now and then in various forms but such differences existed in all nations between all communities. This did not imply that the League did not stand for freedom of the country and for a radical change in the status of India.[175] The differences which existed, if they were not politicized and used for accentuating and perpetuating them, according to Rajendra Prasad, could be solved by statesmanship.[176]

Rajendra Prasad was also dismayed at the fact that whenever the British Government sought India's cooperation and announced some programme to show their supposed magnanimity, it fell much short of the nationalists' expectation. The proposals of the British at the Round Tables Conference, 1919, Dyarchy, announcement of 1929 proposals followed by Communal Award, Government of India Act of 1935, Cripps Mission, Cabinet Mission and

[173] Ibid.
[174] Ibid.
[175] Ibid., 264.
[176] Ibid.

Simla Talk were all 'their window dressing—and none too concealed attempt to take advantage of such differences and deficiencies as exist in this country for most of which the British government themselves are responsible'.[177]

According to Prasad, the British treated the League as a bulwark against the Congress.[178] Its demand for dropping the provision regarding Federation from the Constitution was therefore accepted by the imperialists most readily.[179] Furthermore, the silence of the Viceroy over the charges in the Pirpur and Sharif report of partisan role of Congress Ministry, not setting up of impartial enquiry committee, as Jinnah was using the issue to settle political scores with the Congress, further confirmed Prasad that 'imperialists' were playing the 'divide and rule' game of politics for their own interest.[180] Their talk of democracy was not meant for India. Their war aim of protecting liberty and establishing peace was meant only for European nations. 'Britain's victory meant continuation of colonial conditions not only for India but for all other exploited and suppressed peoples outside Europe. The war was meant to strengthen Britain's imperial position.'[181]

ON THE LEAGUE AND MUSLIM COMMUNALISM

Rajendra Prasad analysed that till the Legislative Assembly elections in 1937, the League was a weak organization. In many Provinces, it did not exist at all.[182] Its dismal performance in the elections of 1937 created resentment among the League members and they with vehemence launched rabid propaganda against the Congress.[183] Prasad blamed the League for the widening of gulf between Hindus and Muslims.[184] According to him, the League followed the strategy of Goebbels,[185] 'of vilifying the adversary by leveling against him baseless charges and the frequent repetition of those charges could not but influence the people.'[186] The propaganda of the League had created bitterness among the Muslims towards the Congress.

---

[177] Ibid., 258.
[178] Rajendra Prasad, *Autobiography*, 506.
[179] Ibid.
[180] Ibid.
[181] Prasad's comment on Viceroy's Statement, 3 November 1939. R.P. Papers, NMML.
[182] Rajendra Prasad, *Autobiography*, 505.
[183] Ibid.
[184] Ibid.
[185] Ibid.
[186] Ibid., 504–506.

This was increased with Congress coming to power in 1937 and forming Ministries in the provinces. The League, frustrated by its defeat, exploited the situation by calling Congress Ministries as 'coming of Hindu Raj' and how it would be once British left India.[187]

Prasad expressed his anguish at the developing political situation in 1938 vis-à-vis the Muslims. 'The Mussalmans as a body have been alienated and in spite of all that Congress Ministry has been doing to be just and even generous to them, there is not only recognition but positive opposition.'[188]

During his talk with Jinnah in 1935 Prasad found arguments of Jinnah reasonable. Writing on his talk with Jinnah, Prasad in his *Autobiography* writes:

> I agreed that the Muslim should get the same number of seats as the Communal Award gave them. Our talks began with this agreement as the basis. Jinnah then put forth another demand that in constituencies where the number of Muslim voters was less than their population warranted, the franchise should be lowered for them so as to increase the number of voters in proportion to the Muslim population. The Muslims, he said, were poor and backward, and where the capacity to pay taxes was the basis of enfranchisement many Muslims would be deprived of the right to vote…. I regarded Jinnah's demand essentially fair in view of our stand on joint electorates and franchise.[189]

But the talk failed and spelt disaster for any future attempt of rapprochement with the League because Jinnah wanted Congress to accept League as the only representative body of the Indian Muslims while he classified the Congress as a representative of the Hindus.[190] This status of the League, only the League and the British Government were ready to accept.[191]

In a letter to Lala Jagannath dated 23 May 1941, Prasad expressed his unhappiness at the behaviour of the League. He wrote, 'although he and Jinnah addressed jointly two meetings at Patna, still it was difficult to work with the League due to the distrust created by their propoganda and they do not care for settlement but are more concerned with their existence and

---

[187] Prasad to Patel, 11 October 1938, R.P. Papers, NMML.
[188] See Rajendra Prasad, *Autobiography*, 401.
[189] Ibid.
[190] Ibid., 402.
[191] Ibid.

continuance.'[192] He blamed the League for inciting violence in Bihar, Sind and Dacca and wrote that he was being attacked by Hindus for condemning alleged atrocities on their part while not condemning the Muslim atrocities.[193]

Reason for the Muslim League's aggression, according to Prasad, lay in

[T]he hymn of hate which has been preached for years past in which not only the two-nation theory had been propounded and propagated with a zeal worthy of a better cause but also direct hatred has been created. All that we have stood for and worked for during our whole lifetime, all that the Congress has been trying to achieve during its history of more than 60 years, has been smashed by this hymn of hate and the result is bitterness of a most intense kind which has been perhaps never known in the country even during the days when the Muslims regarded themselves as conquerors and were ruling the country. There can be no doubt that there has been long and widespread preparation, whether under the guidance of the Muslim League or independently by Mussalmans, in various parts of the country. Searches have discovered large quantities of arms and ammunition in the United Provinces, in Bihar, in the Central Provinces and in the Delhi province.[194]

Prasad tried to strike at the root of the communal violence while blaming the League for being the major culprit in instigating it. He wrote to Nehru on 17 September 1947:

[S]o long West Punjab cities were denuded of Hindu and Sikh population where they were in majority it will not be possible to bring about normalcy in Delhi soon. One-sided action will not bring about the desired result. Therefore, while we should deal firmly with all disorderly elements on our side of the border we should insist that the same should be done on the other side also.[195]

He told Congress leaders that their apologetic attitude had created an impression that all the atrocities had been committed on the Indian

[192] Prasad to Lala Jagannath, 23 May 1941. See R.P. Papers.
[193] Ibid.
[194] Draft of letter of Dr. Rajendra Prasad to Sir Robert Hutchings, 12 October 1947. See Choudhary, *Dr. Rajendra Prasad*, Vol. VII, 372.
[195] Ibid.

side and all the sufferings had been borne by people on the other side.[196] Prasad, an astute politician, knew that any hard line adopted on the issue of Muslim communalism would further push the Muslims into the camp of the League. He knew that feudal values were deeply entrenched among the Muslim community and for a Muslim religion pervaded all his life, including his politics. Therefore, it would not be easy for the Congress to dislodge the League and take its place as the League was playing the religious card. A review of the Congress policy towards Hindu–Muslim question was thus necessary to avoid further alienation of the Muslims.

Rajendra Prasad had inherent dislike for all variants of communalism. Therefore, he did not approve of RSS, too. If he blamed the League for vitiating social environment, he was equally harsh on RSS for indulging in loot, arson, rioting and killing of Muslims in Delhi and other Hindu majority areas.[197] He warned Patel that in Delhi, RSS was reorganizing itself in a big way and indulging in violence. They had planned to dress up as Muslims and create problems in Hindu areas. They also planned to attack Muslims to create problems in the Muslim areas. Their aim was to create conflagration among Hindus and Muslims, and therefore, he requested Patel to take stiff action against the RSS.[198]

He called RSS a Maharashtrian Brahmin movement whose aim was to establish Peshwa Raj after the withdrawal of the British. He further said that its activities and functions were secretive; it used violence and promoted fascism. No regard was paid to truthful means and constitutional methods. The organization had no constitution; its aim and objectives had not been clearly defined. The general public was usually told that its aim was only physical training but the real aims were not even conveyed to the rank and file of the RSS members. Only the inner circle was taken into confidence. It had consequently developed along fascist lines and was definitely a potential menace to public peace.[199]

Like Rajaji's, Prasad's secularism too was rooted in the Advait philosophy and in the philosophy of Karma of Gita, and in the value of truth, honour and other-worldliness of the Epics and the Upanisads.[200] He believed that

---

[196] Prasad's letter to Nehru, September 1947. Ibid., 471.

[197] Prasad's letter to Patel, 14 May 1948. Ibid., Vol. IX, 72.

[198] Ibid.

[199] Prasad's letter to Patel, 12 December 1948, ibid., Vol. X, 182.

[200] Prasad's Convocation Address, delivered on 12 December 1947 at Allahabad. Ibid., Vol. VII, 427–431.

'all human life is sacred and does not become less so because a person holds a different faith.'[201] He further elaborated:

> creative urge and moral will distinguish man from the rest of the animals and it is in the complete fulfilment of these attributes that the victory of human spirit lies. However, lust for power has degraded human spirit, as it had happened in the political sphere in the country. The lust for power led to disastrous consequences uprooting hundreds and thousands of men and women from their ancestral homes.[202]

Drawing from Tulsidas' Ramayana and Gandhiji's concept of Ahimsa, Prasad elaborated on his concept of secularism and communal harmony. He stated:

> If violence is resorted to in a country inhabited by people of different religions, languages and views that country will not find peace even for one day. In India, if various sections of the people do not show cordiality and tolerance towards each other and stress only each other's rights and concentrate on those rights being accepted by the others, forgetting each one's duties to the others it can result only in tension and bloodshed.[203]

He further wrote, while attacking the communalists of both the communities:

> Many can be callous enough to say that Hindu–Muslim unity should have physical force as its basis and not mutual goodwill. That means they think one of the two communities should be suppressed by force. Some Muslims think that they kept the whole of India under subjugation for centuries when their number was much smaller and that they can do the same thing again. On the other hand, there are Hindus who say that the days when the Muslims dominated are gone forever. At that time the Hindus were not wide awake but now they are not only in a majority but are more educated, wealthier and more powerful. The country they say belongs to the Hindus; others are unimportant minorities who should be content with fair treatment.... If we think that the Hindu–Muslim question can be

---

[201] Ibid.

[202] Rajendra Prasad, *Autobiography*, 144–147.

[203] Prasad's address at Allahabad, 12 December 1947. Choudhary, *Dr. Rajendra Prasad*, Vol. VII, 429.

solved by violence, it will only mean more violence and the ultimate destruction of both communities. Only a policy of live and let live, mutual goodwill and respect and non-violent behaviour can solve the problem and usher in an era of Hindu–Muslim unity.[204]

Analysing the Hindu–Muslim question rationally, further, Prasad wrote in his *Autobiography*:

Muslims might have come to this country from outside and added to their members, but they are as much Indians as Hindus are and there is no other country for them. While they may sympathise with Muslims living in other countries and on certain issues may side with Muslims of other lands, it cannot be denied that they will have to live and die in India, that they have to enjoy and suffer here.[205]

Rajendra Prasad further emphasized:

Muslims belong to this country and are its citizens. When it is admitted they are not foreigners, it follows that they have the same rights and privileges in the country as other communities and they should have a share in every thing along with others. Their political rights cannot be ignored, as the denial of this fact will only mean that we want to deprive them of their just rights and to suppress them.[206]

A protagonist of communal harmony, Prasad supported Communal Harmony Movement launched in Punjab in 1946, which was based on the glorious tradition of India where people 'agreed to differ'.[207] He complained that such movements were not given as much importance as it deserved and instead 'politics of conflict' was occupying too much time and space.[208]

Prasad gave an outline of what should be the Congress policy towards Hindu–Muslim question. His note not only laid the foundation of Congress's approach to Hindu–Muslim question but also highlighted the secularism of Prasad. It laid emphasis on establishing mutual trust and faith between the communities through the programme of Muslim mass contact.[209] The note clarified that Muslim mass contact did not mean

---

[204] Ibid.
[205] Rajendra Prasad, *Autobiography*, 142.
[206] Ibid.
[207] Prasad's letter to Maulvi Mohammad Ibrahim Ali Chisti, 12 March 1946. R.P. Papers.
[208] Ibid.
[209] Rajendra Prasad, *India Divided, Bombay, 1946*, 70–75.

hostility towards any Muslim organization nor making them members of the Congress but by serving them in the ways open to the Congress and acceptable to the Muslims, e.g., All India Spinners Association had been serving Muslims by organizing carding, spinning and weaving amongst them.[210] Rajendra Prasad showed interest in cow protection, which apparently seemed to be obscurantist but in reality it did not mar his secularist status. He participated in the Cow Protection Conference in Wardha in 1946 on the advice of Gandhiji. Explaining his position as to why he participated in the conference, Prasad wrote in his *Autobiography*:

> I did not take interest in the subject because of its religious aspect but because the goshala institution was necessary for our peculiar rural economy. If the economic aspect is emphasised we can have the cooperation of everyone even those who do not look upon the cow with the same feeling of reverence as the Hindus. To inject religion into the question provokes the Muslims and makes Hindus fanatical and the real work suffers. I explained the importance of the cow in the economy of a predominantly agricultural country and showed how because of our blind faith and ignorance we were damaging rather than helping the cause of cow uplift and antagonising others instead of enlisting their co-operation.[211]

In his note on the Congress's policy on the Hindu–Muslim question, Prasad elaborated how the Congress should view the cow slaughter issue. Elaborating on the Congress policy, Prasad wrote that Hindus had horror of cow slaughter and Muslims desired perfect peace in and about their house of worship. These two issues were root cause of many deadly feuds between the two communities. But respect for other faiths could not be forcibly cultivated; therefore, no forcible attempt should be made either to prevent cow slaughter or taking out processions before mosques. These should be matters of mutual adjustment between parties. The general rule, however, should be that custom as to cow slaughter or procession should be respected and it should have the force of law. Where no custom could be proved Muslims should have the freedom to slaughter cows so long as slaughter was not made purely with a view to offend Hindu susceptibility. Similarly, in the absence of custom, Hindus might play music before mosque during prayer times and loudly at no times. Arti in Hindu

---

[210] Note of Prasad on Congress Policy on Hindu–Muslim Question, undated in R.P. Papers, NMML.

[211] Rajendra Prasad, *Autobiography*, 579.

temples could not be interfered with except when it was done so boister-
ously as wantonly to offend the devotees in neighbouring mosques.[212]

Not to offend the Muslim sensibility, Rajendra Prasad stated in 1939
that singing of the *Bande Matram* could take place at purely Congress
gatherings and even there it should be left open to individuals whether
they would stand up when the stanzas were sung. In the Local Board and
Assembly meetings where members were obliged to attend, the singing of
'Bande Matram' should be discontinued.[213]

Prasad was also against the 'banning' of any religious book and regarded
it as an encroachment on the religious right of the people. He asked the
people that such action should not only be resisted by the people whose
book was banned but by all who would not regard the book as their own
but who maintained that every religion had a right to propagate itself.[214]

ON PARTITION

Despite the efforts of Congress leaders like Prasad to promote communal
harmony and build confidence among the Muslim minority through programmes of Muslim mass contact,[215] the scale of violence which erupted on
16 August 1946, on the Day of Direct Action in support of Pakistan, shook
the faith of all nationalist leaders in the noble intention of the League leadership to peaceful solution of the communal question.[216]

In a letter to Sir Robert Hutchings dated 12 October 1947, Prasad
explained his position on the issue of Pakistan. He categorically stated that the
decision for Partition was accepted as the best amongst the bad alternatives.[217]

> We were opposed to partition but then we found that it was not pos-
> sible to carry on without some sort of settlement with the League.

---

[212] Rajendra Prasad's note on Congress Policy on the Hindu–Muslim Question, 1939,
undated in R.P. Papers.

[213] See Choudhury, *Dr. Rajendra Prasad*, Vol. VII, 92.

[214] Prasad to Shivachandraji of Satyarth Prakash Defence Committee, 21 August 1945.
See ibid., Vol. VI, 18.

[215] Prasad received reports from Bihar sent by Anugrah Narayan Sinha on the success
of Muslim Mass Contact in August 1939 especially in districts of Bhagalpur, Chapra, Gaya,
Purnea and Dhanbad, although no evidence was found of implementing mass contact programme for Muslims on a wider scale. See ibid., Vol. IV, 181–182.

[216] Rajendra Prasad, *Autobiography*, 579.

[217] Prasad to Sir Robert Hutchings, 12 October 1947, in Choudhary, *Dr. Rajendra
Prasad*, Vol. VII, 370.

We ultimately decided to give in to purchase peace. In this decision we were strengthened by the attitude of those who were most
affected by the Partition namely the Sikhs in the Punjab and the
Bengalees in Bengal. They were originally dead opposed but seeing
the situation came forward with the proposal that Partition should
be accepted.... We accordingly accepted the position and agreed as
the League had always declared that that was the only way of settling
the communal question and in the hope that as a result we would be
free to carry on the many project of reforms and reconstruction that
we have been dreaming about in our part and leave the League free
to do whatever it liked within its own parts.[218]

Although Prasad and others were compelled to accept partition of the
country, he regretted saying, 'It is an irony of time that the very people
who fought against the Partition of Bengal and got it reversed should now
demand that it should be divided and that demand should be conceded.'[219]
However, in a letter to Sachidananda Sinha dated 5 June 1947, Prasad
summed up the political developments culminating in Partition.

Considering all that was happening and viewing the future, we felt
that there was no escape from division unless we were determined
to have a long period not only of uncertainty and instability but
of strife, conflict and even bloodshed spread over large tracts of the
country. I do not know if that is altogether eliminated. That will
depend upon the attitude of the League and its supporters. We hope
however that we shall be able to carry on the great constructive work
of nation building in an atmosphere of peace, if not good will.... In
all this, we have not got all that we wanted. That was not possible but
I trust that on the whole we have got a workable plan on which we
can proceed. I am feeling that Pakistan will soon discover the utility
of a union with India and reconsider its position and when that hap-
pens, we shall all be happy.[220]

Thus, Patel, Prasad and Rajaji saw the communal question as a game
of power politics that the League unleashed with latent support from the
British. To them, the communal question and Hindu–Muslim discord

---

[218] Ibid.
[219] Ibid.
[220] Prasad to Dr Sachidananda Sinha, 5 June 1947, ibid., 46–47.

were political issues, which the British were determined to exploit for their benefit.[221] In contrast to this position of the 'Right' leaders on communalism, Nehru, the forefront leader of the Left faction in the Congress, believed that communal problem was due to economic backwardness prevailing among the Muslim community. He believed that both Hindus and Muslims were dominated by upper class groups who were feudal and who in association with the British Government, in services, professions and as owners of land, came into prominence and became the upper class.[222] Meanwhile the masses of the country, both Hindu and Muslim, became poorer and unemployment grew. This domination had essentially been economic although the upper class dominated both culturally and educationally. Therefore, a group which was economically in a bad condition usually deteriorated culturally and educationally and could be exploited by others.[223]

However, during the by-election of Hamirpur, Jhansi and Jalaun in 1939, Nehru issued this Press statement:

> The leaders of the Muslim League have issued many leaflets and appeals. I have read some of these, but in none of them have I found any reference to a political and economic issue. The cry raised is that Islam is in danger, that non-Muslim organizations have dared to put up candidates against the Muslim League…. Mr. Jinnah has capped the sheaf of Muslim League leaflets and statements by his appeals in his capacity as the President of the Muslim League. He appeals, in the name of Allah and the Holy Kuran, for the support of the Muslim League candidates.[224]

This press statement of Nehru confirmed how correct the understanding of the three senior leaders of the Congress was of the communal problem. Not supporting the power politics of the League, Patel expressed the feelings of his two colleagues too, when he said:

> Nothing will be accepted merely to secure the immediate elimination of British Power from India which would endanger the future security and well being of the country. As far as the Congress is

---

[221] Prasad's statement on Communal Question. Ibid., Vol. IV, 267.
[222] Ibid., 154.
[223] Ibid.
[224] Gopal, SWJN, Vol. VII, 468.

concerned it will not be a consenting party ... to any such arrangement of dividing India into religious groups....[225]

The three leaders did not accept that the Muslim culture and traditions were in dissonance with those of the Hindus, or foreign in nature. They rejected the League's concept of two-nation theory as the basis of Pakistan. Unlike the League they supported composite culture and favoured establishment of free India as a secular state, unlike Pakistan, which was a theocratic state, with right to self-determination and complete freedom of religious practices to all communities.[226]

The thoughts and ideas on religion and secularism of Rajaji, Patel and Prasad were rooted in Hindu culture and tradition. Their idioms and metaphors were drawn from Hindu mythologies. Their view to live and let live in an environment of religious harmony and mutual respect emerged from their belief in the ephemeral existence of man. It had roots in the philosophical thought of Gita, which greatly influenced the thinking of Patel, Rajaji and Prasad. Therefore, young Left leaders within the Congress found them to be obscurantists, soft communalists and conservatives. The Left in the Congress were used to the Western paradigm of socialism and understood its scientific and 'rational' language of enlightenment. They failed to understand the traditional idiomatic language of secularism and rationalism of an indigenous and ingenious kind, rooted in the ethos of the Gita and the tradition of the Bhakti movement. The secularism of these leaders was no less revolutionary, but the only difference was that whereas the secularism of Patel, Rajaji and Prasad was realistic, the secularism of the Left was academic.

[225] See Patel's Speech at Bombay, 29 November 1946, in Patel, *Sardar Patel Ke Bhashan*.
[226] Patel's Speech at Travancore, 13 May 1949 in Nandurkar, *Sardar Patel*, 100.

4

Economic and Political Ideology of the Congress 'Right'

A new way of life, a new culture is what is aimed at. This cannot be achieved by coercion but only by a heart change. The doctrine of enlightened selfishness of the nineteenth century utilitarians should be refined into a doctrine of immanent trusteeship.

—Rajagopalachari[1]

I know that it is necessary that the system should be ended. But is the Zamindar entitled to the price he asks? Is he entitled to any price, seeing that he held only an office? Zamindari had grown iniquitous and you do not compensate for ending iniquitous systems.

—Rajagopalachari[2]

A strong centre, a well equipped modern army, economic contentment and responsible citizenships and a firm administrative fabric are the essential requisites as well as expression of that unity and strength.

—Sardar Patel[3]

ANTI-COLONIAL IDEOLOGY OF THE 'RIGHT'

The Congress 'Right' accepted the exploitative and underdeveloping nature of colonial economy as articulated by Moderate leaders such as Dadabhai Naroji, G.K. Gokhale, Surendranath Bannerjee, M.G. Ranade and G.V. Joshi. The Congress 'Right' proceeded forward in their understanding of colonialism from where Moderate and Extremist leaders had left. Therefore, the Congress 'Right' did not attempt to articulate on

---

[1] See *Swarajya*, 18 December 1960, in *Satyam Eva Jayate, A Collection of Articles from Swarajya and Other Journals, 1956–1966*, Vol. I (Madras, 1961), 321–322.

[2] Rajaji's Speech in the Assembly, 26 January 1939, *Madras Legislative Assembly Debates*, Vol. IX, 700.

[3] Patel's Speech dated 2 November 1948 in *Sardar Patel*, 241.

anti-colonial ideology vis-à-vis drain because they accepted the Moderates' theorization on economic drain of India in toto, and concentrated on carrying out the political aspect of anti-colonial ideology, i.e., political movement for the attainment of India's independence from British imperialism. Now, the phase of analysis was over; what was required was action and mobilization. The 'Right' leaders were engaged not just in analysis but were basically ardent proponents of political praxis.

The focus of this chapter would be on examination of the views and beliefs of Patel, Rajaji and Prasad on the economic enslavement of India, the economic programme for its rejuvenation and their political, economic and social vision for independent India. These issues would be discussed under various sections and subsections, while discussing the position taken by the individual leaders on these issues. Since nowhere in their writings or in their speeches did the 'Right' leaders explicitly indulge in detailed and systematic discussion over drain and de-industrialization as the Moderate leaders had done earlier, the conclusions drawn here are largely based on the analysis of their views over the issues of economic development, role of *charkha* in rejuvenating the economy, khadi, *swadeshi* and revival of cottage and village industries.

According to Patel, 'Our position is that of a milch cow, we are not properly looked after even though we provide milk.'[4] Patel in his public address at Godhara on 25 March 1935 attacked the British government as being the cause of India's poverty. He said:

British people want to rule over us because they want to continue their trade with India. They want to strengthen their trade with India and to do that they play all sorts of games with us. We are fools that we don't understand their tricks and thus they take away our gold from India. Thus day by day we are becoming poorer and they grow fat at our own expense. As long as the British remain in India we are not going to be happy.... A time will come when the British will have to give the reins of the kingdom in our hands and they shall have to go back from where they had come and according to me that time is now imminent.[5]

---

[4] Patel's Speech at Ahmedabad on 4 March 1935 in Chopra, *The Collected Works*, Vol. V, 47.

[5] Patel's Speech at Godhara, 25 March 1935, *Home Department (special)*, Maharashtra State Archives (MSA), NAI, New Delhi.

Patel further reiterated the reason for India's poverty by making indirect reference to drain of India's wealth. He said at Uttar Pradesh Kisan Conference on 28 April 1935:

> Regardless of the hunger which is the constant companion of millions of Indians, the Government is spending crores of rupees on its army and is looking after its own people. Its officers, the members of the ICS are the highest paid in the world and they are spread throughout the country.[6]

In another speech to Gujarat peasants dated 2 November 1935, Patel mentioned how purchase of foreign cloth was causing poverty among the kisans. Here too, reference was to adverse trade relations of India imposed by British colonial rule, implying drain.

> Instead of using home made khadi, if we cast our eyes on the foreign cloth, it amounts to abandoning home made food and to look with greedy eyes on the dust of unknown persons ... foreign cloth should never be used because foreign cloth and liquor are the causes of our downfall.[7]

Speaking on the ruin of indigenous cottage industries, Patel in his speech to kisans of Uttar Pradesh at Uttar Pradesh Kisan Conference on 28 April 1935 said:

> There was a time when in their free time the farmer could find some cottage industry or the other which could help him to supplement his income. The main cottage industry was the production of cloth. In millions of home of farmers the charkha was plied daily and yarn was spun. That gave employment to millions of weavers. That gave employment to craftsmen who manufactured charkhas, looms and carding machines. The foreign rulers have through diverse ways encouraged their own industries and have in the process taken away

---

[6] Patel's Speech at Uttar Pradesh Kisan Conference at Allahabad on 28 April 1935. See Chopra, *The Collected Works*, Vol. V, 81–89.

[7] Patel's Speech at Gandhi Chowk, Saraspur, on 2 November 1935. Ibid. Also See *Bombay Chronicle*, 3 November 1935 and Patel Papers, File No. Lot 1-35, cuttings of Sardar's Speeches, Ahmedabad.

the employment of million of farmers and craftsmen and have placed them in a position where they have nothing to do.[8]

Similarly in his letter to G. Natesan in January 1939, Rajaji expressed his opinion about the British rule and said, 'I cannot give in to Britain's arrogance or be victimized by her trickiness.... I see no greatness of conduct in their present attitude towards India, I see only a desire to loot and exploit.'[9]

Speaking on poverty in 1934 in Madras, Rajaji said that the problem of hunger would not be solved by industrializing India but by making it industrious.[10] In this way, he told the people of Madras, 'Your own unemployment will end and with it that of the poor people.'[11]

Writing in September 1939 to Shankarlal Banker, Rajaji wrote that 'the problems of Indian politics will no doubt be solved sometime and be forgotten thereafter, but the reborn spinning wheel is a thing that will live for ever in the cottage of India.'[12] Thus, though Rajaji did not make any direct reference to underdevelopment of Indian economy on account of colonialism, one may draw inferences from his views as to how *charkha* and khadi through their regenerative role could revive the Indian economy and challenge colonialism.

Rajendra Prasad too instructed Sri Krishna Babu, dated 4 March 1938 that:

Congress Ministry in Bihar should insist upon all purchases to be made in India of swadeshi goods. I may mention for example stationery, furniture for furnishing offices or hospitals, houses for government officers and so forth. All cloth purchases should be of khadi and, where not practicable, from swadeshi mills.[13]

Thus, Prasad's statement was a reiteration of the Moderate viewpoint on colonization of the Indian economy, although the veteran leader did not make any direct reference to drain or de-industrialization as the Moderates had done. In fact, with the exception of Left leaders such as Nehru within

---

[8] Patel's Speech at Uttar Pradesh Kisan Conference at Allahabad on 28 April 1935. See Chopra, *The Collected Works*, Vol. V.

[9] Rajaji to Natesan, January 1939. See Rajaji Papers, NMML.

[10] Rajaji's Speech at Madras, 1934. Ibid.

[11] Ibid.

[12] Rajaji to Shakarlal Banker, 15 September 1939. See Rajaji Papers, NMML.

[13] Rajendra Prasad to Sri Krishna Sinha, 4 March 1938. See R.P. Papers, NMML.

Congress who articulated the economic critique of colonialism during 1920s and 1930s, the 'Right' leaders such as Patel, Rajaji and Prasad accepted the Moderates's analysis of the colonization of Indian economy. The 'Right', however, laid more emphasis on the political critique of colonialism, although they always spoke on how the policy of the British Government was injurious to the interests of Indian people, especially kisans and the labour.

The anti-colonial ideology of the 'Right' hinged on their concept of socio-economic and political vision of the movement which would be realized by achieving *swarajya* and establishing a democratic, civil libertarian, welfare state based on social, political and economic equality. For them, *swarajya* could not be real for the masses unless it made possible the achievement of a society in which democracy could extend from political to the social and economic sphere and in which there would be no opportunity for the privileged classes to exploit the bulk of the people, nor for gross inequalities as it existed then.[14]

Sardar Patel, in his speech at Bombay on 30 December 1935, said that the mission of the Congress was twofold. On the one hand, it was carrying on its struggle for independence. On the other hand, the Congress was building up national institutions in times of peace.[15] Further elaborating on what kind of national institutions he envisaged during peace time, Patel said on 17 October 1935 that for the people of British India as well as for the people of Indian states, he supported establishment of responsible government ensuring fundamental rights of citizenship like freedom of person, speech, association and the press.[16]

Theoretically, the three leaders accepted the relevance of the Gandhian vision of parliamentary *swarajya* based on the panchayat system.[17] It would

[14] Opening Speech by Kriplani, the Congress President and a Right-wing leader at a meeting of the All India Congress Committee (hereafter AICC) in Delhi on 15 November 1947. This view of Kriplani was supported by Patel, Prasad and Rajaji. See Choudhary, *Dr. Rajendra Prasad*, Vol. VII, 386–389.

[15] Patel's Speech at Bombay 30 December 1935. See *Bombay Chronicle*, 31 December 1935, in File No. Lot 1-35, Cuttings of Sardar's Speeches, Patel Papers, Ahmedabad.

[16] Patel's Speech at Congress Working Committee at Madras, 17 October 1935. See Chopra, *The Collected Works*, Vol. V, 170–173.

[17] See the writings of Patel, Prasad and Rajaji. For Patel see his speech on 'To Protect Civil Liberties, Arbitration—A Sovereign Remedy and under the New Order' in Nandurkar, *Sardar Patel*, 143, 175, 179. For Prasad see his letter to Sir B.N. Rao, Constitutional Advisor, dated 10 May 1948. He wrote,

> I like the idea of making Constitution begin with the Village and go up to the Centre and then go down to the Provinces leaving the still lower bases to be dealt

represent the sovereignty of the people based on pure moral authority and devoid of violence. The tools with which such a system would be perpetuated were: the concept of Panchayati Raj, of trusteeship, *charkha*, village industry, basic education, removal of untouchability, communal harmony, prohibition and organization of labour as *Majur Mahajan*.[18] However, for practical purposes, the three leaders accepted the British parliamentary system during the ministry period in 1938–1939 and 1945–1946 and even later. The Congress did not have to build its political system from the scratch as the existence of civil service and judiciary facilitated their shift towards British Parliamentary system. Prasad wrote in his *Autobiography*:

> So long as we were wedded to democratic system of Parliamentary government and accepted the British, we did nothing in thought or deed to infringe those conventions. It is a different matter if one thinks that we should not have followed the British system and should have developed our own convention. No one suggested it at the time. I do not think the idea that India should have a system of government other than democratic ever crossed anyone's mind unless it be that of Muslim League. I do not believe India would ever agree to forsake democracy. If she did so, it would mean entrusting the fate of the country to the hands of a single individual or a group of people.... No political party has ever expressed the view that

---

with by the Provinces.... The idea is to reverse the process and start with the village which has been and will ever continue to be our unit in this country ... there is also the idea of utilizing the adult franchise only for the Village Panchayat and making the Village Panchayats the electoral college for electing representatives to the Provinces and the Centre. I strongly advocate this...."

See Choudhary, *Dr. Rajendra Prasad*, Vol. IX, 51–52. Rajaji too supported political decentralization. He was opposed to the idea of a majority by strength of its number oppressing people and suppressing their rights under the constitution, because of its voting strength in Parliament and State legislature.

People should have confidence in the rightness of democratic governments' policies and democratic government must have faith that it is working for the welfare of the masses. No democratic government should consider all opposition to its programme as hostile. After all democracy goes from strength to strength where there is a healthy opposition acting as a check on its activities which are not in the interests of the nation.

See *Swarajya*, 18 December 1960 in *Satyam Eva Jayate*, Vols. I–IV.
[18] Ibid.

democracy is not possible in India or that another system of government should be introduced here.[19]

Rajagopalachari too, agreed with Patel and Prasad that only democracy could be accepted as a political system for India. He laid great stress on the character of the people for its success. While criticizing the socialists in 1938, Rajaji said that the omnipotence of the state worked havoc with the freedom of the individual and reduced to a minimum all chances of his enjoying happiness or harmony of life. According to him, 'It is the citizen that is a reality and the tangible and unalterable fact.'[20]

Expressing his view on his kind of democracy, popular control and self-government, Rajaji on 27 September 1937 said, It is a well known and well appreciated fact that self-government is not possible, unless we trust all our people. On what is the Government based? This is a great moral movement and we may well trust a little more, the village community.[21]

Patel summarized the opinion of the 'Right' leaders on the kind of political system to be established once *swarajya* was achieved. In his speech at Delhi on 2 January 1949, he said:

In free India there would be no distinction of caste, creed or religion or of classes resulting in the domination of one section over another. There may be rich and poor, happy and unhappy, but there would be no difference in stature between one citizen and the other.'[22]

---

[19] Rajendra Prasad, *Autobiography*, 447.

[20] Rajaji in his letter to Rev. Maclean dated 31 May 1940 expressed his love for democracy and self-government. He also reiterated that people of India did not vote for Congress because Congress lured them by making attractive promises, but because the people too preferred self-government and democracy. Rajaji said:

> Your argument that the people in India can never be expected wisely to answer such a question and therefore they are incompetent to give such a mandate cannot be accepted by one who believes that the people have a 'right' to decide their own future and they generally do well in trusting their own intelligence in such matter....

Rajaji Papers, NMML.

[21] Rajaji's Speech in the Madras Legislative Assembly, 15 September 1937. Ibid. Also see *Madras Legislative Assembly Debates*, Vol. VIII, 142.

[22] Patel's Speech at Delhi, 2 January 1949. Nandurkar, *Sardar Patel—In Tune with the Millions-II*, 56.

Patel, speaking at Ginning Factory at Viramgam on 4 January 1935, had already articulated that by *swaraj* he did not mean removal of white sahibs and placing black sahibs but it meant establishment of *majoor raj* or *raj* of the farmers, reviving spinning wheel and village industries and preparation of khadi 'in every village home' to help the starving millions.[23]

There were two options before the three leaders regarding the *swaraj*, either to opt for Gandhian egalitarian, non-violent, non-exploitative humane society or the society based on Western civic culture. The 'Right' were struggling to amalgamate the best of both. Clarifying their position, Patel further stressed:

> If we want to carry on government, there are only two ways of doing it. One is the path laid out by Mahatma Gandhi. That is the establishment of Ram Raj in which there is complete peace, freedom from crime and coercion of any kind. All of us should try to achieve that consummation; but undoubtedly we cannot reach to that goal overnight. The alternative to it is a firm government backed by a strong Army, strong Navy, strong Air Force and a strong Police; but ultimately governed by the will of people.[24]

The representatives of all the main political currents in the Congress too voiced support for a democratic system of government. On this issue, there was unanimity of opinion between the two main contenders for ideological hegemony over the Congress. Nehru, Bose and socialists were as much supporters of democracy as Patel, Prasad, Rajagopalachari or Pant and Kriplani. On this issue even liberals were not far behind; both Jayakar and Sapru were ardent supporters of the British parliamentary system.[25]

Thus, from 1934 to 1947, British Parliamentary system influenced the thinking of the 'Right' leaders. The features of Gandhi's parliamentary *swaraj*—Panchayati Raj—were finally incorporated in the Constitution of independent India along with khadi and village Industries. Yet during the formation of Ministries in 1937 and 1946, the 'Right' leadership looked upon the British Cabinet as a model and wanted to follow British

---

[23] Patel's Speech at Ginning Factory at Viramgam, 4 January 1935. See *Home Political (special)*, MSA, 4 January 1935, NAI, New Delhi.

[24] Patel's Speech at Calcutta, 3 January 1948. See Nandurkar, *Sardar Patel—In Tune with the Millions-I*, 18.

[25] See the preceding pages of this chapter on democracy. Also see 'Jaykar and Sapru Correspondence, 1938–1939' in Jaykar Papers, File No. 480, NAI, New Delhi.

conventions and traditions.[26] No members of other political parties like those of the Muslim League were taken into the ministry in the provinces where Congress had come in a majority, as it would not have been in accordance with the British democratic principles, according to Prasad.[27]

The 'Right' had empathy with Gandhi's concept of parliamentary *swarajya*. The heart of the three leaders beat in unison with Gandhi's vision but their mind, remembering the history of the nation, favoured strong Central government. Patel stood for strong centre and army, based on industrialization and Prasad and Rajaji went along with Patel's view. Prasad and Rajaji nowhere in their public career expressed disagreement with Patel's viewpoint on this issue. Speaking in favour of a strong state, Patel said, 'I am prepared to admit that if the Indian Government is to be run today on the basis of Gandhian philosophy without army I am prepared to change the whole thing.... Tomorrow the whole of India will be run over from one end to the other if you do not have strong army.'[28]

Patel had been clear about the need for a strong central government. In his speech at Hyderabad on 2 November 1948, he said, 'A strong centre, a well equipped modern army, economic contentment and responsible citizenships and a firm administrative fabric are the essential requisites as well as expression of that unity and strength'.[29]

In practice, this was to be the guideline for the construction of political and administrative institutions for the governance of the state, to which all the three Gandhian leaders agreed. And the fact that the basic administrative structure of the British colonial government was incorporated with some modifications into free India and with the three leaders occupying positions of responsibility and influence is proof enough as to what kind of political system they preferred.

Inner-party Functioning within the Congress

The question of democracy was also related to the inner-party functioning within the Congress. Congressmen were given enough freedom to discuss and voice their opinion over any resolutions of the Congress during local, provincial or AICC meetings or in the Working Committee or in discussion with each other. But they were discouraged from voicing their differences

---

[26] Prasad, *Autobiography*, 446.

[27] Ibid.

[28] Patel's Speech, 10 October 1949 in the Parliament. Nandurkar, *Sardar Patel—In Tune with the Million-II*, Vol. II, 126.

[29] Patel's Speech at Hyderabad, 2 November 1948, ibid., Vol. II, 241.

from the official platform of the Indian National Congress for the sake of maintaining unity. As Satyamurti in his letter to Prasad and Patel wrote:

> I claim every individual Congressman has the liberty to educate Congress opinion so long as he does not compromise the Congress point of view in any case, but the Congress could not allow even a very eminent Congressman to rebel against the Congress; he would then have to go out of the Congress.[30]

Despite voicing such statements, internal differences and bickering did exist within the Congress both at provincial and central levels, like in any other democratic organization. They were, however, resolved within the party. Patel wrote to Bhim Sen on 9 February 1946, 'No man is perfect. Everyone has his own fault but in a common cause if Congressmen could not learn to co-operate, how could we hope to cope with the immense responsibilities of Free India which are going to fall on our shoulders'.[31]

Similarly, the Kher episode too was an outcome of personal ambition and ego, clashing with the party decorum, discipline and national interest. The unfortunate outcome of these episodes was that consciously Patel was made the target of attack by the Left sympathizers within the Congress, although their very existence in the party was due to the democratic nature of the party which was zealously guarded by the so called 'Right' leaders of the Congress.[32]

During the Ministry period too, Patel complained on 31 December 1937:

> There are parties organized within the Congress who form the greatest stumbling block in the Ministries' work. They criticize the Ministries day in and day out and place enormous obstacles in their way of doing good to the masses. A sympathetic and friendly criticism is welcome. But hostile ones are likely to make the Ministries

---

[30] Satyamurti to Patel, 27 June 1939, Satyamurti Papers, NMML, New Delhi. Nehru through his letter to Nariman dated 21 April 1937 warned the Congressmen,

> [I]t is our view that at this time no important Congressmen should make any statement contradicting another Congressman in this particular matter. If any contradiction is necessary, either the Working Committee or the Parliamentary Sub-Committee or President or General Secretary will do that.

AICC, File No. G-39/1937, NMML.
[31] Sardar's letter to Bhim Sen, 9 February 1946. Nandurkar, *Sardar's Letters*, Vol. IV, 61.
[32] See Gandhi, *Patel: A Life*.

capable of doing no good. Ultimately the responsibility is of the electorates and they are the final judges. The moment you feel the Ministries are acting against your interests and are no more useful recall them from office.[33]

The existence of the Congress Socialist Party and other Left sympathizers within the Congress was a reflection of the democratic nature of the Congress. Speaking at Ahmedabad on 18 July 1934, Patel commented on the socialists:

We should welcome the new ideas as well as new parties, if they are helpful in leading us nearer towards freedom. If they prove hindrance to our goal of achieving freedom, we should not hesitate to leave them. No nation has achieved freedom easily without paying its price. Though we should be proud of our penance and sacrifices but our sufferings appear too meagre in comparison to other nations who have sacrificed both for achieving and sustaining their freedom. Those who think that we have not gained anything in relation to our sufferings are mistaken.[34]

Yet the Congress remained liberal enough to allow the Congress Socialist Party to exist within the Congress even when its aim was to dominate the Congress and convert it from national into class organization.[35] Patel said:

I have no dispute with socialism or the Congress Socialist Party, but I cannot help bitterly criticizing our youth, who without giving a proper thought to the prevailing attractive sentences of the western ideology, want directly to adopt them as their own. I am neither learned nor possess any knowledge about the ideologies. But I do have some common knowledge to believe that a certain ideology is not without any defects.... I am afraid that the so-called slogan of socialists to 'March Forward' is nothing but hollow talk. If socialist or any other party comes forward and points out to me some radical

---

[33] *Bombay Chronicle*, 1 January 1938, Bombay.

[34] Patel's Speech, 18 July 1934, in Chopra, *The Collected Works*, Vol. IV, 164.

[35] Patel's Speech at Benaras Vidyapith on 1 August 1934. Ibid., 173–175. In this long speech, Patel clarified his opinion about the socialists, their political methods and why they should be in the Congress. By this speech he also put at rest the allegations that he was determined to root out socialists root and branch.

programme which they have courage to implement immediately,
I am ready to enroll myself in their ranks.'[36]

Both Patel and Nehru believed that democracy did not mean shouting
loudly, taking to violence and defying party discipline, but it meant responsibility, self-discipline and certain standards of behaviour.[37]

Civil Liberties

Democracy as a political system thrives on and draws its rationale from civil
liberties. Being true democrats, all prominent Congress leaders regarded it
as an essential creed for establishing democracy. In the Congress resolution on fundamental rights and duties, civil liberties occupied a position
of immense primacy.[38] Civil liberties were as important to the 'Right' as
to Nehru who said, '[w]hen civil liberties were suppressed a nation lost all
vitality and became impotent for anything substantial.'[39] In fact, in a letter
dated 24 July 1948 Prasad wrote to Nehru, 'The question of civil liberties
stands on an altogether different footing. I do not think there will be any
difference on that point as between conservatives and progressives. In fact
most of the so-called "conservatives" are concerned about it than the so-
called "progressives".'[40]

Nehru in 1936 established an Indian Civil Liberties Union on non-
party lines, with members of all shades of political opinion and even
from outside the party. It had the support of the 'Right' leaders also.
Its Constitution specified that there should be freedom of thought,
expression and assemblage. The aim of the Union was to protect these
rights from all encroachments and infringement by executive and judi-
cial authority, by the issue of ordinances and the enactment of so-called
emergency laws, as well as the detention, internment, externment and
imprisonment of persons without due trial and by the tendency of government and other agencies to use their power to curtail the few remaining
liberties of the people.[41]

---

[36] Ibid.
[37] For Patel's view see ibid. For Nehru's view see his article 'Where Are We?' in S. Gopal,
SWJN, Vol. IX.
[38] P. Sitaramayya, *The History of the Indian National Congress*, Vol. II (New Delhi, 1969)
(reprint), 99.
[39] S. Gopal, SWJN, Vol. IX, 208.
[40] Choudhary, *Dr. Rajendra Prasad*, Vol. IX, 241.
[41] S. Gopal, SWJN, Vol. IX, 113.

Although Rajendra Prasad, Patel and Rajaji agreed with the principles of the Indian Civil Liberty Union, they were opposed to the Leftist interpretation of civil liberties.[42] For the 'Right', civil liberty meant free expression of opinion, right of free association and combination, equality before law as long as the purpose was not opposed to law or morality.[43] But the Leftists discerned a class bias in the definition of civil liberties given by the 'Right'. According to the Left, the civil liberty offered by the 'Right'-supported Congress ministers was conditional.

> The people will have full civil liberty on condition that class war and violence are not preached.... The people of India do not want civil liberties with conditions attached to them. On the contrary the people of India, especially the workers must have the unconditional liberty of association, of going on strike, of making speeches and of issuing newspapers. In the whole of civilized world this indeed is the meaning of civil liberties on which depends our freedom.[44]

The Gandhian leaders were of the view:

> if civil liberty means the liberty of association with a view to molest and even to assault ... then our country at least had better remain without the pale of the civilized sphere. Civil liberties for which the Congress pledged to truth and non-violence mean liberty conditioned by the use of truth and non-violence.[45]

Patel made hard hitting attack on the 'Leftists' viewpoint of civil liberties. He favoured duty-bound civil liberty. According to him:

> It would be a poor return for those sacrifices and sufferings if we fail to preserve the liberties which we have won after so much struggle and to surrender them to the merciless and ruthless tactics of a comparatively small number of persons whose inspiration, methods and culture are all of a foreign stamp. When we think of civil liberties of the extremely small number of persons concerned, let the House

---

[42] Ibid.

[43] Ibid.

[44] The quote is taken from Mahadev Desai's exposition in *Harijan* on civil liberties. In his exposition, Mahadev Desai has criticized the Communist viewpoint of civil liberties. AICC, File No. G-8-1937/38, NMML.

[45] Ibid.

also think of the liberties of the millions of people threatened by the activities of individuals whose civil liberties we have curtailed. I am using the words 'civil liberties' in connection with these individuals with some reluctance because for them liberty is synonymous with license and there is hardly any difference between civil and criminal.[46]

Patel not only regarded civil liberties as cornerstone of democracy but considered freedom of press as life and blood of civil liberty. 'The freedom of Press is an ideal that we cherish as it is a concomitant of democracy. If we want a democratic rule, we must have freedom of press, freedom of speech, freedom of expression and the freedom of association.'[47]

However, Patel was against unconditional freedom which was the demand of the Left. According to him,

All kinds of freedom are good, but if in this big assembly one or two youngsters try to frighten people by hurling bombs or crackers at them what are we to do? Can we allow them freedom? Can we ask policemen not to handle them? Should we call it freedom? It is not freedom but lunacy and asylum is the only proper place for him.[48]

In his instruction to the Ministries on civil liberties Patel stated:

Civil Liberty must have the full scope in Congress regime. Please note the adjective civil before 'liberty'. The moment your drop the word 'civil', 'liberty' will then mean license. No responsible government can allow license or unlimited liberty to the people. If the criminal liberty of a few persons should be restrained for exercise of the civil liberty of lakhs of law-abiding citizens and if the Congress Ministries fail to impose restrictions on those few, then they will be failing in duty.[49]

Patel advocated civil liberty tempered by a sense of duty and responsibility. In a letter to S.K. Patil dated 28 June 1937, he highlighted this aspect categorically.

A newspaper in the hands of an office bearer of an important Congress organization is a dangerous weapon and can often be successfully used

---

[46] Nandurkar, *Sardar Patel: In Tune with the Millions-II*, 145–148.
[47] Ibid.
[48] Ibid.
[49] *Bombay Chronicle*, 31 December 1937.

to mislead public opinion by suppressing the truth and also by propagating untruth, unless the man holding that office has the courage to face unpopularity, risk his office and even incur the displeasure of his colleagues for the sake of standing by the truth and exposing fraud, hypocrisy and untruth. This is a difficult task. I frankly confess that you are not according to my judgement an equal to that task.... My advice to you would be, resist the temptation of taking the responsibility of running a newspaper, until you are mentally, morally and financially equipped adequately for the task which to my mind is not so easy as is supposed to be.... I hope you will not take this amiss. I understand your difficulties and your delicate position but we who have braved hardships and borne sufferings have not done so far, depriving our soul, and we are expected to have greater moral courage than the normal run of people to stand by truth in spite of difficulties and embarrassments.[50]

Thus, in the notion of Congress 'Right' on civil liberties, there was no space for acts of violence, incitement to violence or promulgation of palpable falsehoods. They supported the measures that might be undertaken for the defence of life, property and democracy.[51]

However, the Congress Ministries were not entirely working on the principles of non-violence, while dealing with the question of civil liberties in the respective provinces. Rajendra Prasad protested on misuse of the Maintenance of Public Order Act and wrote to Patel, dated 18 May 1948:

I object to the suppression of expression of public opinion by the use of extraordinary powers under the Maintenance of Public Order Act in such matters on which public opinion should be not only allowed to be expressed but welcomed.... As I have indicated in my last letter Governments are only too prone to take recourse to extraordinary powers. In recent months it has been seen that the High Courts have upset more orders of Government than perhaps they did in former regimes. It is not in the interest of our governments that they should be exposed to criticisms that High Courts have had to intervene for the protection of people from illegal arrests and detention. In our regime the people should have no ground to go to High Courts

---

[50] Patel to S.K. Patil, dated 28 June 1937. See Patel Papers, F. No. 1-33-3, SPNM.
[51] *Bombay Chronicle*, 26 September 1938.

against our Governments, and if they did go the orders should be
such that the High Courts would not interfere.[52]

During the Ministry period, there was an upsurge of strikes and violent
demonstrations from 1937 onwards. Like agrarian troubles, it was widespread but also localized within each province. Except for the North-West
Frontier Province and Orissa which had no large industries, no province
was wholly free from strikes during the short spans of Congress Ministries.
Especially in Bihar, UP, Madras and Bombay, there were breaches of peace.
Rajaji was greatly alarmed by labour disputes during his tenure of office.
He blamed the communists for causing disruptions in the functioning of
industries and producing antagonism in the relationships between capital
and labour. He was of the opinion that certain amount of thoughtlessness
and confusion of principles, and the propaganda and wrong leadership of
some men, who had love of a class revolution for their own sake, made
them blind to the starvation and misery of actual human beings. He further
said that the transition from slogans to certain forms of dangerous violence
would ruin all industries long before a class revolution could ever be conceivably brought about and before the state and its resources were strong
enough to bridge the gap between capital and labour. This the revolutionary young men who maintained their influence over industrial labour did
not realize. Forcible occupation of the workshop and physical seizure of
machinery were forms of disorder and violence that were a mockery of the
methods of non-violence, of peaceful methods of picketing or non-cooperation, which were associated with the name of the great leader the magic of
whose name gave to the classes strength and prestige they now commanded
in India. Rajaji also said that the revolutionaries brought about a situation
whereby authorities of the state were compelled to use force far out of proportion to the original mischief and thereby rousing public attention, and
such act would not succeed except very temporarily.[53]

The Congress Ministries on their part were well aware that the
outbreak of strikes was not only a challenge to their authority but

---

[52] Prasad to Patel dated 18 May 1948, Choudhary, *Dr. Rajendra Prasad*, Vol. IX, 76. Also
see Prasad, *Autobiography*, 689.

[53] Copley, *The Political Career of C. Rajagopalachari, 1937–1954*, 159–160. At Haripura
Congress in 1938, the Civil Liberty resolution that was passed deplored the violence and
arson carried out in the name of class war and supported the measures taken by Congress
government in defence of life and property. Also see Sinha, *Left Wing in India, 1919–1947*,
Muzaffarpur, 1965, 447. See B.N. Pande, ed., *A Centenary History of the Indian National
Congress*, Vol. III (New Delhi, 1984), 182.

also an attack on the policies till now followed by the Congress. The Ministries, backed by Sardar Patel, at once took steps to strengthen the forces of law and order. The Bombay government adopted a Trades Disputes Act in November 1938 to prevent lightning strikes and lock-outs. The Communists declaring that the rights of labour had been violated set themselves to organize demonstrations. They were joined by Dr Ambedkar's Independent Labour Party and the Bombay's branch of Trade Union Congress. However, the response to the Communists' call was very feeble; out of 77 mills, communists succeeded in closing only 17 mills. Similarly, in Kanpur, labour unrest was brewing but with the intervention of Pandit Nehru and setting up of Labour Enquiry Committee it was averted.[54]

The 'Right' leadership of the Congress was worried over the propaganda carried out by the communalists and communists against them in the name of civil liberties. They were forced to make statements that the designs of the opponents of the Congress could be stalled if Congressmen behaved in responsible way and did not get carried away by the propaganda of their opponents who claimed to fight imperialism or agitate for civil liberties or the economic rights of the peasants or the labourer. Rajaji said: 'Congressmen should have the confidence that they are the best guardians of the economic and political interests of the country and the masses.'[55]

Patel, Prasad and Rajaji in a truly democratic manner refused to participate in Congress Legislative Assembly elections in April 1945, when other organizations were still under ban.

Free and fair elections are hardly possible when several organisations like the Congress Socialist Party, the Forward Block and Kisan organisations are still under ban, when thousands are still held in detention without trial or are undergoing sentences of imprisonment with political activities, when in many places public meetings cannot be held without previous permission of the authorities and when many persons are labouring under the qualifications arising out of their convictions for political offence.[56]

---

[54] R. Coupland, *The Constitutional Problem in India* (London, 1944), 127–129.
[55] A.R.H. Copley, *The Political Career of C. Rajagopalachari, 1937–54: A Moralist in Politics* (Madras, 1978).
[56] Patel's Speech, 2 April 1945, in Patel Papers, File No. Lot 1 to 3, SPNM, Ahmedabad.

EXTENSION OF DEMOCRACY TO THE
SOCIO-ECONOMIC SPHERE

The socio-economic vision of the 'Right' leadership for independent India
was based on social equality and justice. The guiding principle for formulating socio-economic policy was:

> Swaraj can not be real for the masses unless it makes possible the
> achievement of a society in which democracy extends from the politi-
> cal to the social and economic sphere and in which there would be
> no opportunity for the privileged classes to exploit the bulk of the
> people nor for gross inequalities such as it exists at present.[57]

However, the extension of democracy to socio-economic sphere should
be seen at two levels within the anti-colonial ideological framework—one
at the level of ideas and value and its dissemination through khadi, *charkha*,
Harijan Seva Sangha, basic education and village industries, and, secondly,
at the operational level during the Ministry period. The legislative measures
on labour, tenancy reforms, position on labour–capital and zamindar–
peasantry issues, etc., may merit special consideration in this regard.[58]

Constructive Programme

In the realm of ideas, Patel, Prasad and Rajaji regarded the Gandhian
concept of Panchayati Raj and trusteeships as two pillars of economic
decentralization. The Congress manifesto influenced by Gandhian ideology touched upon the crucial aspects of economic decentralization. It gen-
erated enthusiasm intermingled with optimism so much so that Erskine,
the Governor of Madras, commented just after the election in 1937:

> The wildest promises in regard to land revenue and other taxes were
> made in the village by Congress and within the greatly enlarged and
> ignorant electorate these promises were for the time being believed
> by the great majority of the voters.... As far as I can make out and
> I have had enquiries made, very little real sedition was talked during
> the election and the Congress victory was won entirely by economic

---

[57] J.B. Kripalani's address at All India Congress Committee meeting on 15 November
1947 in Choudhary, *Dr. Rajendra Prasad*, Vol. VII, 386–389.
[58] See Chapter 5 titled 'Strategic Issues'.

promises and the general idea was engendered of a sort of utopia in which nobody need in future pay any taxes and where hospitals, wells etc. would spring up like mushrooms in the night.[59]

The framework for democratization of economy and society as visualized by the three leaders was based on Gandhi's constructive programme. However, while analysing the views of these leaders individually one may notice their nuanced differences. In consonance with the Gandhian constructive programme of decentralization of economy and society, Patel exhorted the peasants of Gujarat on 27–28 December 1934, while visiting various districts of Gujarat like Broach, Ras, Rampraja, Kareli, etc., to forsake drink, gambling and untouchability. They should use *khaddar* to help the peasantry and support home industries. He said *swaraj* could be achieved with the help of the village or home industries.[60] Patel further elaborated that for India hand spinning and hand weaving were appropriate as it was impossible for a country like India to seek a solution to its question of village reconstruction or rehabilitation through industrial development.[61]

According to Patel, economic power would come to the villagers by strengthening village industries. Village industry would need a village organization. It would give rise to accumulation of money which till now was being sent to the cities. Thus, peasants would become independent of government as they would be able to generate resources at the village level.[62]

In his speech to the women members of the Jyoti-Sangh, Ahmedabad on 2 October 1934, Patel explained what he meant by *swadeshi* and how it would strengthen the peasantry and give them economic power to make them self-reliant so that they could meet the difficulties imposed by the British government on them. He said:

One definition given by you that Swadeshi is mill made cloth may be correct in one sense. But in a broader sense it is a great stigma. It is not necessary for us to popularize the mill cloth. Mill owners are monetarily in a very sound position. They would be able to dispatch

[59] Erskine to Zetland, 20 April 1937 in Copley, *The Political Career of C. Rajagopalachari*, 118.
[60] Patel's Speech at Jambusar, 27 December 1934, *Home Department (special)*, MSA, Bombay.
[61] Patel's Speech at Ras, 30 September 1934. Ibid.
[62] Patel's Speech at Nadiad, 29 December 1934. Ibid.

their goods in every village without your help … when many varieties of khadi are available then why help the mills. I do not want you to hear the complaints of Bombay and Ahmedabad mill owners. When a number of persons had courted imprisonment at that time the mill owners of Bombay had entered into a contract with Lancashire and mortgaged the nation. How can we assist those who care for their own business and have no feelings for the nation's welfare? The factory owners shall indulge in flattery to the Government. In that sense if we use only khadi we would have the satisfaction of doing enough.[63]

Similarly, Rajaji too actively participated in making Gandhian programme of economic and social decentralization popular and successful. Like Patel, he too regarded that spirit of sacrifice, spirit of unity and self-confidence would be built up among the Indian masses through *charkha*, khadi, removal of untouchability, removal of drinking and temple entry of Harijans. These he saw as a vehicle to forge unity among the various social groups of India, an essential condition for the success of *swarajya*.[64] As early as in 1923 to make constructive programme a success, Rajaji had supported foundation of Gandhi Sewa Sangh and Tiruchengode Ashram.[65] Rajaji regarded production and sale of khadi, trusteeship, harijan upliftment, prohibition of liquor and Hindu–Muslim unity as a process of self-purification and decentralization of society, the only path to attain swrajya.[66] To quote Rajaji on trusteeship:

A new way of life, a new culture is what is aimed at. This cannot be achieved by coercion but only by a heart change. The doctrine of enlightened selfishness of the nineteenth century utilitarians should be refined into a doctrine of immanent trusteeship.[67]

Rajendra Prasad too in his writings *At the Feet of Mahatma Gandhi* and *Autobiography* discussed his belief that the decentralization of economy and

---

[63] Speaking at Bhadra in Gujarat in October 1934, Patel, however, spoke on not making khadi wearing and weaving an essential condition to become a Congress member. His anxiety was due to influx of socialist members within the Congress. Although Patel accepted that unless wearing of khadi was made compulsory nobody would use the spinning wheel. *Bombay Chronicle*, 2 October 1934.

[64] Gandhi, *The Rajaji Story-I*, 155.

[65] Ibid.

[66] Rajgopalachari, *Satyam Eva Jayate*, Vol. I, 321–322.

[67] Ibid

society was essential for the wholesome growth of the basic constituent of the society, i.e., the individual. He highlighted through his writings and speeches his faith in khadi, *charkha*, Panchayati Raj and Wardha Education Scheme for whose promotion he made considerable efforts during the Ministry period through the All India Talimi Sangh.[68]

At the operational level, the three leaders used the Ministry period to put into practice what they were articulating through the Congress's Constructive Programme. Despite many social and political convulsions of kisan movements focusing on no rent, labour strikes or increased political activities of the socialists and communists occurring in the name of civil liberty, the three leaders were in favour of debt relief, streamlining tenancy and rent act and settling labour–capital disputes through arbitration. The focus of the three leaders was on averting labour–capital or kisan–zamindar conflict. A class war, in their view, might have been necessary in other countries under other historical conditions. In India, the struggle for national independence was all inclusive. It included and transcended the class war. It had within itself the seeds of every necessary revolution and readjustment.[69]

Patel, Rajaji and Prasad considered building of zamindar–peasant and labour–capital relationships on the Gandhian principle of co-operation, compassion and arbitration. Realizing that the Congress Ministry had little time at hand, Prasad wanted to put into action many of the Gandhian schemes incorporated in the election manifesto of the Congress. In a letter to Sri Krishna Babu, Prime Minister of Bihar, on 4 March 1938, Rajendra Prasad wrote:

> I do not know when the next constitutional crisis will arise. It may come as suddenly and unexpectedly as the last one. I am therefore anxious that the Ministry should get through as many legislative and administrative measures as possible within the shortest possible time so that when the next crisis comes, the country may have before it a record of good work done by the Congress Ministry.[70]

In the same letter, he instructed Sri Krishna Babu to include village industries in the department of industry besides introducing the Tenancy Bill, Prohibition, Wardha Education Scheme and amendments of

---

[68] Prasad, *At the Feet of Mahatma Gandhi*.
[69] Prasad's Letter to Sri Krishna Sinha, Prime Minister, Government of Bihar, 4 March 1938 in R.P. Papers, NMML.
[70] Ibid.

municipal, local self-government and village panchayats. The amendments that Prasad suggested were the reservation of seats for Muslims on the basis of joint electorates and increase in the number of seats for scheduled castes and tribes. The power should be conferred on village panchayats for dealing with village disputes and village uplift work. The cooperative movement needed overhauling and the Act might also need to be amended.[71] Prasad in the same letter mentioned that in the election manifesto of the Congress there was promise of introducing collective farming. He wanted it to be introduced on an experimental basis without hurting the property rights of individuals. His suggestion was that the Ministry should make this experiment in two or three suitable places where the agricultural department should cooperate with a non-official organization like the Congress. It could only be on a voluntary basis, i.e., the owners of land should agree amongst themselves to have collective farming and to distribute the produce in proportion to the land belonging to each after deducting the cost of cultivation. Prasad suggested that in the beginning the experiment should be made for three classes of crops, i.e., paddy, sugar, maize, arhar, wheat, etc.; a detailed survey of plots and keeping a complete record and paying wages to the very men whose land had been taken could be some of the measures effected in this direction. He also suggested to Sri Krishna Babu that repressive laws, police and jail rules and regulations too needed repeal and reform and they required urgent attention.[72] The agrarian question

---

[71] Ibid.

[72] In a letter dated 20 April 1938, Rajendra Prasad wrote to Sir Kameshwar Singh stating,

> After much discussion and a great deal of deliberation we have managed to come to an understanding on many points relating to tenancy law and the Agricultural Income Tax Bill. Speaking from the point of view of the large body of tenants and the government ... I have no doubt I shall come in for a great deal of criticism from not only the Kisan Sabha but Congressmen in general and even perhaps from our High Command, But I have taken the responsibility.... More important than the law is its administration and more important than the understanding is the way in which it is given effect. I am anxious that the tension that now subsists should be eased and the people at large made to feel that they have got some relief as a result of the understanding.
>
> I suggest that the following steps may be taken without delay:
>
> (i) All abuses and illegal exactions should cease, e.g. no Zamindar or his amla should realize anything in excess of the legally ascertained rent and cess. No abwab in any form should be realized.
> (ii) Tenants should not be compelled to sell any articles without price or at less than the market price, e.g., oil, ghee, milk, dahi, vegetables, shoes, bamboo baskets, earthen pots, goats, young buffaloes, etc.

being the most important issue, the Bihar ministry, under the guidance of Rajendra Prasad, put into action the relief programme for the kisans. It implemented the Bihar Tenancy Act of 1938, Bihar Restoration of Bakasht Lands and Reduction of Arrears of Rent Act of 1938 and Bihar Moneylenders Act of 1938. These acts were reformative in nature.[73]

The leadership realized that the formation of the Congress Ministry would not herald coming of the Congress Raj. The Ministry was nothing but a lame experiment of the government to dilute the anti-colonial movement. And it had to function within the colonial framework with all its attendant constraints. Therefore, no radical reforms were to be expected from this experiment.[74]

Rajaji while replying to criticism that the Ministry had not done enough said on 24 February 1939:

I admit that judged from our own standards, we have done nothing. The troubles, the segregation, the ex-communication all that is a Himalayan fact which remains there. We have not shaken it. I am not satisfied with what we have done, I admit. But yet, give the devil his due; it is not right to refuse even the devil his due.[75]

The way in which the three leaders handled the agrarian and labour problems reflected their democratic and libertarian approach towards development. They also stood for building up social relationship among classes on democratic principles which would blunt the spirit of conflict and create a congenial environment in which the seeds of anti-imperialism would bloom and flourish.[76]

    (iii) No payment should be accepted without grant of a receipt in the prescribed form.

    (iv) Tenants should not be required to render to any service without wages or at less than the prevalent wages, e.g., Hari, begari, should not be demanded...

    (v) Any complaints against amlas should be promptly inquired into by the zamindar concerned and whenever found justified relief should be given and suitable action taken against the amla if necessary....

Rajendra Prasad to Sir Kameshwar Singh, 20 April 1938, Choudhary, *Dr. Rajendra Prasad*, Vol. II, 1984, 40–41.

[73] Ibid.

[74] Patel's Address to the peasantry of Boriavi, dated 29 December 1934, *Home Department (special)*, MSA, Bombay.

[75] Rajaji's Speech on 24 February 1939 in Rajaji Papers, NMML.

[76] J.B. Kriplani's Speech in New Delhi, 15 November 1947. See Choudhary, *Dr. Rajendra Prasad*, Vol. VII, 387.

They were highly critical of the centralized economy of communist or fascist states. Patel, speaking at Rani Praja Conference in Vira Teshsil, Baroda Estate on 3 March 1935 said:

> Our aim should be to see that no injustice is done either to the big landholders or to the sowkars and at the same time to see that no one's fundamental rights are ignored. We may give this much assurance to everybody that however great our difficulties and whatever the injustices perpetuated on us, we do not wish to be unjust to anybody or to act in a spirit of vengeance. At the same time we must state firmly that we do not wish to surrender our rights. If anyone still thinks in terms of living like a parasite … we would say to him that we do not propose to tolerate it. Anyone who allows another to live on him is not a man but an animal and we ought to be free from that condition. Our welfare does not lie in the hands of the king or on the merchants. Our welfare lies in our own hands. If you can grow your own food requirements from your soil and if you can also produce your other requirements no one could be happier than yourself.[77]

The three leaders were aware that some moderate agrarian reforms were immediately required. The antiquated and repressive land tenure and revenue system needed reform, and burden of rural debt needed attention. But it was equally essential to remove British imperialistic exploitation. In his first budget speech, Rajaji laid down the direction the reforms would take. Speaking in the Assembly, on 1 September 1937, he said that immediate steps would be taken to provide relief from indebtedness. Also, steps would be taken to provide clean drinking water for every village, adequate drainage system for all towns, medical relief, centres for healthy entertainment and culture in all villages and establishment of cottage industries throughout the land.[78] Defining the direction the relief measures of the Ministry should adopt, Rajaji on 1 September 1937 said in the Assembly:

> We are fully aware that the burden of the land revenue assessment is heavy but the grant of relief on a scale which would be of material assistance to the individual small ryot would involve such a dislocation that not even a beginning could be made with other ameliorative

---

[77] Patel's Speech at Rani Praja in Vira Tehsil Baroda Estate, 3 March 1935 in Parikh, *Sardar Vallabhbhai Patel*, Vol. II, 201.

[78] Rajaji's Address to the Assembly dated 20 December 1937, ibid., Vol. IV, 80–85.

measures and reforms for the well being of the masses which in the opinion of the government are of great and urgent importance and which it would not be right thus for the government to disable itself from undertaking. While on the question of the relief of the land revenue burden, my colleagues and I consider that of even greater urgency and value to the agricultural population is the adequate relief of indebtedness and immediate steps will therefore be taken in this direction, which will release the cultivators in our Province from the strangle-hold of unredeemable insolvency and despair and we hope make a man of him.[79]

Providing relief to the village was high on the priority list of Rajaji. His wish was articulated in his speech on 1 April 1939, 'I do want I admit and I repeat to shift the burden from the village to the town.'[80]

Focusing on the losses a kisan faced and how it should be checked, Rajaji continued:

Agriculture has been admitted to be uneconomic industry. The agriculturist produces the grain in that uneconomic way. He brings it to the bazaar. At once pounce upon him parasites, other people, honest people, conduits ... and all the intermediaries. None of them suffers a loss. Instead of allowing for this unfortunate state of affairs, merely as a misfortune of our country, we want to remedy this position. We want to see that the producer is really in the position that he ought to be and that the intermediaries really got what they deserve ... we want to shift the burden not so to say geographically from the village to the town, but we want to shift it a little bit from the producer to the intermediary.[81]

This could only be achieved by implementing social justice but in a non-violent manner. Arguing for the elimination of economic inequality, Rajaji said on 1 April 1939:

The choice before the people is whether they want common management by abolishing the system of individual property or whether they hope to stem the tide of that flood by heavier and heavier taxation on

[79] Rajaji's Speech in the Assembly dated 1 September 1937, *Madras Legislative Assembly Debates*, Vols. I and II, 120–126.
[80] Rajaji's Speech in the Assembly dated 1 April 1939, ibid., Vol. VII, 177.
[81] Ibid., 179–181.

those who are able to bear it and by distributing the proceeds of that taxation in such common management as will distribute amenities of life to all people. There is no other philosophy behind this proposal or any other similar proposal. It is impossible to stem the tide of communism if I may use an easily available word unless businessmen and capitalists and those who stand for individual property are ready to realize the need and the emergency for imposing upon themselves heavier and heavier taxation, fair but yet heavy taxation, and distributing the proceeds, so far as benefits go, over the whole of state.[82]

Rajaji accepted the major proposals of the Prakasam report which examined the conditions in the zamindari areas in 1938. The Committee put forward the proposals against usurpation by the zamindar of the states' right to enhance the rent.[83] He further argued that the zamindars had raised their standards of life to a level which was not contemplated by Sir John Shore or Lord Cornwallis. 'I know that it is necessary that the system should be ended. But is the Zamindar entitled to the price he asks? Is he entitled to any price, seeing that he held only an office?'[84]

Rajaji's Madras Debt Relief Act of 1938 came under much criticism from within and without the party. Yet the recommendations of the Prakasam's Zamindari Abolition Committee were radical by the standards of his followers and contemporaries. Rajaji's emphatic rejection of compensating zamindars at the market price was not liked by many. Rajaji's argument was, 'Zamindari had grown iniquitous and you do not compensate for ending iniquitous systems.'[85] He said:

---

[82] Ibid., 174–175.

[83] In 1938, a Committee of the legislature was appointed with Prakasam the Revenue Minister as chairman to enquire into relations between zamindars and tenants in permanently settled estates and to make recommendations for legislation. Its report was signed on 7 November 1938. The majority report proceeded on the assumption that the *raiyat* and not the zamindars were the owner of the soil and that (in spite of various legal decisions to the contrary) the intention of the Permanent Settlement of 1802 was to fix rents (as well as the sums–*Peshkash*–payable by the zamindars to the government) for all time. See *Quarterly Survey of Political Constitutional Position in British India*, No. 6, Surveys 1 to 6, April 1937 to 31 January 1939, NMML, New Delhi. In an interview to *The Indian Express* dated 26 September 1939, Rajaji told the correspondent that if he continued as Prime Minister, Mr Prakasam's Zamindari Bill would come into force within three months. Rajaji Papers, NMML.

[84] Rajaji's Speech in the Assembly, 26 January 1939, *Madras Legislative Assembly Debates*, 700.

[85] See Rajaji's speech in the *Madras Legislative Assembly*, 13 January 1939, Rajaji Papers, NMML.

In the other hemisphere they once had very valuable properties. Slaves they had. Was compensation paid when slavery was abolished? As far as I know even though money had been paid in the year previous to abolition to purchase thousands of slaves, no compensation was given when slavery was abolished.[86]

Thus, Rajaji was not only in favour of ending zamindari without compensation but he was also inclined towards giving protection to the landless labourers. He argued that landless labourers should be:

protected by being attached to the land as inseparable material as is mentioned in the Tanjore document: 'the land is sold with trees, with the birds, and with the men on it, with the wage earner on it.' Ultimately, we will have to come round the circle to this position that the man who works on a piece of land should stick to that land and should not be driven out of it.[87]

Rajaji further expressed his view on ameliorating the condition of the rural artisan through the means the Ministry provided. He believed that no policy for the agrarian economy would be complete if it did not assist the rural artisans.[88] Therefore, he allocated 2 lakhs of rupees for the hand-spinning movement.[89] He subsidized khadi and remained loyal to the constructive programme.[90] Defending his position in the Assembly on the issue of protecting village industries, Rajaji said on 27 September 1937:

The 2½ lakhs of handlooms are crying for help. How shall we help them? … Any protection given to the Indian mills is welcome as against the foreign cloth. But what has it done in fact? It has strengthened a giant against a giant, then it has also strengthened the giant against the worm. The handloom. This protection that is offered to the Swadeshi mill industry—whether European or Indian owned it makes no difference—this protection that has been given to the Indian mills has enabled the mills to sell their cloth cheaper than

[86] Ibid.
[87] Rajaji's Speech in the Madras Legislative Assembly, 26 January 1939. See *Madras Legislative Assembly Debates*, Vol. IX, 703–705.
[88] Ibid., 24–25.
[89] Ibid., 1 September 1937, Vols. I–II, 122.
[90] Ibid.

the rate at which the hard worked handloom weaver is expected to put his cloth in the market.[91]

Rajaji further explained his position on the issue:

It does hurt me to have to legislate in this manner, but we have to see who is worse hit. I have lived in those villages where live hundreds of weavers, weaving day and night; I have heard the tick-tick of their flying shuttle; but when the next morning the cloth is taken they see another load, the hawkers' load with Japanese cloth and mill cloth and they have to take back their load unsold. So is it wrong, is it bad to pity the weaver and do something to help him?[92]

Rajagopalachari regarded that the Ministry should involve itself in reviving and protecting rural craft industries, integrating rural craft industries and rural artisans to the economic development plan in future and providing immediate relief for the time being. In his speech on 1 October 1937 Rajaji reiterated, 'Power had been accepted to realize these principles.'[93]

Similarly, in the case of labour, Rajaji preferred settlement of labour disputes through arbitration. He employed this method in settling labour–capital disputes in January 1938 in Madura Mills at Madras and Papanasam.[94] The Madras ministry also provided non-lapsing fund for taking water to dry villages and building roads and dispensaries. They remitted land revenue in the areas hit by cyclone or drought, halved grazing fees, launched Tungabhadra scheme, initiated thermal plants in Bezwada and Vizag in the Telegu districts and took power from the hydro systems of Pykara and Mettur to eight additional Tamil districts. The Ministry, for the first time, introduced a Public Health Act in the province, and funds were allocated for drainage, purification of water and prevention of disease in towns.[95] The most important financial innovation Rajaji's ministry made was of imposing sales tax to make up for financial constraints, with central finances resting with the British. The new tax was put on the sale of tobacco, petrol and electricity. Rajaji's explanation was:

---

[91] Rajaji address to the Assembly on 27 September 1937. See ibid., Vol. III, 906–907.
[92] Ibid.
[93] Ibid.
[94] Copley, *The Political Career of C. Rajagopalachari*, 158.
[95] Ibid.

We cannot however maintain our standard of government giving up the victimization of the drinking classes without agreeing to be taxed in some way or other. The tax on petrol and electricity will fall on those who are comparatively well-off. The incidence of the general sales tax and tobacco tax will be light and the former will be a progressive source of revenue as trade and industries in the province improve. At present all the big businesses almost completely escape taxation so far as the province goes. The policy of the government in getting rid of the drink revenue will increase the spending powers of the masses by no less than Rs. 15 crores per annum, the effect of which being a considerable rise in the standard of living of masses will automatically lead to an increased demand for consumption goods thereby benefiting the trading classes all round as well as agriculturalists. I hope therefore that a long and patriotic view will be taken and our proposals given support by all classes.[96]

The Congress leadership was not seeking structural change. To bring about democratization in society and also not hurt the on-going struggle for independence, the leadership was seeking in fact attitudinal change. This could be possible by popularizing Prohibition and Temple Entry programme which formed the core of the social democratization programme of the Congress during the ministry period of 1937–1939.[97]
Defending his Temple Entry Bill on 1 December 1938, whereby Malabar temples were to be opened to the depressed castes, Rajaji said:

They want food, they want raiment, they want shelter, they want education and they want employment. In short they want a betterment of their economic condition.... Let me now come to the utility of a legislation of this nature and deal with the purposes it serves. When once the Harijan was allowed to enter the temple with his head erect, having nothing to doubt or fear then untouchability will at once vanish, ... when once entry into temples of the Harijan is recognized—he may go or he may not go to the temple; he may get darshan of the God or not he will no longer be an untouchable; and he will have all the facility to which any other Hindu is entitled.... Orthodoxy permits entry into the temples of all caste Hindus.... What the reformers want is that this tolerance should also be shown to the Harijans.

[96] Ibid., 153–154.
[97] Ibid., 145–147.

In this respect, the disability imposed upon the Harijans in regard to temple entrance is different from the other disabilities they suffer from. The distinctions in regard to social equality with reference to the various castes and communities, sub-castes and sub-communities are carefully and obstinately maintained; but these very classes are allowed on fairly equal terms entry into the innermost places of the temples. That is the reason why I said that temple entry might be the first step in the uplift of the depressed classes and not the last step.[98]

Rajaji further argued on 2 December 1938 saying:

It is true that the intellectuals amongst the Harijans may not agree for such things as temple entry and the like. They may care for more things like bread, water, services, posts and the like, but I maintained that there is no doubt whatsoever that if the temples are opened the hearts of a mass of the harijans will rejoice.... Because this country is a deeply religious country, we cannot succeed in lifting the status of the Harijans unless we touch the religious aspect of their condition. It is because our people are a deeply religious people that it is not enough if we give the Harijans schools, appointments, hospitals, hostels and sanitary conditions and roads to go about, but it is necessary to give them religion also which we have denied, which it was wrong to deny and which we seek to remove by this measure, if the people will agree and if the people will cooperate. Therefore it is because our country is truly and deeply religious that this measure is important.[99]

Thus, the three leaders stood for a democratic Kisan Mazdoor Praja Raj which would provide work to all through weaving, hand spinning and other cottage industries like gur making, etc.[100] They believed in minimum wages for all, through the All India Spinners Association. They supported associations for both the workers and peasantry. The Congress, according to them, aimed at reducing the gap between the rich and the poor. To reduce inequality of sexes, the organization of the Kasturba National Trust

---

[98] Rajaji's Speech in the Assembly, 2 December 1938. See *Madras Legislative Assembly Debates*, Vol. VIII, 469–470.

[99] Ibid., 2 December 1938 and 8 December 1938, 469–470, 661.

[100] Rajendra Prasad to Sri Krishna Sinha, 1 May 1938 in Choudhary, *Dr. Rajendra Prasad*, Vol. II, 43.

was an addition to the long list of services rendered by the Congress to the women's cause.[101]

The three leaders thus did not believe in proletarianizing the peasantry. They favoured organization of the village on Gandhian line where town would exist as the distributing and organizing centre for the villages. They wanted the Congress not only to be the representative of peasantry but an instrument for mitigating violence against them by supporting zamindari abolition in a non-violent manner.[102] Furthermore, the Congress being a national organization, the three leaders believed that its first and foremost objective was national freedom and all other freedoms could flow from this freedom. Therefore, it concentrated all the energies of the nation on achieving this goal by providing a common anti-imperialist platform for the various interests in the country. For them,

> [s]waraj could not be real for the masses unless it made possible the achievement of a society in which democracy extends from the political to the social and economic spheres and in which there would be

---

[101] See Chapter 2 of this work.

[102] Shankarao Deo, General Secretary of Congress was close to the three leaders. In his foreword to P.P. Lakshmanana's brochure on Labour for Economic and Political Research Department, All India Congress Committee in 1947 he answered the accusation of the Left both within and without Congress that Congress cared for the interest of propertied class. Shankarrao Dev wrote:

> The Congress has been practically from its very birth very solicitous for the interests of the workers and has always tried its utmost to safeguard them from the foreign government as well as the Indian capitalists. Of course, the Congress being a national organization, its first and foremost objective was national freedom. It knew that all other freedoms could flow from this freedom only and therefore it concentrated all the energies of the nation on achieving this goal by providing a common anti-imperialist platform for the various interests in the country. It could not in the very nature of things, like a class or communal organization, to confine its activities to the furtherance and safeguarding the interests of a particular class or community to the exclusion of others. It had necessarily to follow the policy of proper adjustment of conflicting interests of different communities and classes and thus try to keep them all on the right path of nationalism. But this does not mean that the Congress sacrificed at any time the interests of the masses. As Mahatama Gandhi puts it very succinctly at the time of the Second Round Table Conference, whenever there was a real conflict between any other interests and the mass interests Congress has always upheld the interests of the masses. This can be easily proved by the history of the last thirty years of the Congress.

See P.P. Lakshmanana's brochure, AICC, LDI/1946-47, NMML.

no opportunity for the privileged classes to exploit the bulk of the people, nor for gross inequalities such as it exists at present.[103]

INDUSTRY AND AGRICULTURE

Village Industries and Agriculture

The three leaders—Patel, Prasad and Rajaji—theoretically accepted the Gandhian plan of decentralized economy founded on agriculture, cottage and village industries, *charkha*, khadi and trusteeship. But for practical implementation they saw industrialization as a necessary force for modernization and increased production. However, one may observe breaks in the beliefs of these leaders before and after 1947. Patel in 1934 and 1935 stated during his various tours in Gujarat that for India hand spinning and hand weaving were appropriate occupations as it was impossible for a country like India to seek a solution of its question of village reconstruction or rehabilitation through industrial development.[104] He blamed the machine age for making millions idle and talked of establishing 'Raj of the farmers'.[105]

Rajaji too in 1939 supported village industries and agriculture as it meant decentralization of the economy, whereas industrialization signified centralization and conflictual social relationship.[106] Prasad in 1939, while discussing the impact of World War II on the economy, said that village and cottage industries did not suffer the same fate as large industries during the war; therefore, to avoid such calamities India should concentrate on 'this item of constructive programme' to make the countryside self-sufficient in basic goods.[107] However, by 1947 when *swarajya* became a reality, a shift could be discerned in the thinking of the leaders on development issues. The most obvious shift was visible in the approach of Patel. Prasad maintained consistency in his view that a balance should be maintained between agriculture and industry and priority should be given to a

[103] Patel's address to UP Kisans at Allahabad, 28 April 1935 in Chopra, *The Collected Works*, Vol. V, 82–90.
[104] Patel's Speech at Jambusar, 27 December 1934. See *Home Department (special)*, MSA, Bombay.
[105] Patel's Speech at Viramgam, 4 January 1935. Ibid.
[106] Rajaji's Speech in the Madras Legislative Assembly, 27 November 1937. See *Madras Legislative Assembly Debates*, Vols. I–II, 122.
[107] Rajendra Prasad's draft of the Working Committee Instruction 1939, (n.d.) in Choudhary, *Dr. Rajendra Prasad*, Vol. V, 299.

village industry, but large industries should also be developed.[108] Rajaji was of the view that whatever be the instrument of development whether large industries or cottage and village industries or agriculture, the economy should be free and it should establish relationship of cooperation between labour and capital.[109] Speaking in the Madras Legislative Assembly in support of agriculture on 1 April 1939, Rajaji said:

> Agriculture has been admitted to be uneconomic industry. The agriculturist produces the grain in that uneconomic way. He brings it to the bazaar. At once pounce upon him parasites.... None of them suffers a loss. Instead of allowing for this unfortunate state of affairs, merely as a misfortune of our country, we want to remedy this position. We want to see that the producer is really in the position that he ought to be in and that the intermediaries really got what they deserve.[110]

Rajaji maintained consistency in his approach regarding the focus of economic development in the later years also. He was aware of the significance of modern industry and he regarded industry and labour as 'modern side of the economy' but he was averse to social conflict accompanying industrialization. Speaking on how modern industries lead to class conflict and thus injure the economy, he said on 20 February 1939:

> There has been a silent but effective revolution and the position of the workers is miles ahead of what it was before we took up office. Their unions and their rights of collective bargaining have been recognised without all these disputations over formulas and conditions of recognition that marked the previous history of this element in the labour movement. The gain is placed on the sure foundation of

---

[108] Ibid.

[109] Rajaji argued, 'it is a great decentralised industry which would really serve to maintain the texture of our rural life and not create slums in the towns along with the problems of housing, health and sanitation with which governments are unable to deal satisfactorily.' Rajaji's Speech in the Assembly, 4 November 1942, *Madras Legislative Assembly Debates*, Vol. V, 138–142. Speaking in the Assembly Rajaji further argued, 'if producer is strangled by rules and regulations or like a thief carries his own produce in order to sell it surreptitiously, he will not have any interest in production.' Rajaji's Speech, 11 December 1952. See ibid., Vol. VI, 727.

[110] Rajaji's Speech on 1 April 1939 in Madras Legislative Assembly. See ibid., Vol. XII, 179–181.

an accepted fact and not on the elusive phraseology of a declaration of rights.[111]

Rajaji gave preferential treatment to agriculture and rural craft against industry because modern industrial capitalism meant centralization of economy and class conflict. He argued that agriculture was the province's most important industry and handloom weaving was its next most important industry.[112]

Defending Rajaji's position, V.V. Giri, minister in Rajaji's cabinet, said in the Madras Legislative Assembly on 28 March 1939 that he would prefer not to have any industries than to have industries which would go to rack and ruin for want of a plan action.[113] Thus during the Ministry period, village and agrarian economy remained the main concern of Rajaji.

Rajendra Prasad too gave preference to agriculture over industry. In a letter to Sri Krishna Babu, the Premier of Bihar, dated 4 March 1938, he advised on what should be the attitude of Congress Ministries towards industries. He wrote that a complete reorientation of the government policy was necessary and it was unwise to depend upon the advice of the departmental head for guidance. He further argued that for the past 17 years the Congress had adopted and preached certain views which were fundamentally opposed to the official view. The Congress ministers should not expect any guidance in introducing village industries of which spinning was the most important part. The officials were incapable of thinking on different lines from what they had followed for so long. But the Congress ministries should promote and develop village industries.[114]

Prasad saw a symbiotic relationship between agriculture and village industries. He repeatedly encouraged the Ministries to implement reforms as early as possible to make agriculture effective, productive and

---

[111] Rajaji's address in the Legislative Assembly, 20 February 1939. Ibid., Vol. XI, 50.

[112] Speaking on how important cottage industries should be to the income of the peasantry, Rajaji said on 1 September 1937,

> It is difficult to overestimate the importance of the hand spinning industry for the well being of rural families in the dry areas of this province. It is essential that this industry should be given some measure of assistance to enable it to be revived and to grow and become again a source of supplementary income to peasant families.'

Ibid., Vols. I–II, 122.

[113] V.V. Giri's clarification in the Assembly 28 March 1939, ibid. Vol. XII, 898–906.

[114] Rajendra Prasad to Sri Krishna Sinha, 4 March 1938 in Choudhary, *Dr. Rajendra Prasad*, Vol. II, 8.

growth-oriented.[115] He believed that the economy of rural India should be strengthened by improving agriculture combined with encouragement, expansion and rejuvenation of village and cottage industries. He advised the ministers to take initiative in popularizing the near forgotten village industries like making *gur* out of palm juice or jaggery through traditional method.[116]

Rajaji argued that dependence on modern industry could bring about situations of helplessness in the event of breakdown, apart from bringing about centralization.[117] Rajendra Prasad was not against industrialization. He favoured industrialization provided it supported agrarian economy.[118] He regarded agriculture as the foundation of Indian economy and large- and small-scale industries should be geared to assist, improve and strengthen the agrarian economy and not the other way round. In his view, industries were the essential evils of the modern time but the state should own and control key industries, services, mineral resources, railways, waterways, shipping, etc. There should be relation of cooperation between cottage and large-scale industries. Where the need was for mass scale production, that job might be transferred to large-scale industries. But wherever there was a conflict between cottage and large-scale industries, the latter would have to give way to the cottage industries. This position of Prasad on industry was different from Patel who viewed large scale industrialization essential for security and prosperity of the nation.[119]

However, in his note to Nehru dated 18 February 1947 on the major task before the interim government, Prasad wrote that the major issue before the government was to increase production and this could be achieved by developing commerce, industry and agricultural sectors. Also by providing coal, steel and iron, improving on transport, maximizing production of consumer goods by making industries efficient and reducing strikes all this together, would lead to the growth and development of economy.[120]

---

[115] Ibid.

[116] Rajendra Prasad to Sri Krishna Sinha, 1 May 1938. Ibid., 43–44.

[117] Rajaji said, 'If all agriculturalists have to depend on the electric wire and the electric power generator, how easy it would be to dislocate the whole thing on any occasion and bring us all into trouble.' Rajaji's Speech of 25 July 1952 in *Madras Legislative Assembly Debates*, Vol. IV, 267–268.

[118] Prasad's Speech in Bombay on 27 December 1935 in Chaudhary, *Dr. Rajendra Prasad*, Vol. I, 271–275.

[119] Rajendra Prasad's note to J.C. Kumarappa in 1939 (date not given). See ibid., Vol. III, 432–433.

[120] Rajendra Prasad to Nehru, 18 February 1947 in ibid., Vol. VII, 24–25.

Generally speaking, the 'Right' leaders gave primacy to agriculture as the fountainhead of Indian economy but they realized the essentiality of industrialization for its forward movement. Patel in particular became more emphatic on the need for industrialization saying, 'this is the age of scientific and industrial research. If we want to achieve our proper place in the community of nations, we should carry on our work of research with speed and efficiency.'[121]

Patel, in general, accepted the role of agriculture and village industries in the development of the rural sector. But for national canvas, the two guiding principles for him were stability and self-sufficiency and these, he held, could not be achieved without industrialization and strong army. He said:

> Many say that we should adopt Gandhiji's programme. But they hardly realise that the government which has to maintain the army must have industrial installations too. For that we must have industrialisation. Some say that we should not industrialise it but build our country on rural life. I spent a lifetime with Gandhiji. I am not a fool to forget his teachings. I also want village self-sufficiency. But what is the position in which you find yourself? Villagers are forsaking the villages for cities. If we do not have industries what will happen? Will villages equip the Army? Will they supply all the transport, guns and ammunitions, petrol, steel, clothing and other things which a well-equipped Army must possess? Instead of looking at the problem one sided we have to do justice to both towns and villages.[122]

Patel, a true Gandhian and peasant by instinct, could not remain apathetic to agrarian problems despite his support for a strong industry. But by 1947 he gave primacy to industry over agriculture for two reasons. First, the history of India made him realise that:

> If the Indian government is to be seen today on the basis of Gandhian philosophy without army, I am prepared to change the whole thing.... Tomorrow the whole of India will be run over from one end to the other if you do not have strong army.[123]

---

[121] Patel's Speech at Ahmedabad while laying foundation stone of the Ahmedabad Textile Research Association on 30 October 1950. Nandurkar, *Sardar Patel*, Vol. II, 227.

[122] Patel's Speech of 4 January 1950, Bombay. Ibid., 20.

[123] Patel's Speech in the Parliament, 10 October 49. Ibid., 126.

Second, strong centre and well-equipped army required strong industrial base; therefore, industrialization of Indian economy came to occupy
position of prominence in Patel's thinking during this period. This shift in
the position of Patel from his earlier stance was dictated by the emerging
new challenges of the statecraft. He insisted that industry meant more production and considering the economic situation of the country the sooner
the agricultural economy transformed itself into a predominantly industrial
one, the better it would be for the country. Patel reiterated his view that
India could be a welfare state like other industrialized nations only when
it had advanced substantially in industrialization.[124] He also emphasized
that agricultural economy should have balance of cash and food crops and
it should be organized in such a manner that it should help in the geometri-
cal progression of industrial development which would increase general
prosperity and thereby secure a higher standard of living for the common
man.[125] Furthermore, Patel categorically stated:

> If the world succeeds in having disarmament all over it then the
> scheme of village sufficiency would be an idle thing to follow. But
> it is a far dream. Therefore we have to plan for our industry and
> agriculture in order to meet our primary and immediate needs. In
> certain directions at least the country has to be industrialised rapidly
> and with all the efficiency needed for it. Otherwise we are doomed in
> the modern context of the world. The modern army is not the army
> of bows and arrows. It is an army which requires many things which
> only machine can produce. Apart from arms and ammunitions, apart
> from the uniform and other things that are needful, it needs a large
> quantity of stores, jeeps, motors, mechanical appliances, aeroplanes
> and petrol and so many other things. And for that purpose, you must
> have industries and they should be developed in our own country.[126]

Planning

Generally, the three leaders believed that in the development of the economy
there had to be a proper integration and balance between rural and urban
sectors. Earlier rural economy had suffered and town and city prospered at

---

[124] Patel's Speech at the Central Advisory Council of Industries in New Delhi on
12 November 1949. Ibid., 197–205.
[125] Ibid.
[126] Ibid., 215.

their expense.[127] This according to them had to be corrected and an attempt should be made to equalize as far as possible the standard of life of town and village. Industry should be developed to give a balanced economy and it should be decentralized without sacrifice of efficiency.[128] In his speech of 3 January 1935, Patel pointed out that machine alone was not going to solve the problems because 'millions of idle hands cannot be employed on machine; machine by its very nature displaces men and socialism lies in the development of the village industries.'[129] According to Patel, therefore, planning for industries in India had to differ from the planning adopted by the industrialized countries. And both Indian States and the Centre should indulge in mutual consultation for achieving satisfactory results. He argued that while planning for industries one should bear in mind that:

India for ages has been looked upon as a predominantly agricultural country. Therefore in the process of industrialisation we have to make up the leeway of decades. There can never be anything like an industrial revolution in this country which would quickly trans-form its agricultural economy into a predominantly industrial one. Of course our industrialization would have to take note of modern ideas of relationship between the employer and the labour and also between them and the general community.[130]

[127] On 1 April 1939, Rajaji spoke in the Madras Assembly of the need of shifting the balance from the village to the town. See *Madras Legislative Assembly Debates*, Vol. XII, 177.

[128] Rajendra Prasad's Speech in Bombay on 27 December 1935 in Choudhary, *Dr. Rajendra Prasad*, Vol. I, 271–275. In this Speech, Prasad criticized,

[H]ow large industries fail to solve the problem of unemployment and what adverse effect the products of large industries has on people like those who are employed in factories and are torn away from their natural and healthier surround-ings; one has to eat sugar, rice, oil without vitamins, to live in houses covered with the sheets which give no protection from heat in summer or from cold in winter and which add only to the noise. During rains one has to depend on aluminium and enamelled utensils which refuse to be kept clean and on crockery and china-ware which break without provocation.

Yet in this very speech he accepted that 'no country dependent only on agriculture can be prosperous. Since large industries can never provide employment to all unemployed, country will have to depend on village industries.' Thus, he nowhere in his speech categorically rejected large industries. Also see Prasad's Note to Nehru on Major Tasks before the Interim Government, 18 February 1947. Ibid., Vol. 7, 24–27.

[129] Patel's Speech at Ahmedabad, 2 1935. See *Gujarat Samachar*, 3 January 1935, MSA, Bombay.

[130] Patel's Speech of 2 January 1935. See *Bombay Chronicle*, 3 January 1935, MSA, Bombay.

Prasad, Patel and Rajaji believed that true socialism lay in the development of village industries. They did not want to reproduce in India the chaotic conditions prevalent in the Western countries, a consequence of mass production. Provincial leaders like G.B. Pant who too had considerable influence over these leaders were of similar opinion. Speaking in the Central Legislative Assembly in 1937 on the question as to how to build up the economic wealth and economic structure of the country, he said that the answer lay in industrialization. But bigger industries should systematically be linked up with the smaller industries, cottage industries coordinated with key industries and thus alone could agriculture and manufacture thrive side by side at one and the same time. Infant industries should be given protection; therefore, imposition of an import duty was essential.[131] The three leaders accepted that the necessity of time was to 'produce or perish' and to 'learn how to produce wealth and thereafter to think what to do with it'.[132]

Patel's view was that the heavy machinery for work of public utility which could not be undertaken by human labour was to be encouraged, but all that would be owned by the state and used entirely for the benefit of the people.[133] The three leaders acknowledged that only such industries were to be promoted which could be founded on conciliatory relationships between capital and labour, where industrialists would concentrate on getting the maximum out of their plant and machinery, and labour would lend their helping hand to the industrialists to exploit the resources to the maximum national advantage.[134]

Patel, speaking on what should be the priority of the nation and the role of capitalists and labour in maximizing the production, said on 13 November 1949:

> The Government, Industry and Labour must all play the game in a spirit of national service ... we must have the fullest sense of national emergency; we must close our ranks as we do in the presence of a common danger.... Who flourishes if the country sinks into

---

[131] G.B. Pant's Speech in the Central Legislative Assembly in 1937. See Pant Papers, NMML.

[132] Nandurkar, *Sardar Patel: In Tune with the Millions-II*, 193, 198–201.

[133] Ibid. For Rajendra Prasad's view see Choudhary, *Dr. Rajendra Prasad*, Vol. VII, 19–25. For Rajaji's view, see his speech in Madras Legislative Assembly, 25 July 1952 in *Madras Legislative Assembly Debates*, Vol. IV.

[134] Nandurkar, *Sardar Patel: In Tune with the Millions-II*.

economic slaving? Who sinks if the country prospers? Let that be our ruling sentiment, let that be our ruling thought.'[135]

Both the factions within the Congress thus favoured industrialization as an answer to the economic malaise which was plaguing the country. And both the groups gave equal importance to cottage and village industries. However, the factions differed on format. Nehru clarified his position vis-à-vis *charkha* and village industries. He regarded khadi and *charkha* useful for creating self-reliance and utilizing surplus manpower. To quote:

I have whole heartedly supported the khadi movement as well as the wider village industries movement for political, social and economic reasons. In my mind there was no essential conflict between the two although there might occasionally be conflict in regard to certain aspects of development of both.[136]

Further developing the argument in his draft of the Working Committee Instructions, dated 30 December 1941, Nehru wrote:

Big scale industries in other countries have suffered heavily on account of the War.... China has largely overcome these difficulties by a widespread development of village industries. India may have to face similar problems; and village and cottage industries afford a solution, desirable in itself, and more particularly suited to the needs of the moment. Such industries can escape to a large extent the effect of dis-location of trade and transport. It is, therefore, necessary that this item of the constructive programme should be widely taken up and worked with vigour and earnestness so that the countryside may be rendered as far as possible self-sufficient in regard to the necessaries of life.[137]

Industry and Socialism

Patel, Prasad and Rajaji too did not believe in a social order which pro-duced 'modern kings of industry'. But neither did they believe in Nehru's European model of socialism since to them Gandhian programme on economy was equally socialistic in nature, if not of the Left variety. If

---

[135] Patel's broadcast to Nation on 13 November 1949. Ibid., 210.
[136] Nehru to Krishna Kriplani, 26 February 1940 in Nehru, *A Bunch of Old Letters.*
[137] Nehru's draft of the Working Committee Instructions dated 30 December 1941 in Choudhary, *Dr. Rajendra Prasad*, Vol. V, 297.

Nehru was against building of predatory industrial cartels, Patel and Prasad were also against such industrial cartels whose fortunes were built on pauperization of the masses.[138] Like Gandhi, the 'Right' realized that mass production would result in mass killing but not in mass wealth.[139] Both the 'Right' and the Left factions of the Congress believed that if attainment of *swarajya* was the central concern of the Congress, equally significant was the problem of economic reconstruction. Nehru did not favour doctrinal position of the other Left leaders within and without Congress.[140] He as well as the 'Right' leaders stood for the establishment of free democratic state based on the egalitarian society which would provide equal opportunity of self-expression and self-fulfilment to all and ensure basic civic rights to all. Yet both he and Patel believed that Gandhian emphasis on cottage and village industries alone would not rescue the dilapidated economy of the nation nor could it survive on its own without being supported by modern industries. The 'Right' advocated decentralized planned economy but were not very clear as to how they were going to put it into practice. Verbally, they all spoke in favour of it but when it came to its implementation, Patel favoured heavy industry on the plea that security of the nation would be compromised if the Gandhian Plan was to be put into action.[141] Similarly, Rajaji too showed signs of shift but only in the late 1950s.[142] Only Prasad stood primarily in favour of the Gandhian Plan, but being an astute politician with feet set firmly on the ground he realized that adoption of a balanced economy based on healthy amalgamation of both heavy and cottage industry would solve the Indian economic crisis.[143]

The three leaders were unanimous that whatever the path of development there would be no confiscation of private property without adequate compensation.[144] Patel in his Presidential Address at Rani Praja Conference in Vira tehsil, on 3 March 1935, outlined that social relationships should be based on cooperation, civil rights and social justice.

---

[138] Patel's Speech on 14 Dcember 1936. See *Bombay Chronicle*, 15 December 1936, MSA, Bombay.

[139] Ibid.

[140] S. Gopal, *Jawaharlal Nehru: A Biography, 1889–1947*, Vol. I (New Delhi, 1975), 246.

[141] See Patel's Speech at Ahmedabad, 13 October 1950 in Nandurkar, *Sardar Patel: In Tune with the Millions-II*, 227.

[142] Gandhi, *The Rajaji Story 1937–1972*.

[143] Rajendra Prasad's reply to J.C. Kumarappa in 1939 (date not mentioned). He said that cottage industries are to be supported by mechanised industries till they are able to stand on their own. See Choudhary, *Dr. Rajendra Prasad*, Vol. III, 433.

[144] See Patel's Presidential Address At Rani Praja Conference, 3 March 1935 in P.N. Chopra, *The Collected Works*, Vol. V.

Our aim should be to see that no injustice is done either to the big landholders or to the sowkars and at the same time to see that no one's fundamental rights are ignored. We may give this much assurance to everybody that however great our difficulties and whatever the injustices perpetrated on us, we do not wish to be unjust to anybody or to act in a spirit of vengeance. At the same time, we must state firmly that we do not wish to surrender our rights. If anyone still thinks in terms of living like parasites upon an industry, we would say to him that we do not propose to tolerate it. Anyone who allows another to live on him is not a man but an animal and we ought to be free from that condition. Our welfare does not lie in the hands of the king or the merchants. Our welfare lies in our own hands.[145]

Class Collaboration

The 'Right' favoured a democratic economic structure which would foster social relationships based on social harmony and cooperation thus eliminating economic exploitation of one class by another. Patel, Prasad and Rajaji were of the opinion that since in India the struggle for national independence was all inclusive, it included and transcended the class war and had within itself the seeds of every necessary revolution and readjustment. Therefore, there was no need to start a conflict between zamindar and kisan, and capital and labour. This line of thought determined the nature and direction of their relationship with various social classes. Hence, they encouraged class collaboration and eschewed class conflict. The 'Right'-wing leaders derived their social and political strength from the peasantry. They being themselves peasant proprietors and peasant leaders were familiar with the problems of the peasantry and its low social status. Whatever stand Patel took on peasantry and issues related to it, it had largely the consent of both the leaders. Patel did not believe in Left jargon and radicalization of peasantry by slogan shouting.[146] He along with Rajaji and Prasad was dedicated to the struggle for securing justice to the peasantry. He did not want peasantry to continue with its dependent psychology that someone from outside would come as their saviour. He wanted to shake peasantry out of its inertia to enable them to become fearless and self-reliant.[147] Speaking at the Kisan Conference at Allahabad on 28 April

[145] Ibid. Also see the *Bombay Chronicle*, 4 March 1935, MSA, Bombay.
[146] Sardar Patel's speech at Allahabad Kisan Conference, 28 April 1935. Ibid., Vol. V, 81–91.
[147] Ibid.

1935, Patel said that he had not come there to teach the kisans to weep over their lot or to teach them hatred against anyone. The kisan was the supporter of the whole country as he produced food material and Patel was pained to see kisans weeping over their plight. He admonished them that they should learn to realize their own weaknesses and remove them. Until that was done there was no hope of their upliftment. Neither communists nor socialists, nor any other body of reformers would reform kisans until kisans themselves realized their shortcomings and made efforts to remove them. One great weakness of the kisans was that they feared everyone. They should learn to be fearless and form a strong *sangathan*.[148]

Patel reiterated in 1935:

I am familiar with the various problems and the pains that the farmers suffer. I have no soft corner for the zamindars. If the kisans can rid themselves of the burden of zamindar and they can improve their lot, I would be the happiest of men....[149]

Patel warned the zamindars and taluqdars that the days of landlordism were over. 'Those who do not cultivate the land themselves must seek another occupation. The land is the mother of the cultivator. It is their right to enjoy the fruit of their land and revenue power of the taluqdars should go to the people.'[150]

However, he was not in favour of class conflict. Class collaboration was the need of the hour to defeat the forces of imperialism and the 'Right' were fully aware of it. Patel said in 1935 that abolition of the zamindari system was something 'to be done in future and if we insist on it today our cause would suffer'.[151]

He also added:

[i]f you plan for the abolition of zamindari, you have other problems coming up before you. Therefore it is not a question merely of abolition of zamindari, but its abolition in a manner as will create no trouble for us. Otherwise all the plans will go to a dung heap. The abolition of the vested interests is a good thing, but indecent haste will nullify everything and delay the thing we want....[152]

[148] Ibid.
[149] Ibid.
[150] Ibid.
[151] Ibid., 91.
[152] Ibid., 87.

Therefore, during 1934–1939, Patel spoke on how government was responsible for the plight of kisans. He, however, purposely avoided any direct attack on the zamindars. In his speech addressed to the kisans at Allahabad he said:

> It is the administrative policy of the government which is responsible for the plight of the kisans. It is only a partial view which makes people believe that it is the zamindari system which is responsible for the plight of the farmers. If one ponders a little, one will come to believe that this is only half truth.... Even so my views on the questions are different from those of others. I am of the firm belief that the main reason why the farmers find them in such straitened circumstances is the administrative policies of government.[153]

Patel blamed the government for the status and power the zamindars enjoyed. He mentioned that Sir Harry Haig had advised the zamindars that they were the natural representatives of the farmers and should try to regain that position. But according to Patel, this advice was not given with good intentions. The British-colonial government and zamindars together had broken the back of farmers and when the administration was not sympathetic to the farmers, the zamindars found it easy to persecute the kisans.[154] To avoid class conflict, throughout in his Allahabad speech, Patel reiterated that a part of the foreign conspiracy was to sow the seeds of discord among the various communities. He said, 'You would love to hear me talk about the evil ways of the zamindars, but it does give me pleasure in telling the farmers to rise and fight against the government and the zamindars.'[155]

In the 1930s, Rajaji too did not favour any structural changes but preferred social and moral reforms within the existing system. He preferred the social relationship between various social groups to be harmonious and co-operative.[156] He argued in 1939, 'I am conservative enough to admit the proposition at once that unless it is necessary to disturb an existing organization you should not disturb it.'[157]

Rajaji regarded the ancient village community as ideal type where harmonious relationship among various classes through social, cultural and economic interaction could be maintained, but not at the cost of hardship

[153] Ibid., 88.
[154] Ibid., 87–89.
[155] Ibid., 91.
[156] *Hindu*, 1 April 1939.
[157] Ibid.

and impoverishment of the peasantry. Realizing that reduction in land revenue and rent was the imminent agrarian problem to be addressed, and addressed in such a way that it might not give rise to conflict, Rajaji suggested of imposing sales tax, which would meet the financial loss due to prohibition and help in reducing land revenue and rent.[158]

Commenting on the disturbances the imposition of sales tax would cause, Rajaji said that the businessmen could well afford these new demands as earlier too they followed the custom of *Mahimai*, the practice of setting aside three pies for charity for each rupee transacted.[159] And thus some relief would be provided to the producer by shifting a little bit of the burden from the town to the village and from the producer to the intermediary.[160]

Accepting the major proposals of Prakasam's zamindari report, Rajaji outlined the ownership rights and based on it the relationships between the tenant and the zamindar.

> I do think that the two cardinal principles which the Committee has laid down, viz, that the ownership of the land is in the pattadar and that the usurpation by the zamindar of the States' right to enhance the rent should be put an end to, because it had not been transferred to the zamindar.... There is no doubt whatever that the original sanad was wrong. There is no doubt, whatsoever, that the position must be put an end to.[161]

Furthermore, Rajaji's strong sense of justice made him adopt a more radical view on the issue. 'The Zamindar has changed his manner of life.... I know that it is necessary that system should be ended. But is the zamindar entitled to the price he asks? Is he entitled to any price, seeing that he held only an office?'[162]

The three leaders were not in favour of the zamindari system but the political exigencies of the period made them adopt the strategic policy of class collaboration against British imperialism. Similarly, their relationship with both the capital and the labour was defined by the parameters of the national movement. Therefore, they laid emphasis on arbitration as the

---

[158] Rajaji's Speech in the Madras Legislative Assembly on 31 March 1939. See *Madras Legislative Assembly Debates*, Vol. XII, 51–52.

[159] Ibid.

[160] Rajaji's speech in the Madras Legislative Assembly, 1 April 1939, ibid., 179–181.

[161] Ibid.

[162] Ibid., Vol. IX, 26 January 1939, 701.

basic foundation of the capital–labour relationship. Rajaji, Prasad, Patel accepted J.B. Kriplani's commentary on the Russian experiment and they all opposed it because for them:

> [S]ociety is not synonymous with the Government and therefore if the administration of means of production is left in the hands of a small group of government officials, such a concentration of power becomes anti-social because the society as a whole will be denied the enjoyment of true freedom. The mass of people in that society will be denied necessaries of physical existence. They will remain slaves so long as production of wealth and the power of distributing it is concentrated in the hands of an all powerful bureaucracy. In Russia, Socialism was shipwrecked because the retention and extension of centralized large scale industries resulted in the emergence of a class of experts and technicians who dominated the economics and politics of the country. If all the wealth in the country is concentrated in the hands of a few, the temptation of these few will be to grab the whole of the surplus value produced by the workers and the workers will be increasingly impoverished and mechanized.[163]

The 'Right' believed that society could develop harmoniously only if social reform introduced were to be gradual, and peacefully planned. It was to be achieved through decentralized economic development and by educating both the haves and have-nots. The former should be assured that there never would be force used against them. The have-nots must be educated to know that no one could really compel them to do anything against their will and they could secure their freedom by learning the art of non-violence. An atmosphere of mutual respect and trust had to be established as the preliminary step. There would then be no violent conflict between the classes and the masses.[164]

Thus, the 'Right' supported an economic system where industry would be decentralized so that the administration of the means of production was not left concentrated in the hands of a small group of government officials. Nor should there be any bureaucratic concentration of control in distribution of wealth and power.[165] Commenting on the role of capital in the development of industries, however minuscule the growth of industries

---

[163] Kriplani's Statement in 1946 in AICC, File No. 26/1946, NMML, New Delhi.
[164] Ibid.
[165] Ibid.

was, given the constraint of colonial economy, Patel applauded the role of industrialists. He said he was glad to say that:

> through the foresight, the spirit of adventure and the nationalistic fervour of our pioneers of industry in the past; and thanks to the interest in our industrialization by a comparatively small band of industrialists we have been able to establish centres of industrial installations here and there which form the nucleus of our industrial effort today.[166]

Similarly Patel favoured labour organizations such as Indian National Trade Union Congress (INTUC) and All India Trade Union Congress (AITUC) to be based on Gandhian principles of *Majoor Mahajan* whereby the labour and capital relationship would be free from friction and animosity.[167] Rajaji and Prasad too approved of such labour organizations and they along with Patel accepted the truth that both labour and capital were the axle of the developmental wheel whose primary duty was to increase the production of the country and 'if any obstruction arises disrupting the production process, it would be considered enemy of the state.'[168] And 'if any disputes arise between labour and capital it should be solved through the panchayats.'[169]

In a long speech at Ahmedabad on 4 October 1934, Patel candidly explained the Congress's approach to labour and capital, his own position regarding these two classes and expressed his distress at the attitude of the Left towards labour, whose basic interest was to organize movement based on 'class antagonism'.[170]

Supporting Ahmedabad Labour Association and advising people to emulate Ahmedabad experiment and support class collaboration, Patel said that since its inception:

Ahmedabad Labour Association had worked for the labourers selflessly and in a true spirit. These labourers are neither credulous nor foolish to get cheated by those abusing the capitalists. There is no parallel to Ahmedabad Labour Association in the whole of India. Let those who desire to abolish

---

[166] Patel's Speech at the Central Advisory Council of Industries in New Delhi, 12 November 1949 in Nandurkar, *Sardar Patel: In Tune with the Millions-II*, 198.

[167] Ibid., 177.

[168] Ibid.

[169] Ibid., 182.

[170] Patel's Public Speech at Ahmedabad, 4 October 1934. See *Gujarat Samachar*, 6 October 1934, MSA, Bombay.

capitalism may organize another superior association like this. If they are able to make it a reality, I am then prepared to work as a sepoy under them.[171]

Commenting on the attempt of the Left to create social dissonance by supporting class struggle, Patel said:

> I am informed that their meaning of labour association is that labourers should proceed on strike everyday and disputes should be whipped up between labourers and management. No benefit can accrue to labourers in such conditions. It is sheer madness to apply foreign experiments in this country.... I am not telling anything to you because your experience is limited. So long as you have not committed to a scorched-earth policy, it is alright. If the mill owners here have destructive mentality, you are sure to gain, not otherwise. But here the mill owners are sensible, here there is love and amity between management and labourers and a feeling of family relationship exists between them. If this is vitiated, then devilish atmosphere will prevail every where ... if you are cherishing the idea of mitigating the Congress or to abolish capitalists and zamindars, so long as I am alive you will not succeed. Congress belongs to the country and everyone is welcome in it. We have not given up hopes of co-operation from capitalists, zamindars as well as native rulers. We shall have to march together to free India from the foreign rule.[172]

Patel was the most vocal spokesman among the three leaders on policy issues vis-à-vis labour. Although Rajendra Prasad was Chairman of the Labour Enquiry Committee, major decisions taken by him were with the consent of Patel. Rajaji too went along with the decisions of the two on most of the issues, including labour. Therefore, when Patel took position vis-à-vis social classes, be it peasantry, landowners, capitalists or labour, it was with full confidence that the two other leaders, Rajaji and Prasad, would support him.

These three leaders regarded that speedier and voluminous progress could be achieved only by coordinated efforts of the government, industry and labour. According to Patel:

---

[171] Ibid.
[172] Ibid.

The need today is that we should all put our heads together, our hands together and our hearts together to achieve maximum production—what is required is not an economic approach to the problem, but the practical view of the action required to implement the economic policy.[173]

Keeping in tune with the above line of argument Patel further argued, 'If the industrial community as a whole is not willing or prepared to shoulder the burden we cannot succeed. I know it well that if we will not utilise your talents and resources the country will not be able to achieve sizable progress.'[174] This was not to the liking of the Left who blamed Patel for being pro-capitalist. Writing in 1949, Ashok Mehta, the socialist leader, criticized Patel for favouring pro-capitalist policies. He wrote:

Sardar's economic policies are leading the country to disaster... The fostering of Birla bees and Dalmia cows has brought no honey or milk to our starving people. His capitalist friends and advisers are taking Sardar Patel along the wrong track. We need an economic wizard but such men do not sit on the treasury benches nor are they to be found among those who perambulate behind the Sardar during his morning walks.[175]

Patel advised labour not to be misled by the propaganda of the Leftists. He advised that labourers should bear in mind that there was no use in

[173] Patel's note to Nehru, 4 July 1948 in Nandurkar, *Sardar's Letters Mostly Unknown*, Vol. 1, 144.

[174] Patel's Speech addressed to the industrialists, 16 April 1949 in Nandurkar, *Sardar Patel: In Tune with the Millions-II*, 195.

[175] Ashok Mehta, *Economic Consequences of Sardar Patel* (Hyderabad, 1949), 12. Mehta realizing the exigency of the time revised his opinion about Patel in 1980,

Sardar was not pro-princes nor was he pro-landlord, he could not have supported landlords because he himself belonged to the sturdy peasantry. As far as the capitalists were concerned he really felt that they were needed. And he felt that he could control them, he could limit their gains in the wider interests. Looking back, perhaps in those very difficult years in 1946, 47, 48, he had a case. It was a question of India surviving or not surviving.... I think we did not, at least I failed to take that fact into account.

See Ashok Mehta, Oral History Transcript, dated 4 December 1980, NMML.

showing hostility towards the millionaires and destroying their own shelter.[176] He further said:

> According to some people, it is Gandhiji who says that the relationship between mill owners and labourers is akin to that between a father and a son. Some others compare it with a mouse and a cat. By indulging in such foolish talks, our strength is not going to be built up. So long as labourers are not aware of their own strength the brave shall overpower the weak. This is the universal law. But when labourers become aware of their own strength no power on earth shall be able to suppress them.[177]

Rajaji too was criticized by the Left for the dictatorial manner in which he handled the labour problem during the Ministry. He was accused of being pro-management during the labour strike at Papanasam and Madura Mills on 27 January 1938. Rajaji's reply to the Leftists' allegations was a significant comment on how he perceived the capital–labour relationship and what sort of relationship he wanted to foster between them for the development of the country and anti-imperialist movement. Rajaji said on 28 March 1939:

> They should know that this Government is charged primarily with a bias in favour of labour. Therefore working on behalf of labour is our primary effort; our greatest effort should be to secure the confidence of the management. Otherwise we shall not be able to take even one step or achieve even one success in the settlement of disputes.[178]

Highlighting the conditions of the workers, how improved it was in comparison to the earlier days and what 'mischief' the Left was playing in instigating the labour to be non-constructive and violent, thus damaging the national cause, Rajaji said in 1939:

> I claim that we have done remarkably well and are grateful to the spirit of reasonableness on the part of managements that has enabled us to achieve what we have achieved. There has been a silent but effective revolution and the position of the workers is miles ahead of

---

[176] Patel's Speech at Gandhi Chowk, Saraspur, 2 November 1935, *Gujarat Samachar*, 3 November 1935, MSA, Bombay.

[177] Ibid.

[178] *Hindu*, 29 March 1939.

what it was before we took up office. Their Unions and their right of collective bargaining have been recognized without all these disputations over formulas and conditions of recognition that marked the previous history of this element in the labour movement. The gain is placed on the sure foundation of an accepted fact and not on the elusive phraseology of a declaration of rights.... But for a certain amount of thoughtlessness and confusion of principles and the propaganda and wrong leadership of some men whose love of a class revolution for its own sake makes them blind to the starvation and misery of actual human beings the situation could be described as very satisfactory. Our large industries are still young. The transition from slogans to certain forms of dangerous violence which will surely kill all industry long before a class revolution can ever be conceivably brought about, and before the state and its resources are strong enough to bridge the gap between capital and labour.[179]

Rajaji regretted that the Left made a mockery of the methods of non-violence, peaceful picketing and non-cooperation, and compelled the state to resort to use of force far out of proportion to the original mischief.[180] He further held that the use of violence both by the Left and the state would not succeed except temporarily, but it would put the clock of progress back and even lead to a total reversal of its direction.[181]

Similarly, Rajendra Prasad as Chairman of the Labour Enquiry Committee in 1937 favoured foundation of labour unions on sound principles, i.e., Gandhian principles of industrial growth, development and peace. He warned the employers that it would be both short-sighted and wrong for the employers to deny to the workers the right of organization and to refuse to discuss with their accredited representatives matters affecting their wages and working conditions. He regarded strong union an insurance against unauthorized irregular and lightning strikes. In his opinion, the intelligent and active co-operation of the workers was an essential prerequisite in the conduct of modern industry. Therefore collaboration rather than conflict should be the foundation of the capital–labour relationship.[182]

---

[179] Rajaji's Speech, 20 February 1939 in *Madras Legislative Assembly Debates*, Vol. XI, 50.
[180] Ibid.
[181] Ibid.
[182] Prasad Rajendra's comments dated 11 September 1937 in Report of Labour Enquiry Committee in R.P. Papers.

The 'Right' faction's insistence on cooperation between labour and capital was seen by the Left as subtle denunciation of those political groups that claimed to be more representative of the peasants and workers than the Congress. The policy of cooperation between labour and capital was regarded by the Left as the Right's attempt to maintain a conservative economic and political structure that would foster measured and orderly progress and restrict popular protest and mass uprisings. The 'Right' leaders were blamed for resorting to repressive measures to deal with the strikers. They were accused of deviating from the Congress Election Manifesto and harbouring intolerant attitude towards the mill workers and favouring conservatism behind the façade of 'wider national aim'.[183] The 'Right' leadership knew that the labour was not disciplined; it had not been trained nor given political education. Therefore, it was easy to gain their sympathy by resorting to popular slogans. Patel criticized the Left for that:

But to stand for their legitimate 'rights' and to serve their just causes is a different thing ... to organize strike just to test the strength of their leadership over labour is to negate the purpose of labour movement. To them such strikes are means to self-glorification and thanks to them; it is the Labour that suffers grievously. Strikes benefit only the leaders, the labourer loses his wages.[184]

Further, 'the technique of communists are foreign to India and although they are now fermenting strikes in the country, they have already betrayed the cause of labour and the country when there was a real time for work of this kind in 1942.'[185]

Conception of Planned Development

Planning in the 1930s was seen as a gift of socialism. Its main purpose was to appraise the resources, organize the smooth running of production process, take account of the weak sectors, prepare for the adversities and increase the production free from profit motive.[186] The 'Right' leaders were aware of the fact that the well being of the people depended upon

---

[183] *Bombay Chronicle*, 11 March 1938, MSA, Bombay.
[184] Patel's message to INTUC workers in May 1949 (date not mentioned) in Nandurkar, *Sardar Patel: In Tune with the Millions-II*, 179.
[185] Patel's Speech at the Annual Session of INTUC, 6 May 1949, ibid., 177.
[186] Gopal, *Jawaharlal Nehru: A Biography, 1889–1947*, Vol. I, 245.

sound planning. Patel, Prasad and Rajaji were concerned about the political, social and economic freedom of the individual. The kind of society they conceived was to be based on truth and non-violence. The Gandhian policies were meant to be adopted by a state whose political, social and economic organizations were based on principles of social justice and economic freedom. It was aimed at healthy living and moral and intellectual development of the individual. To this end and to secure social justice the state should endeavour to promote small-scale production carried on by an individual or cooperative effort for the equal benefit of all concerned. All large-scale collective production would be eventually brought under collective ownership and control.[187] To achieve it, these leaders supported the *charkha*, *Gram Udyog* and the *Talimi Sangha*s. They were incorporated in the constructive programme, and during the ministry period 1937–1939, each leader tried to implement it within the constraints of colonial economy and governance.[188] The Gandhian plan, followed by the three leaders for reconstructing the society and economy, proposed decentralization of agriculture and industry and to achieve this, proliferation of cottage and village industries on the basis of limited private property was suggested.[189] Gandhi and his colleagues doubted the fact that classless workers' society could be built around centralized big industry.[190]

The Left within the Congress regarded this view of the 'Right' as 'muddled humanitarianism'. For them the need of the hour was to establish a classless society organized on a planned basis for raising the mankind to a higher material and cultural level. Influenced by the Russian concept of human welfare and not motivated by profit, Nehru wanted Congress to adopt a congenial program of national planning, within a democratic structure. Nehru on 4 June 1939 gave an outline of what the planning stood for.

> The ideal of the Congress is the establishment of a free and democratic state in India. Such a free democratic state involves an egalitarian society in which equal opportunities are provided for every member for self-expression and self-fulfilment and an adequate minimum of a civilized standard of life is assured to each member so

[187] Ibid., 246.
[188] Ibid.
[189] For Gandhian view on Planning see D.G. Tendulkar, *Mahatma: Life of Mohandas Karamchand Gandhi*, Vol. II (Bombay, 1951), 499.
[190] Ibid.

as to make the attainment of this equal opportunity a reality. This should be background or foundation of our Plan.[191]

In a letter to Shankar Lal Banker, dated 24 February 1940, Nehru criticized the Gandhian viewpoint that industry was an evil in itself. In Nehru's view for the survival of cottage industries, back up of heavy industries was essential. And both of them were to be supervised, controlled and co-ordinated to the general plan.[192] Misuse by capitalists was to be checked, private ownership and acquisitiveness of the society were to be restrained.[193]

Nehru's explanation that planning did not mean abandonment of *khaddar* and cottage industries did not mitigate the alarm of the 'Right'. The proposition of state-controlled industry and agriculture also aroused the opposition of the 'Right'. The 'Right' opposed the Nehru's cult of planning as it perpetuated foreign socialistic doctrines.[194] Gandhi wrote to Nehru, expressing his failure in understanding the efforts of the Planning Committee:

> I have never been able to understand or appreciate the labours of the Committee. I do not know that it is working within the four corners of the resolution creating the Committee.... It has appeared to me that much money and labour are being wasted on an effort which will bring forth little or no fruit.[195]

The 'Right' were not impressed by the Russian experiment. To them, society was not synonymous with the government and therefore if the administration of means of production was left in the hands of a small group of government officials, such a concentration of power would become anti-social because the society as a whole would be denied the enjoyment of true freedom. The mass of people in that society would be denied the opportunity of self-development and often even the bare necessaries of physical existence. They would remain slaves so long as production of wealth and the power of distributing it was concentrated in the hands of an all powerful bureaucracy. In Russia, socialism was shipwrecked because the retention and extension of centralized large-scale industries resulted in the emergence of a class of experts and technicians who dominated the

---

[191] Gopal, *Jawaharlal Nehru: A Biography, 1889–1947*, 246.
[192] Nehru to Shankarlal Bankar, 24 February 1940, ibid., 246.
[193] Ibid., 247.
[194] Ibid.
[195] Gandhi to Nehru, 11 August 1939 in Nehru, *A Bunch of Old Letters*, 378–379.

economics and politics of the country. If all the wealth in the country was concentrated in the hands of a few, the temptation of these few would be to grab the whole of the surplus value produced by the workers, and the workers would be increasingly impoverished and mechanized.[196] The social and economic growth of the nation as visualized by the 'Right' was to be achieved through planned development but the nature of planning was not to be communistic. Prasad in his letter to Kriplani dated 8 August 1939 raised his doubts on the acceptability of the concept of national planning due to its implied foreign socialistic tenor. He wrote:

Since 1920 Congress has laid down stress on hand-spinning and hand weaving and that emphasis continues. In May 1929, the All India Congress Committee passed a resolution to the effect that 'In order to remove the poverty and misery of the Indian people and to ameliorate the condition of the masses, it is essential to make revolutionary changes in the present economic and social structures of society and to remove gross inequalities.' This resolution indicates an approval of socialistic theories, but apart from this general approval and some further advances in subsequent resolutions, the Congress has not, in any way, accepted socialism.[197]

Prasad questioned the Chairman of the National Planning Committee, Nehru's note and whether Nehru's interpretation of the Congress resolution was correct. Did it mean acceptance of socialistic theories? Prasad further quoted from the Chairman's note, in his letter to Kriplani, dated 8 August 1939,[198] and raised further relevant questions regarding the nature of planning, thus not only expressing his own apprehensions but also those of Patel and Rajaji. Prasad, quoting from Nehru's note, stated:

What is planning? Planning under a democratic system may be defined as the technical coordination by disinterested experts, or consumption, production, investment, trade and income distribution in accordance with social objectives set by bodies' representative of the Nation. Such planning is not only to be considered from the point of view of living but must include cultural and spiritual values and the human side of the life. In the paragraph above referred to, mention is made of bodies'

[196] Kriplani's Speech delivered in 1946 (date not given) in AICC File No. 26/ 1946, NMML.

[197] Prasad to Kriplani, 8 August 1939, in Choudhary, *Dr. Rajendra Prasad*, Vol. IV, 20.

[198] Ibid.

representative of the Nation. So far as we are concerned the Congress is the representative organization of the Nation. Had it set forth any definite social objective for planning? If so what is it exactly? It is necessary to have a clear and comprehensive exposition thereof so that there may be no room for any doubts or misunderstanding.[199]

Since before the articulation of the 'Right's plan there was the Gandhian Plan of rural reconstruction which dealt with the social and economic issues in a manner causing least anxiety of any kind, the 'Right' leaders were not very enthusiastic about Nehru's concept of Planning. Prasad accepted the fact and so did both Patel and Rajaji that the well being of the people depended on sound planning and the committee constituted to guide and decide the plan of the country should have people who have 'living and intimate knowledge' of the life and condition of the people.[200]

Further, clarifying his position vis-à-vis the ideology and planned economy, Prasad on 10 December 1947 said:

We have not been thinking of the Marxist theory or of any other theory ... but we took facts as they are, the difficulties that we have to face and the further difficulties which we anticipate and we came to certain conclusions ... if we want to have planned economy the first step is to scrap the haphazard growth and then think of the planned economy. I should not like planned economy to be introduced by the backdoor in this way. Let the country, let this House, let Government make up their minds about planned economy; let them prepare a scheme of that planned economy and then introduce it. That may be something worth having, not this pseudo planned economy which has neither its birth—illegitimate birth—nor is going to have its end in anything like planned economy. If there is going to be a disturbance generally in our economic life we should be prepared for that; only it should not be allowed to go up to such an extent as to upset our whole economy, I think in this country grey is the best colour for all things.[201]

Rajaji too equated planning with 'controlled economy'. He was a protagonist of free economy, and rejected planned economy, saying 'Even

[199] Ibid.
[200] Ibid.
[201] Speech of Prasad, 10 December 1947, ibid., Vol. VII, 405–406.

members opposite who swear by communism and a planned economy believe that we must give an interest in the land and the produce to the farmer if we expect the farmer to produce more.'[202]

Patel accepted relevance of planning but his focus was on preserving the internal and external security of the nation so that the measures in other fields, such as strengthening economy, improving living conditions, providing livelihood and health services, could be carried out smoothly.[203]

Clarifying on what should be the priority areas while planning, Patel said that planning for India should differ from the planning of industrial countries which were highly developed. India being an agricultural country with a large population the focus for planning should be confined first to industry and then to agriculture.[204]

The three leaders by and large accepted the usage of planning but they differed in their emphasis. If Prasad was doubtful about the socialistic tenor of the language in which planning was defined by Nehru, the Chairman of the National Planning Committee, Rajaji disliked reference to imposition of controls through planning. Patel adopted a pragmatic approach towards Planning, accepting it for integration of the country. He being a realist knew what was possible and what was not. He was apprehensive over both the approaches on planning—the Gandhian and the Socialist.[205] He was aware of the fact that many extraneous factors governed in the success of the planning. Firstly, he laid great stress on realizing internal and external security for the implementation of plan, saying 'You cannot plan anything, you cannot work on any plan, if there is no internal and external security. Therefore I took to planning for the integration of the country.'[206] Secondly, Patel believed that 'Planning howsoever good would not work unless we realize our responsibilities and unless we think that it is our obligation to implement the schemes that have been planned.'[207] Thirdly, he believed that industry should increase employment and not reduce it. Therefore,

Our planning must necessarily differ from the planning of industrial countries which are smaller in dimensions or are highly developed

---

[202] Copley, *The Political Career of C. Rajagopalachari, 1937–1954*, 299.

[203] Patel's 'My Concept of Planning', in *Sardar Patel: In Tune with the Millions*, ed. G.M. Nandurkar, Vol. II, 215–18.

[204] Ibid., 216.

[205] Ibid.

[206] Ibid.

[207] Ibid., 27.

industrial countries…. Ours is primarily an agricultural country
and in a country so thickly populated as ours, idleness is the greatest disease…. If you want to employ millions of the idle hands they
must be employed in spinning and weaving cloth and in other village
industries…. So difficult it is to plan purely on a non-industrial basis!
We must, in certain directions, at least, industrialise our country
rapidly and with all the efficiency needed for it. Otherwise we are
doomed in the modern context of the world…. We have, therefore,
to plan for our industry and agriculture in order to meet our primary
and immediate needs.[208]

Daridranarayan

The concern of the Gandhian programme of social, political and economic
regeneration was focused on the poor. The poor peasantry represented
the node of development and anti-imperialist movement in the scheme of
the 'Right' for national reconstruction. The leaders adopted constructive
programme, khadi, *charkha* and panchayat system as tools for the regeneration of the poor. From the Congress platform, they launched the Karachi
resolution of 1931, Faizpur resolution of 1936, Election Manifesto of 1936
and 1945, and Meerut resolution of 1946, in support of the poor. The
reform programme for people's amelioration adopted during the Ministry
period too was centred around the poor.

There were three ways of looking at poverty. The first view was the
Marxist view which regarded the poor as 'wretched of the earth', with
orientation on class struggle and socialistic economy. The second was the
utilitarian view according to which the solution to overcome poverty lay
in capitalism and industrialization. Both the views regarded poverty as a
stigma.

The third view was the Gandhian view, which the three leaders
assimilated. This view regarded the poor as the extension of the divine
and to be in his service was to be the calling of all. The poor was called
Daridranarayan—God in the poor or divinity in poverty.[209] Patel in his
broadcast on 30 January 1949 said, 'Gandhiji saw the glimpses of the
Divinity among the poor and the depressed whom symbolically he called
Daridranarayan. In the service of *Daridranarayan* lay his unique way of life.

---

[208] Ibid., 218.
[209] Ibid., 258.

He inspired us to follow the same path.'[210] This approach did not regard poverty as stigma but as something to be empathized with. It did not imply celebration of poverty either; it meant that the poor had grace of God and society should perform its duty towards them.

The 'Right' did not condone the situation that created poverty in society. They used the concept of *Daridranarayan* to invoke society's commitment for the removal of poverty, because for them the poor was not to be seen as a marginalized category but the centre around which all political, economic, cultural and social policies and programmes were to be focused.

[210] Ibid.

5

Strategic Issues

In these circumstances those who have not fully understood Gandhiji's principles, find themselves surrounded by a dilemma. But they should understand that the Gandhian Era is an era of tide and ebb. Those who fully understand Gandhji's principles have realized what tide and ebb means. We know the universal law of nature that the ebb, which succeeds the tide, generates a powerful and deadly energy.

—Sardar Patel[1]

MASS POLITICS VERSUS CONSTITUTIONALISM

In this chapter, the questions and debates raised over the issue of suspending extra-constitutional form of agitation and acceptance of Council entry, and the option put at the doorstep of the Congress by introduction of the Government of India Act 1935, will be examined. In the process of analysing the strategic shift, focus will be on why the issue of suspending extra-constitutional form of agitation and acceptance of Council entry arose? Why leaders like Patel, Rajaji and Rajendra Prasad, who made their career as mass leaders by participating in extra-legal forms of agitation, agreed for Council entry programme and under what circumstances? Was it due to consolidation of Left forces within the Congress with the emergence of the Congress Socialist Party (henceforth CSP) in 1934 and the threat felt by Gandhian leaders of their leadership being usurped by the Left if they revived civil disobedience? The question of Subhas Chandra Bose's re-election to the post of Congress President would also be discussed in this section. Of specific interest would be the examination of Bose's challenge to the accepted strategy of the Congress which so far had remained confined within the Gandhian boundary. These questions will be analysed in relation to each leader in the context of the anti-imperialist movement.

---

[1] Patel's Speech at Ahmedabad on 25 August 1935. See Chopra, *The Collected Works*, Vol. V, 157.

A no-changer of 1922, Patel remained a no-changer at heart even in 1934. When in April 1934, Gandhi announced the suspension of selective disobedience and added that he himself would retain the right to disobey and the Congress should permit a Council entry to members desiring it, Patel called it 'Bapu's bombshell'[2] and said to Gandhi that he was troubled and pained as it would amount to the 'revival of *Swarajya* Party', and that Gandhi had thus snatched away the weapon with which he had armed the people.[3]

Patel, who in 1937 went along with the Congress programme of office acceptance and later Ministry formation, at the time of his release from Nasik Jail in July 1934, was strongly opposed to Council entry.[4] Neither the steady consolidation of Left forces, i.e., the emergence of CSP in May 1934, strengthening of the trade union movement after the Red Trade Union Congress rejoined the AITUC in April 1935, the formulation of a United Front strategy by Moscow and formation of the All India Kisan Sabha in 1936, presidentships of Nehru and Bose in 1935, 1936 and 1938, nor provincial factionalism within Provincial Congress Committees (PCCs) could influence Patel for acceptance of Council entry.[5] After coming out of Nasik jail in July 1934, in an interview to the correspondent of *Bombay Sentinel*, Patel expressed his view regarding the question of Council entry. His answer to the journalist's question showed that he was clear regarding his view on Council entry but gave evasive answer to the correspondent, as he was not confident about what programme the Congress would adopt. Patel's reply to the correspondent was that he had never approved of the Council entry programme, but he would support any programme accepted

<hr/>

[2] See Patel's letters to Gandhi, 23 April 1934 and 3 May 1934 in M.K Gandhi, *Letters of Vallabhbhai Patel*, Ahmedabad, 1957. In a letter dated 18 April 1934, Gandhi wrote to Patel:

> I can see from your letters the pain you have felt.... Have patience and you will see that everything will turn out well in the end.... It should be quite easy to understand the revival of the Swaraj Party. Don't you think it is better for someone who is always dreaming of jalebi to eat it and find out its actual taste for himself? Those who daily attend the councils in spirit should be permitted to enter them in fact. I have not snatched away the weapon. I have only postponed its use to prove its efficacy.

See ibid., 56–59.

[3] Ibid. In a letter to Manibehn dated 16 April 1934, Patel expressed his misgivings, 'The decision is somewhat difficult to understand, but those of us who are in jail need not waste time in trying to resolve such puzzles—when we are out of jail we too will have to interest ourselves in what is taking place....' See Parikh, *Sardar Vallabhbhai Patel*, 158.

[4] Ibid.

[5] Rajmohan Gandhi, *Patel: A Life* (Ahmedabad, 1990), 240–241.

by the Congress because he was against imperilling the prestige of the Congress at a very psychological moment like the present one, by creating differences within the Congress ranks.[6] Asked specifically if he approved of the Council entry, Patel said that he had never approved of the Council entry programme, but he was not prepared to say categorically as to what he would do before he discussed and consulted his colleagues. He could not say whether he would support or oppose the Council entry programme but he was definite about one thing and that was that he would support any programme of the Congress if it meant saving the prestige and honour of the organization.[7]

Questioned about the socialist group and their offering alternative programme, Patel categorically stated:

> [d]ifferences of opinion should not decide the Congress at present as it would be unfair to those who have burnt their boats in their loyalty to the Congress. As long as the socialists, for that matter any group had any programme, which would maintain the prestige and honour of the great organization and would not imperil it any way, he would welcome them and support them, but if the programme of such group meant the lowering of the Congress prestige he would oppose them.[8]

In July 1934, statements of Patel reflected the confidence he felt in handling the socialists[9] but it also brought out his unease with the Council entry programme. His discomfort with the subject of Council entry persisted throughout the period, but he was brought to accept it when its relevance for the time being was brought out by Gandhi's letter to him.

---

[6] See *Bombay Sentinel*, 14 July 1934, MSA, Bombay.

[7] Ibid.

[8] Ibid.

[9] Patel had a dismissive attitude towards the Socialists and did not see them as a threat to Congress, describing them as 'there are 84 castes among Brahmins, whereas it would seem there are 85 different types of socialists.' Secondly, 'they are wasting time speculating about the social and political organization in the future independent government of India.' Thirdly, 'some socialists hereby talk, with such persons I shall never be able to get on.' See Parikh, *Sardar Vallabhbhai Patel*, Vol. II, 198–199. Sardar in his address to the Congress Workers at Bhadra, Gujarat on 1 Octobe 1934 said, 'Socialists can indulge in propoganda about socialism, but they should not interfere in the work of the Congress … to follow the resolutions which are passed by a majority in the Congress is an act of discipline. Socialists should be ready to act according to Congress discipline, otherwise they may carry out their programme on their own.' See Chopra, *The Collected Works*, Vol. IV, 210.

In answer to Patel's anguished cry that by withdrawing Civil Disobedience Gandhi had snatched away the weapon with which he had armed his people, Gandhi replied that suspension would give 'much needed respite to civil resisters who are today tired, and enable them to emerge stronger and more equipped for the next battle whenever it comes.'[10]

Realizing that a situation of flux existed, about which nothing could be done except to wait for people's response and carry out other non-confrontationist activities, Patel reassured the followers of Civil Disobedience at Ahmedabad on 25 August 1935:

> In these circumstances those who have not fully understood the Gandhiji's principles, find themselves surrounded by a dilemma. But they should understand that the Gandhian Era is an era of tide and ebb. Those who fully understand Gandhiji's principles have realized what tide and ebb means. We know the universal law of nature that the ebb, which succeeds the tide generates a powerful and deadly energy.[11]

He was convinced not only by Gandhi's explanation but also by Rajaji's reasoning:

> [w]ithdrawing a movement of sacrifice is often necessary and should not be deemed a matter of shame. The situation now is different from what was in 1922. We should now go into the elections on behalf of the Congress. Nobody can prevent the adoption of civil resistance by the Congress at any future time.[12]

Patel, when he toured Gujarat during the latter half of 1934 and 1935, realized that people were tired of agitation and weary of government repression. The Council entry programme would be a welcome break from the non-constitutional agitation in order to recuperate, strengthen and reinvigorate the flagging spirit of the people. It would never be an alternative strategy replacing non-constitutional agitational strategy for the rest of the period of anti-imperialist movement, as proclaimed by the Leftists.[13] As the reality sank in, Patel's initial opposition gave way to acceptance. In all

---

[10] Rajmohan Gandhi, *Patel: A Life*, 241.
[11] Patel's speech at Ahmedabad on 25 August 1935. See Chopra, *The Collected Works*, Vol. V, 157.
[12] Gandhi, *The Rajaji Story I: A Warrior From the South*, 265.
[13] Ibid., *The Rajaji Story 1937–1972*, 243–245.

his speeches throughout Gujarat after his release from jail on 14 July 1934, Patel forcefully reiterated on how people should strengthen the Congress by making its programme successful, whether it was constructive programme or Council entry.[14] He stated:

> [T]he tactics might have changed, the fight for freedom once started would never cease till the goal was reached.... It was well known that he was a staunch opponent of Council entry, but now that the Congress had decided on that programme he would loyally abide by the decision. It was no use questioning the step that had already been taken by the Congress. The people themselves were responsible for creating a situation, which necessitated the step. If the situation was different then nobody would have dared to talk of Council Entry. Now the issue was a clear cut one. Having decided to contest the election it was now then duty to see that they captured the Legislatures. Their prestige was at stake. Government had thrown out a challenge and Congress had accepted it. It was not the time to consider whether they had taken the right or wrong step. Exercise your vote to the fullest extent and see that as many Congressmen as possible are returned to the legislature. Then come to me and I will show you the way.[15]

However, Patel advised the Socialists Party in Congress not to create a split within the Congress.[16] 'We should welcome the new ideas as well as new parties, if they are helpful in leading us nearer towards freedom. If they prove hindrance to our goal of achieving freedom we should not hesitate to leave them.'[17]

Patel told the socialists that he would expect of them to have their loyalty to the Congress first and foremost. If he were a socialist today, he would show his loyalty to the Congress by sending Congress candidates to the Legislatures; at this stage when they were themselves in bondage, true socialists should concentrate their energies in maintaining firstly the solidarity of the struggle which was now being carried on by the Congress.[18]

---

[14] Patel's Speech at Bombay, 16 July 1934 in Chopra, *The Collected Works*, Vol. IV, 160–161.
[15] Ibid.
[16] Patel's Speech at Bombay, dated 16 July 1934. Ibid., 161.
[17] Patel's Speech at Bombay, dated 18 July 1934. Ibid., 164.
[18] Ibid., 160–161.

Patel ultimately accepted Council entry programme neither because it would divert the attention of the people from the radicalism of the socialists, nor did any threat to Congress unity from Left radicalism motivate him to accept a programme that he had originally frowned upon.[19] In fact, in his speeches if he insisted that socialists in the Congress should unitedly work for the success of Congress programme as need of the time required, he also threatened in the same breath that if at any point they posed hindrance to the Congress programme, they would be thrown out of the Congress. He warned the socialists that they were 'free to leave Congress when they felt remaining inside Congress put a strain upon their political conscience.'[20]

The position of the Left too in the Congress was such that they could not leave Congress and survive in isolation at the same time, whatever policy the Congress might adopt. If Patel was warning the socialists and their sympathizers, Acharya Narendra Dev too was warning his socialist colleagues to be tactful and not precipitate a crisis by advocating a full socialistic programme before the Congress or by defying the official policy of the Congress. In a letter to Gandhi dated 6 August 1934, Narendra Dev requested, 'Please correct our mistakes and take work from us. Do not regard us as separate.'[21] M.R. Masani, at Annual Conference of All India Congress Socialist Party, at Meerut on 20 January 1937, articulated the practical strategic approach the Socialists should adopt, thereby indicating the actual strength of the Congress Socialist Party. 'We should on no account alienate these right wing elements by intolerance or impatience. The Congress constructive programme should not be obstructed or interfered with.'[22] Achyut Patwardhan too confessed the weak position of the Left forces within Congress. 'I am convinced that no socialist can keep out of Congress howsoever much he may charge at one or the other of its ideological drawbacks.'[23]

Thus, the argument that the threat of Left consolidation influenced the three leaders to adopt the constitutional programme which does not seem to be supported by historical evidences. The very fact that although the Kisan Sabha, AITUC, CSP, Royists and Communists were active in the nationalist politics, Congress too from 1935 to 1938 had Left-leaning

[19] Ibid., 164.

[20] Ibid., 255.

[21] Narendra Dev to Gandhi, 6 August 1934 in Gandhi, *The Rajaji Story 1937–1972*, 245.

[22] Masani's Speech, 20 January 1937. See File No. 1936–1947 in Jayprakash Narayan Papers, MSS, NMML.

[23] *Congress Socialist*, Vol. I, no. 9, 27 January 1935, NMML.

Presidents, yet all these forces could not make any dent in the status of the three leaders nor did their hold over Congress slacken. Instead the Congress, as the election results showed, consolidated itself and emerged as the most popular mass party.

The acceptance by no-changer Patel of Council entry programme of the Congress emanated primarily from three considerations. First, Congress as an organization was in disarray due to government repression. It required time to reorganize and consolidate itself. Though the Civil Disobedience movement was withdrawn, the government repression continued. Distress warrants were still executed to recover fines imposed on active participants of the struggle. The peasants residing in Indian States were still forbidden to enter the British territory. The government bans on educational institutions like Gujarat Vidyapeeth were not removed. Several ashrams in the Bardoli *taluka* and Karia district were in the government's custody and efforts to revive or reform village Congress Committees were looked upon with suspicion.[24] Patel told his colleagues of Bardoli, 'I am not happy about the existing circumstances.... At present there are quarrels all along in the Congress. Everywhere there is confusion.'[25] Therefore, the job before them was 'to revive the Committees of Congress and strengthen it, since now that the bans were removed.'[26] Patel regretted in not being amongst them and an almost Bardoli-like struggle situation forced him to be in Bombay.

I know that you are all waiting for my return to Gujarat. I am no less anxious myself to meet you at the earliest possible moment; indeed I am impatient. Yet I must bow to circumstances which render it impossible for me to be in your midst immediately.

Nearly 125 of our comrades still remain imprisoned. A number of our institutions are still under Government control or restrictions. Buildings of educational institutions such as the Gujarat Vidyapeeth, Patidar Hostel, Anavil Hostel, Sunav Rashtriya Shala (National School), Baraiya Vidyalaya of Bochasan etc. are still in Government hands.... Efforts to revive or reform village Congress Committees are looked upon with suspicion. Names and other particulars of those enrolled as Congress members are being made the subject of police enquiry. All this gives one, not unreasonably, the impression that hostilities have terminated on one side only.... The immediate task

[24] Patel's Speech at Bombay, 15 July 1934. See *Bombay Chronicle*, 16 July 1934.
[25] Parikh, *Sardar Vallabhbhai Patel, 1971*, 192.
[26] Ibid.

before you is twofold: (1) to help the distressed farmers and (2) to revive the Committees.[27]

Therefore, the task Patel put forward before the Congress was just to strengthen and revive the organization and to ameliorate the condition of the farmers. His advice to Congress workers of Gujarat was:

> Houses and household properties of farmers are still being auctioned by the Government in order to realize the fines. Confiscated lands, too, are being similarly auctioned.... If we do not help and support those who have lost their homes, their cattle and their fields and who have literally been turned out on to the streets, we could firstly be charged of failing in our duty.[28]

Realizing the exigency and imperative of strengthening the Congress and raising the morale of the masses, Patel asked them to avoid any kind of confrontation with the Government. Since Civil Disobedience could not be revived considering the existing situation, focus was to be placed on constructive work to keep the fire of anti-imperialism alive in the hearts of the people through Council entry. He said:

> You have therefore to work under difficulty circumstances. It will tax your patience and will put you to the most severe test. Yet do not be impatient. Do not get exasperated, but carry on whatever work may be possible avoiding all conflict with the authorities. In our programme we have nothing secret or surreptitious to execute. All our cards are on the table. If you are harassed in the course of your purely constructive activities, avoid a clash, withdraw for the time being, while acquainting your district leader with facts and let your further actions follow his directions. Guard against the temptation of offering resistance even under the gravest of provocations or harassment.[29]

Patel felt despondent at the withdrawal of civil disobedience and revival of Council entry programme, but he was also aware of the constraints of the situation. Therefore, to explain about the shift in strategy, he carried

---

[27] Patel's Speech at Bombay, 25 July 1934. See Chopra, *The Collected Works*, Vol. IV, 166.

[28] Speech of Patel at Bombay dated 25 July 1934, ibid., 167–168.

[29] Ibid., 168.

out extensive tour not only in Gujarat but also in other parts of the country, throughout the election period.[30] He explained to the peasants:

> At present there is terrorism in the public and the Government thinks that its repressive policy has proved successful so they should not discontinue it. Mahatma Gandhi and other Congress leaders also thought upon this question and have wisely come to conclusion that it is quite imperative to change the battlefront, looking to prevailing circumstances. Under the Ordinance Raj the public is not bold enough to say or show their loyalty towards the Congress. Wide powers have been invested into the hands of the Police under the Ordinance.... You are tired of fight and so the Congress has put before you constructive programme so that you can do your work by remaining within the four corners of the law and you may not have to come into clash with the Government. When you are tired you can take rest for a while but wise persons never retire without reaching the destination. It is also no good to continue going along when one is tired. It would surely bring sickness.[31]

Patel concluded that to remove the fear, 'the Congress leaders thought to change the ways of fight...the Congress therefore to gauge the situation preferred to send our candidates in the Assembly.'[32]

As early as 1935, in a meeting with the Governor of Bombay, Sir Roger Lumbey, Patel who had then replaced Ansari as Chairman of the Congress Parliamentary Board, did not reveal his thought over the issue of office acceptance. But he did not deny to the Governor that no Congressmen would be Bombay's Premier and he warned Sir Lumbey that the lands of the peasants would be returned to them soon.[33] Thus, Patel had made up his mind that Council entry programme would commensurate with providing relief to distressed farmers.

---

[30] Ibid., 167–170.

[31] Speech of Patel at Boriavi, 29 December 1934, ibid., 257.

[32] Speech of Patel, dated 4 January 1935 while touring Gujarat. See File No. 800 (98) Home Special Department, MSA, Bombay.

[33] On Patel questioning Sir Lumbey, Governor of Bombay, over returning the confiscated lands to the peasantry, he answered, 'I don't see how those lands can ever be returned.' And Patel replied, 'I will give it to you in writing that the lands will come back to their right owners', suggesting the likelihood of Congress accepting provincial power under the new Act to provide relief to the farmers. See Gandhi, *Patel: A Life*, 251–252.

Thirdly, Patel's acceptance of Council entry emerged out of strategic reasons. Patel like Rajaji and Prasad had deep affinity towards mass struggle.[34] Yet they realized that without people's enthusiasm and spirit of sacrifice no mass movement could be sustained for a prolonged period. Mass struggle always had to be short-lived, and it needed periods of rest to recuperate, consolidate and to gather strength for the next phase of the struggle.[35] Elaborating on the Congress strategy Patel said:

Changes have taken place in the political conditions of the country. The person who wants to cover a particular distance, starts moving, takes a pause on getting tired, but he does not go back. He would take his lunch, have some rest as well as sleep for a while and resume his onward journey, as soon as he feels fresh.[36]

Elaborating on shift in the strategy Patel said:

We have not given up the fight for freedom. We have merely changed the mode of fight. It is no use now going to jail or conducting a No-Tax Campaign. We have to fight our own weakness without coming into conflict with government so that we may acquire the strength to fight when it is resumed.[37]

Patel accepted Council entry as a challenge and conveyed the spirit under which he accepted the challenge to the people through his speeches and campaigns:

The coming election is a trial of strength and loyalties for the Congress. Government has thrown a challenge at us that the Congress has gone down in the estimation of the people. Congress has accepted that challenge by consenting to run candidates for the Assembly elections and prove to the world by the triumphant return of these candidates that although physically suppressed for the time

[34] Ibid., 241.
[35] See Bipan Chandra et al., *India's Struggle for Independence*.
[36] Patel's Speech at Valsad on 24 December 1934. See *Gujarat Samachar*, 27 December 1934.
[37] *Bombay Chronicle*, 4 January 1935.

being the Congress is still the greatest representative organization in the country and the mass opinion is solidly behind it.[38]

In full knowledge of the lack of genuineness of the Government's intention in offering new constitution, Patel forged ahead like a galley in full sail, with provincial elections and ministry formation. During 1936–1937, he was at the helm of affairs. Despite being the electoral boss and securing electoral success for the Congress, he never harboured any illusion about the true nature of the Constitution of 1935.

We know that we are not going to achieve much by going in the Councils and Assembly. We want to send our men there with a view to remove the obstacles that are coming in our way. We don't want to give a false promise and hopes to the peasants that after entering the Councils we will be able to reduce their taxes. By all means we will do everything to make the masses happy. The government says that we have given you Provincial Swaraj. Well, let us see how far it is true. If it is a toy we will break it. And if it is real Swaraj we will know when the Collector and the Commissioner become the servants of the people. When these officers become our servants, it will be real swaraj.[39]

If socialists and Nehru were against the shift of Congress strategy from mass struggle to constitutional politics, Patel too consistently emphasized that the Council entry programme, its implementation and working of the Government Act of 1935 never figured in their schema of strategy. The 'deliverance' of the nation from imperialist subjugation lay in mass struggle. In his speech at Bombay in 1936 Patel spoke:

I know that nothing can be done except through the power of the people. Fortunately we have learnt what non-violent, non-cooperation can do. When people learn the art of withdrawing their co-operation from the forces of evil, it will perish for want of nourishment. However as Pandit Jawaharlal stresses, and rightly too, our present purpose is to free India from foreign subjection and thus destroy imperialist exploitation root and branch.... One thing, however, is

---

[38] Patel's Speech at Shivaji Park, Dadar, Bombay on 7 October 1934. See Chopra, *The Collected Works*, Vol. VI, 227.

[39] Patel's Speech at Suraj, dated 6. November 1936, in File No. 800 (98), Patel Papers, SPNM, Ahmedabad.

the immediate issue—the parliamentary programme and its implications. There is again no difference of opinion about the objective. All
of us want to destroy the imposed Constitution. How to destroy it
from within the legislatures is the question. It will depend upon the
resources and resourcefulness of those men and women who enter the
legislatures under the Congress banner....

The question of office holding is not a live issue today but
I can visualize an occasion when taking office may be desirable to
achieve the common purpose. There may then be a sharp division
of opinion between Pandit Jawaharlal and myself or rather among
Congressmen. We know Pandit Jawaharlal to be too loyal to the
Congress to disregard the decision of the majority even if it lays
down a policy repugnant to him. I am no more wedded to the
Parliamentary programme than to acceptance of office. I only want
to say that we may in the course of events be driven to such acceptance. But it shall never be at the loss of self-respect or a compromise
of our objectives.[40]

Rajaji at the Gaya Congress in December 1922, acting as the advocate
of Patel and Prasad forcefully argued against the Council entry programme
as favoured by the *Swarajists*. '(a) By contesting elections even with the
avowed object of non-cooperating from within the Congress was, in
essence, accepting the reform's scheme and enhancing the prestige of the
councils, (b) by causing deadlocks in the councils the country could not
possibly be brought closer to the Congress goal—*swaraj* and (c) by altering
Gandhi's programme only two years after its adoption Congressmen had
not yet given it a fair trial.'[41]

In 1923, Rajaji pronounced that 'Councils and Civil Disobedience are
irreconcilable.'[42] But by 1934 he changed his stance. Seeing the condition of the erstwhile *satyagrahi*s who were tired of government repression
and agitation, he felt that they needed some respite and relief. The senior
Congress leadership gleaning the mood of the masses realized that a change
in the tactics was needed. In Madras too, spirit for Civil Disobedience
among the people had dampened. Moreover, by 1933 Madras had gained
some benefits from the implementation of the dyarchy, which had created

---

[40] *Times of India*, 28 November 1936, MSA, Bombay.
[41] Report of the 37th Indian National Congress, Patna, 1923, 77.
[42] Ibid., 111.

a 'mind set' for acceptance of more reforms.[43] Also the weak organizational status of the Congress, with its banning, dwindling finances and slackness in spirit to fight created an environment which too influenced Rajaji for the acceptance of Council entry. Rajaji believed that in a movement of such magnitude as Congress was fighting, various turns, twists and influences played role in the making of a strategy.[44]

Like Patel, Rajaji also believed that in any movement phase of tide and ebb would come.[45] He said 'Congress would have to carry on many campaigns before we can reach our goal.'[46] And Satyagraha would be the progressive wave of Congress which would take it to its goal but in between it would be divided by troughs during which Congress would recuperate, recover its breath and build its organization.[47] The 'no-changers' had thus realized that the civil resisters were tired and to enable them to emerge stronger and more equipped for the next battle whenever it was to come, they needed rest.[48] Rajaji said:

I do not think we look small at all. Withdrawing a movement of sacrifice is often necessary and should not be deemed a matter for shame. The situation now is different from what it was in 1922. I think we should now go into the elections on behalf of the Congress.... Nobody can prevent the adoption of civil resistance by the Congress of any future time.[49]

Besides this, the other significant consideration for Rajaji was the growing political violence in the country in 1932. He realized that it was more important to halt, rally all forces behind a common national front and then renew Civil Disobedience. As acting president of the Indian National

[43] Dyarchy had brought in some improvement in Madras, e.g., secondary education had expanded threefold between 1920 and 1930. Increase in the education of untouchables was seen. Irrigated areas through state-financed projects and agricultural credit societies were being established. Cottage industries were revived during the 1920s and a commercial outlet, the Victoria Technical Institute was established. Local Bodies were more widespread in Madras than elsewhere in British India. And there were more Indians administrative officers than Europeans in the Madras province. See M.R. Dove, *Forfeited Future: The Conflict over Congress Ministries in British India 1933–1937* (Delhi, 1987), 29–30.

[44] Gandhi, *The Rajaji Story 1937–1972*, 260–265.

[45] Rajagopalachari, *Jail Diary* (Madras, 1922), 108–109.

[46] Ibid.

[47] Gandhi, *The Rajaji Story 1937–1972*, 260–265.

[48] Ibid., 264.

[49] Ibid., 265.

Congress in September 1932, Rajaji spoke against the violence threatening the Congress strategy:

> I deplore the increased activity of the violent revolutionaries. I say this is not to deceive anyone, not merely to reiterate a creed, but as a sincere expression of what even as a practical politician I strongly feel. I admit that the increased activity of the party in Violence is due to the increased provocation of repressive measures.... Not only is our creed but our whole strategy is built on non-violence. As practical men therefore we cannot permit a weakening of that strategy. Our campaign will collapse and all its items be turned into futility if we divorce them from non-violence.[50]

Having once decided in favour of Council entry, Rajaji tirelessly worked for the 'self-purification' programme by adopting the constructive programme centring on sale and production of 'khadi,' harijan upliftment, prohibition of liquor and attainment of Hindu–Muslim unity.[51] He insisted that these measures should be adopted by supporters if constitutionalism was to be the strategy for the time being. According to him, this would keep the space open for the revival of the non-constitutional form of agitation.

> I hope they will adopt measures to see that the Congress constructive movement receives active support from them namely, khadi, removal of untouchability, abolition of liquor, drugs traffic. Any laxity on these points is unthinkable.[52]

Rajaji did not like any fanatical approach to any particular strategy. He was supporter of the view that political exigencies determined and made strategies essential. He said, 'If it is satisfactorily proved that the boycott of legislatures will do immense harm, the Congress will not boycott the legislatures. It is never to be imagined that the Congress will hold to any policy fanatically.'[53]

---

[50] See AICC File No. 1, 932, Part II, NMML.

[51] Ibid. Also see Rajendra Prasad to Nehru dated 19 December 1935. See Nehru, *A Bunch of Old Letters*, 157.

[52] See Minutes of the Congress Parliamentary Board (undated), R.P. Papers, File III/36 AICC, NMML.

[53] Gandhi, *The Rajaji Story 1937–1972*, 248.

Also unlike the *Swarajists*, Ansari, Satyamurti and others, he did not accept the shift to constitutionalism easily. Rajaji was initially hesitant and wanted any shift in the strategy to take place under the supervision of the Congress and Gandhi only. 'It is my own personal view that the new Swarajya Party to which Mr. Gandhi offered welcome and friendly help should await the decision of the AICC and proceed only if it is found necessary thereafter....'[54]

Keeping in mind the disaffections, demoralization and disorganization which had set in within the Congress with the withdrawal of the Civil Disobedience movement, Rajaji insisted that the parliamentary programme would be carried out only under the supervision of the Congress; if not, it would lead to corruption, disharmony and disunity. In a long letter to Gandhi in April 1934, Rajaji wrote that the parliamentary programme should be done in the name of the Congress and through Congress machinery and not in the name of a separate party affiliated to the Congress. The magic of the Congress name would check the difficulties that might crop up due to 'Hindu Mahasabha' and 'terrible corruption' that had been introduced in the country as incidental to election work. According to him, if Congress did not take part directly in the parliamentary work, a loosely affiliated *Swarajya* party would lead to the formation of independent groups based on various independent policies all claiming to be equally important.[55]

Rajaji saw constitutionalism, office acceptance and later ministry formation as a:

> question of political strategy ... there is no question of creed involved in it. The question is whether it is desirable to settle this matter at the time of the issue of the manifesto or keep it open after election results are known. This is also a question of electoral strategy.[56]

And once the strategy was adopted, unlike the socialist approach,[57] Rajaji was of the firm belief that 'no futile wrecking should be attempted

[54] See *Hindu*, 7 April 1934.

[55] Intercepted letter dated 4 April 1934. Rajaji to Gandhi, Government of India, Home (Political) File 4/4/34, NAI.

[56] See *Bombay Chronicle*, dated 8 July 1936.

[57] Jayprakash Narayan in his *Towards Struggle*, 129 wrote:

When we go to the legislatures our purpose should be not only to inflict constitutional defeats on the Government, but also to raise fundamental slogans for the purposes of propaganda, to relate the work within to the day to day struggles of the masses outside, to expose Imperialism, to obstruct its working.

but as much benefit should be wrung out of the Councils as possible for strengthening the prestige and position of the Congress.'[58]

He warned the socialists that they were mistaken, 'if they thought that parliamentary activities could bring about revolution. Under the limitations of the constitution, they could not expect the party to achieve more than they actually did....'[59]

Prasad too was aware of the limitation of the parliamentary programme and knew that it alone could not lead the nation to *swarajya*. Moreover, Prasad was of the opinion that a party engaged in mass struggle should not accept the position of honour, responsibility and profit until it had succeeded in capturing power. The reasons were that such acceptance 'creates personal jealousies among the members, raises hopes among the masses while the party is unable to fulfil and thus a reaction sets in.'[60]

The objective condition during 1930–1934 demanded review of the ongoing strategy. The Congress Civil Disobedience of 1930–1933 was a mass protest against the British refusal to grant anything more than Dominion status to India.[61] Its culmination in Gandhi–Irwin talk of 1931 enhanced the status of the Congress as being the sole representative of Indian opinion. It evoked large-scale enthusiasm among the people, making the first phase of Civil Disobedience a success. But enhancement of Congress prestige by Gandhi–Irwin talk was not seen in a favourable light among the imperial circles.

> The highest authority of the British Government in India and the representative of the Crown had entered into an agreement with the renowned leader of the proscribed organization who by a complex mental process, created an illusion of triumph and a concomitant Halifax and spirit of defiance.[62]

Therefore during the second phase of the Civil Disobedience 1932–1933, the attempt of the Congress to raise popular grievances crumbled under heavy repression of the government. The mood of the Government was to crush all attempts of the Congress to raise popular grievances. Mass scale arrest of leaders broke the tempo of the movement and leaders who

---

[58] Rajagopalachari to Prasad, dated 24 February 1936. See File No. VIII/36, Collection I, NAI.

[59] See *Hindu*, 25 April 1935.

[60] Rajendra Prasad to Nehru dated 26 December 1934 in R.P. Papers, NMML.

[61] B.R. Tomlinson, *The Indian National Congress and the Raj 1929–1942* (London, 1976), 35.

[62] Birkenhead Halifax, *The Life of Lord Halifax* (London, 1965), 299.

were outside the jail, were by 1933 convinced that Civil Disobedience could not be carried on.[63] Wholesale preventive arrests, declaration of Congress as illegal organization, seizure of Congress offices and properties, punitive fines and confiscation of properties of the protesters by 1934 led to strategic crisis leading to debate as to what should now be the strategy of the Congress.[64]

This led to hectic debates amongst various ideological groups within and outside Congress as to whether to engineer a new course of action such as constitutionalism or continue to follow the non-constitutional path. Rajendra Prasad regarded Council entry useless because the rights provided by Constitution of 1920 or 1935 were inadequate. According to him, 'Entry into Councils would only create illusions and difference.'[65] A sagacious politician, Rajendra Prasad could foresee that once provincial legislatures were dissolved and provincial autonomy inaugurated, competition for seats would intensify giving rise to all kinds of caste and communal jealousies—once provincial elections were in sight. And the contest for power would be fiercer if Congressmen went in for ministerships.[66] Therefore, Prasad had been skeptical about the Congress shift towards constitutionalism.[67]

Soon after the 1934 central legislative election, he expressed his disagreement:

> I am one those who believe that a party engaged in a mass revolutionary movement should not accept positions of honour, responsibility and profit until it has succeeded in capturing power ... (because) such acceptance creates personal jealousies among the members, raises hopes among the masses which the party is not able to fulfil and thus a reaction against it sets in.[68]

Under the given situation, the answer according to Prasad lies in constructive work. Yet, complete independence was the goal and for that 'The method, too, is crystal clear. It is active, dynamic, non-violent mass action ... we may fail once, we may fail twice; but we are bound to succeed

[63] Tomlinson, B.R., 'India and the British Empire, 1935–1947' *IESHR*, 13, no. 3 (July–September 1976).

[64] Prasad, *Autobiography*, 263–267.

[65] Ibid., 245.

[66] Ibid.

[67] Ibid., 245–250.

[68] See Prasad to Ansari dated 26 December 1934 in R.P. Prasad Papers, NMML.

one day.'[69] Prasad cogitated and reflected on the complexity of the situation arisen due to debilitating effect of low morale and low enthusiasm of the masses. He entered into dialogue with various leaders both the *Swarajist*s and non-*Swarajist*s such as Ansari, Dalvi, Bhulabhai and Nehru to seek an answer for himself and find a way out of the situation of political flux.[70]

In a long letter to Dalvi dated 25 September 1935, Prasad tried to objectively place before the liberal group the actual political scenario, the only way out to tackle it and in the process getting himself reassured that what he thought about Council entry in 1922 still held true in 1935.[71] He wrote to Dalvi, explaining in what manner the constitution should be worked upon, its merits and demerits and how unitedly it should be dealt with.

As you have noticed there are two schools of thought. Any decision in favour of office acceptance will be such a big departure from the policy that has been pursued by the Congress for the last fifteen years that it would not be right for the Working Committee or even for the AICC to come to it. It has therefore been left over for the Congress....

We realize that while Congressmen and advanced liberals are more or less in argument as regards the merits or rather demerits of the new Constitution, the way in which they would like to bring about the destruction is not likely to be the same. Even those Congressmen who advocate acceptance of office indicate no intention to work the Constitution. They say they will use their positions and opportunity for implementing the Congress resolutions of rejecting the Reforms. The fundamental difference between a positive attitude of rejection and a passive attitude of non-acceptance makes any programme of combined action very difficult.

I know that reactionary forces are combining together and preparing to fight against the progressive elements in the country....

The difficulties in the way of the progressive is undoubtedly great but they have to depend on the inherent strength and justice of

[69] Rajendra Prasad's Presidential Speech at Bombay Congress on 26 October 1934. See Choudhary, *Dr. Rajendra Prasad*, Vol. I, 232.

[70] In his *Autobiography*, Prasad writes about his position in 1922, 'My own view had always been that if we entered legislatures at all we should do whatever we could under the constitution.... But, of course, I considered council entry useless.' See Prasad, *Autobiography*, 245.

[71] Ibid.

their cause. I am personally anxious to bring about a rapprochement among all the progressive forces. Could we not ask the liberals who hold the opinion expressed in the 'Servants of India', to
devise some method whereby they may combine with us in making
this Constitution invalid and thus force the hands of the British
Government to revise it? Whether the Congress decides for or
against offices this will be the basic idea and I would ask you to
look at it from that point of view and suggest ways and means. I
am not suggesting anything in the nature of direct action. The ways
and means must be in reference to action within the Legislatures.
we could get the Congress and the liberals to join in this, the liberals
may leave direct action to the Congress without involving themselves
in it, if and when the Congress resorts to it, it would expect them to
maintain benevolent neutrality if not of active sympathy.[72]

For Prasad, the acceptance of parliamentary programme was tactical
rather than a political commitment. His letter to Dalvi indicated that
Council entry was merely a tactical sojourn in the long struggle for liberation. He assured Nehru in December 1935 that the matter of taking up
offices was a question of formulating a strategy to deal with the situation
created by the introduction of the Constitution.

You are undoubtedly dissatisfied with the present condition of
things. Not one amongst us here is satisfied with them. But the

[72] Prasad to Dalvi, dated 25 September 1935, AICC Papers, File No. G 43 Kw(i),
NMML, New Delhi. Bhulabhai Desai wrote to his son dated 2 April 1935 explaining why
Congress should accept office,

> [I]f Congress did not get a majority in most provinces and did not accept office,
> the pro British Ministries will continue the operation of all repressive laws and
> measures (including Ordinances) and crush or at all events suppress the Congress
> organization and the mass will be separated from the Congress and probably
> alienated....

See M.C. Setalvad, *Bhulabhai Desai* (New Delhi, 1968), 168–169. Similar views were
expressed by Saytamurti during Delhi session of AICC meeting. He said:

> Acceptance of office is a wrong term. It is no acceptance of office but capture of
> power from the enemy. Congress leaders want to prevent reactionaries occupying
> the positions of power. They do not accept the Act, instead want to destroy it. We
> want to prevent the Government of India Act from functioning and we want to
> use it partially to serve our people and mostly to prevent the mischief of others.

See AICC, File No. G-25-26-1936, NMML.

difficulties are inherent in the situation and it seems to us that it is not possible to force the pace or cause any wholesale change. In all big struggles we have to come across such situation and however we may chafe and fume, we have to lie low and work and wait for better times. We are passing through one of such crises.[73]

Prasad further elaborated to Nehru that mass struggle was the basic strategic character of the Congress and the Gandhians.

The spirit of freedom is not crushed nor is there anything like a spirit of resignation and helpless submission. I do not believe that anyone has gone back to pre-non-cooperation mentality. I do not think we have gone back to 1923–28. We are in 1928–29 mentality and I have no doubt that better days will soon come. We have been carrying on to the best of our might and ability and no one can do more.[74]

Prasad knew that there could be no simplistic answer to the complex issue of entering legislature, accepting office and finally forming ministries. He was also aware of the limitations of the parliamentary programme.[75] Therefore, he chose to keep an open mind on the question. Prasad's understanding of the political situation in 1935 was:

As it strikes me, it is not right to put it as if it were a question of acceptance or non-acceptance of office. So far as I can judge no one wants to accept offices for their own sake. No one wants to work the Constitution as the Government would like it to be worked. The question for us is altogether different.... It is really a question of laying down a positive programme for dealing with the situation created by the introduction of this Constitution in the light of circumstances as they exist. It is not a question to be answered apriori on the basis of preconceived notions of a so-called pro-changer or no-changer, cooperator or obstructionist. There has been some amount of mudslinging but that is inevitable and we have to consider and decide the question irrespective of everything except the good of

---

[73] Rajendra Prasad to Nehru dated 19 December 1935. See Nehru, *A Bunch of Old Letters*, 159.
[74] Ibid.
[75] Ibid.

the country and the effect of our decision on the great objective we have in view.[76]

Prasad knew a united protest of all political groups and communities would be a befitting answer to the imperialist design of dividing the anti-imperialist forces by offering constitutional reform of Government of India Act 1935.[77] Therefore, if he was seeking support from the liberal Dalvi he was also writing to Hasan Imam, a Muslim leader from Bihar to think 'about what Congressmen and non-Congressmen disgruntled alike by the proposals should do.'[78] He also approached Srinivas Sashtri,[79] leader of Liberal Federation, whether his party and Congress might 'chalk out a common line of action for the limited purpose of meeting the situation created by this report without in any way expecting or insisting on either to abate its ideal [sic] or alter its methods?'[80]

Accepting that political situation of 1934–1935 being different characteristically from the situation prevailing during 1920–1922, Prasad emphasized on the commensurate response to the present political challenges.[81] Believing in Gandhi's assessment of the situation that 'the masses have acted bravely and have suffered much wherever they have responded to the national call. But ample evidence is forthcoming to show that they are not able any longer to suffer the prolonged torture of the Ordinance Rule.'[82] Therefore, Prasad, aware of the decline in the response of the people for mass struggle and existing dissensions and fission in the party confided in Patel, as early as December 1934, that despite the talk in the air about 'concerted action, I am afraid concerted wordy protest may be possible, but concerted action appears impossible.'[83] He concluded 'it seems to me that at present we have only to register a protest and devote ourselves to constructive work for organizing the country.'[84]

---

[76] Prasad to Nehru dated 19 December 1935 in Nehru, *A Bunch of Old Letters*, 159.

[77] Intercepted letter Prasad to Hasan Imam, 11 December 1934, G1 Home Political File 145/34, NAI.

[78] Ibid.

[79] Leader of the Liberal Federation and head of the servants of India and friend of Gandhi.

[80] T.N. Jagdisan, ed., *Letters of V.S. Srinivas Sastri* (Madras, 1944), 336.

[81] Rajendra Prasad to Nehru dated 19 December 1935 in Nehru (ed.), *A Bunch of Old Letters*, 159.

[82] See *Collected Works of Mahatma Gandhi*, Vol. 55 (Ahmedabad, 1971), 296.

[83] Prasad to Patel, 24 December 1934, Intercepted letter, G.I. Home (Political), File No. 145/34, NAI.

[84] Ibid.

Prasad being the Congress President during the turbulent period, when report of the Joint Select Committee was made public, was kept busy trying to keep Congressmen away from quarrelling over this issue. He maintained public neutrality, as he had to manage the CSP, Swarjists and Gandhians. In 1934, he persistently told the Congressmen not to make any public statement whether for or against office acceptance as the question of office acceptance had not yet been discussed by the Working Committee.[85] He told Satyamurti that his statements were causing him embarrassment. He bluntly asked Satyamurti, 'to desist from statements on points about which there is bound to be serious controversy.'[86] He was also distressed when Ansari signed a joint statement with B.C. Roy, Asaf Ali and Khaliquzzaman, favouring the acceptance of Congress ministries. Prasad mildly reprimanded Ansari, 'those who like you not only guide but also represent us should stay neutral; otherwise, it creates a feeing as if that decision has already been reached by the Congress and I am anxious that should not be the impression created.'[87]

As the dissensions were prevalent at the PCC and lower units of the Congress in the major provinces, Prasad could not ignore the factional politics plaguing the Congress while considering the issue of adoption of constitutionalism followed by office acceptance and ministryship.[88] As early as 1934, he could foresee that if the Congress went in for Council entry, ministry formation would result inevitably. Therefore, he was of the opinion that if Congressmen entered legislatures, they should do whatever they could for the constructive programme instead of causing deadlocks.[89] But he also forewarned his fellow colleagues that entry into council would

[85] Prasad to Satyamurti 28 May 1935, AICCP, File No. G-43, (KW)(ii) 1935, NAI.
[86] Ibid.
[87] Prasad to Ansari, 13 July 1935, R.P. Papers, NMML.
[88] Rajendra Prasad, *Autobiography*, 242–251.
[89] Prasad was in agreement with Gandhi over not causing baseless deadlocks. Ibid. Gandhi's view was,

> To enter the Councils with a view to obstructing and creating deadlocks after taking the oath of allegiance is like entering the house as a tolerated guest and trying to pull it to pieces…. It is not working the Councils but playing with them in a frivolous way. It may be politics, it may be good tactics, it may be necessary and inevitable but it is not dharma.

See *Mahratta*, File No. III/35, R.P. Papers, MSS, NAI. Rajaji too wrote to Prasad in February 1936 that 'no futile wrecking should be attempted but as much benefit should be wrung out of the Councils as possible for strengthening the prestige and position of the Congress.' See Rajgopalachari to Prasad, 24 February 1936, File VIII/36, Coll. I, R.P. Papers, MSS, NAI.

create illusion and differences while non-cooperation would awaken the constructive strength of the people.[90] To Ansari he wrote, 'In spite of this conviction, out of deference to friends and co-workers we have not only acquiesced in but have given a whole-hearted and full-throated support to the Council programme....'[91]

Visualizing that 'all kinds of personal, caste and communal jealousies' would arise once the provincial elections were in sight,[92] his concern now was how to neutralize and minimize the negative implications of the Council entry programme. He was of the view that the main strength of the Congress was service and sacrifice rendered by thousands of the Congress workers. Therefore, he emphasized:

> To harmonize by equalization, as far as possible, the position of the legislators with that of the ordinary workers ... it should be made clear that positions in the Assembly and the Councils are sought for service and sacrifice and people going there are as much under discipline as the humblest worker in the Congress ranks. Service, sacrifice and discipline are ought to be our watchwords whether we are engaged in sweeping and cleaning a Harijan village or are seated on a ministerial gaddi exercising what may appear to be extensive powers.[93]

A no-changer of the 1920s, Prasad now tried to blend Congress legislative work into the conceptual framework of the constructive programme to make it a vanguard of Congress activities.[94] He suggested that the Parliamentary Board should collect all allowances and emoluments given by the government. It should support the members out of Board funds, thus creating a, 'kind of kinship with the humble workers' and making legislators subservient to the dictates of the Parliamentary Board and in turn to the AICC.[95]

Prasad weighed all consequences of a strategy before making his position definite. Therefore, though by December 1934 he was convinced of the possibility of formation of Congress ministries, he was not fully converted to the idea as late as September 1935. The cautious, unhurried

[90] Prasad, *Autobiography*.
[91] Prasad to Ansari, 26 December 1934, R.P. Papers, File No. III/35, AICC, NMML.
[92] Ibid.
[93] Ibid.
[94] Ibid.
[95] Ibid.

and accommodating approach of Prasad could be gleaned from his letter
to Sardar Sardul Singh Caveesher so far as ministries were concerned. 'I am
honestly in the position of one who has not yet made up one's mind.... It
depends upon circumstances, upon balance of profit and loss, upon probable effect on our struggle; and it is precisely because all these have to be
taken into consideration that I am unable to make up my mind.'[96]

Prasad never made any public statement in haste, which he would regret
or withdraw later. He maintained the image of public neutrality so as to
keep the channel of communication open with all ideological variants
within and outside the Congress. He had been dealing with the mundane
affairs of the Congress, and was aware of the capabilities of his Congress
workers and being a major provincial leader, he was equally in close touch
with his people and knew the extent to which the revolutionary zeal of the
people could be stretched. Prasad perceived that there was no context for
civil disobedience; by accepting office Congress could prevent reactionary
takeover and their efforts to erode Congress base; it would enhance civil
liberties and boost the morale of the masses.[97] In his view, 'People today
want small good things done for them, they would not like complete
deadlock.'[98]

Prasad argued that the danger of the Congress getting habituated to
routine administration could be avoided by using the Constitution as
Congress wanted. They could still be revolutionary by accepting office and
rigidly implementing Congress programme. He believed that the right of
Congressman in authority controlling the state apparatus would restore

[96] Prasad to Sardar Sardul Singh, 7 September 1935, R.P. Papers, NMML. This view of
Prasad is same as Gandhi's who said:

> I know that my opposition to going into Legislatures had now considerably sof-
> tened. But there has been no loss of principle here.... My response is generally in
> conformity with the atmosphere—If it rains I use an umbrella, if it is cold I can
> wrap myself in woolens and in summer there is muslin to cover me. There has
> been no change in my ideas. But I express them in keeping with the prevailing
> wind—Non-cooperation is not something I have accepted for all time. When
> I find that India can advance through cooperation, I will accept cooperation ...
> today we are going into the Legislatures not to give but to take cooperation.

Speech of Gandhi at Gandhi Seva Sangh Meeting, 17 April 1937, *Collected Works of
Mahatma Gandhi*, Vol. 65, 99–100.
[97] Rajendra Prasad, *Autobiography*.
[98] See All India Congress Parliamentary Board Manifesto, File 1/36 Collection-2, R.P.
Papers, NAI.

the low morale of the people and lead to better implementation of Civil liberties.[99]

He agreed with Rajaji that no futile wrecking should be attempted by the legislatures, but as much benefit should be wrung out of Councils as possible for strengthening the prestige and position of the Congress.[100] But he also agreed with Nehru that real work lay outside the legislature.[101]

A no-changer who made his foray into the central political scene through non-constitutional form of agitation, Prasad could never accept constitutionalism as the basic strategy of the Congress. The Secretary of State's report of January 1936 on Prasad's tour to Madras pointed out that:

> Rajendra Prasad is optimistic about the result of his tours in Madras and he is now convinced that the country is ready for a new civil disobedience movement, when the Congress High Command decides to commence it. He feels however that another year should be spent in preparation and when the new Constitution is working and the country has seen the inherent defects in it, the appropriate moment to commence the civil disobedience movement will arrive. Apparently the provincial leaders concur in this view.[102]

Thus, Prasad's political maturity and pragmatic firmness put at rest the squabble over the issue of the entry to legislature and office acceptance. His firm and objective statements echoed in the corridors of Congress guided the Congress in an unobtrusive way, commensurating with Prasad's personality. Commenting on Nehru's view over office acceptance, with a note of finality he said:

---

[99] Ibid. K.M. Munshi too was of similar opinion. He mentioned that by accepting office, the Congress would establish itself as the successor of the British. Secondly, the spirit of resistance would not be lost but it would be kept burning through an uncompromising administration. Thirdly, establishment of Congress in the seat of power would remove the mystique of state, make it more organic, humane and approachable.... The sense of frustration which had taken hold of the public mind at present could only be removed by a steady and laborious process of building up hope, faith and power. This could be done much more easily by a political party which worked both through public activity and administrative channel. See K.M. Munshi on Office Acceptance in R.P. Papers, NMML.

[100] Rajaji to Prasad, undated in Intercepted Letters, G.I. Home (Political), File No. 145/36, NAI.

[101] See All India Congress Parliamentary Board Manifesto, File 1/36 Collection 2, R.P. Papers, NAI (Manifesto was drafted by Prasad).

[102] See Secret Reports by 'S S', 4 December 1935–1 January 1936, G.I. (Home political) File Nos. 4/13/35 and 4/18/36, NAI.

[W]hilst Pt. Jawaharlal Nehru holds that the Congress should definitely decide not to take office under new Constitution, we think
that the time has not yet arrived to decide the question and we are
not prepared to rule out office acceptance all together and under
all circumstances at this stage. We can conceive of circumstances in
which office acceptance may become necessary for the very object we
both have in mind.[103]

In short, the view that the shift in the strategy of the Congress was
dictated by the fear of the Left takeover is not borne out by the existing evidences. The morale of the masses at that historical juncture predominantly
determined the shift in the strategy of the Congress.

THE TRIPURI CRISIS

By 1939, the Left groups in the Congress had made their presence felt in
the form of Congress Socialist Party. The Left's semantic militancy gave
the impression that they were the most vocal members of the Congress,
and that they had the support of the rank and file. The impression the Left
conveyed was that with the coalescence of the Left in the Congress, the
'Right' in the Congress felt threatened. Therefore, the issue of re-election
of S.C. Bose as Congress president, leading to Tripuri crisis, was regarded
as a manifestation of the struggle between the two factions—'Right' and
'Left'—to establish hegemonic control over the Congress as an anti-imperialist organization.

Related thus are the issues:

1. Why should the Tripuri crisis be seen as re-affirmation of Congress
   ideology and strategy and not as a defeat of the Left and the victory of
   the 'Right'?
2. Why should the Tripuri crisis not be seen as the result of conflicting
   ideologies but as a result of conflicting strategies?
3. Why should it not be seen as struggle between regionalism and nationalism for dominance over Congress either?

---

[103] Prasad's Speech at Lucknow Session of All India Congress Committee, April 1936, in
R.P. Papers, File No. VI/1936: Correspondence with Nehru, NMML.

The rift between Bose and Gandhian leaders was given a colour of conspiracy of the 'Right' against the Left by Bose himself.[104] Keeping 'federation' issue as the central theme to rally support for his president-ship, Bose insinuated that Gandhi and 'the Right-wing of the Congress' were attempting a compromise with the British government on the federal scheme incorporated in the Government of India Act of 1935. He further held that they had also drawn a prospective list of members for minister-ship. Explaining the 'conspiracy', Bose in his press statement on 27 January 1939 said:

> It is widely believed that there is prospect of a compromise on the Federal scheme between the Right Wing of the Congress and the British Government during the coming year…. This impression may be erroneous, but it is there all the same and nobody can deny its existence. Not only that, it is generally believed that a prospective list of Ministers for the Federal Cabinet has been already drawn up.[105]

Bose alleged that Congress had been electing a Leftist president since 1934, with the support of both the Right wing and the Left wing. The departure from this practice in 1939 and an attempt to set up a 'Rightist' candidate for the office of the President was not without significance. Since the senior Congress leaders were seeking compromise with the British on the federal scheme, they did not want a Leftist president who would be a 'thorn in the way of compromise and may put obstacles in the path of the negotiation.'[106]

---

[104] In his letter to Gandhi dated 6 April 1939, Bose accused the 'Right' leaders of conspir-ing against him and getting him out of the Congress intelligently by dragging in the name of Gandhi. Bose wrote:

> If your personality is not dragged into the picture, I shall continue to have their support, the 'Old Guard' notwithstanding. At Tripuri, the Old Guard cleverly dropped out of the picture and more cleverly pitted me against you. (But there was no quarrel between yourself and myself.) Afterwards they said that Tripuri was a great victory for them and a defeat for me. The fact of the matter is that it was neither a victory for them nor a defeat for me (without any cause for a fight with you at all), but a Pyrrhic victory—a victory purchased by a certain loss of prestige.

See Bose's letter to Gandhi dated 16 April 1939 in R.P. Papers, NMML.
[105] Bose's Press statement on 27 January 1939. See *Indian Annual Register*, Vol. VI, January–June 1939, Calcutta 1934–1946, 314–315.
[106] Ibid.

It is curious to note that the strong sentiment of rejection of federation expressed by Bose was also the unanimous view taken by the Congress in general and the 'Right' leaders in particular.[107] Not only Patel and Prasad expressed their anguish at the false allegation of Bose of their conspiring with the imperialist for 'few crumbs' but even Nehru expressed his surprise at the allegation.[108] Patel complained to Nehru, dated 24 December 1938, 'It pains me to find Subhas Babu imputes motives to the signatories and majority of the Working Committee. I can only say that I know of no member who wants the federation of the Government of India Act.'[109]

Prasad too in his Press statement dated 27 January 1939 stated that it was not fair to sidetrack the real issue by reference to an imaginary difference on the question of Federation between Subhas Bose and certain other members of the Working Committee. On that point there was absolutely no difference of opinion. It was easy to understand that there were differences between Subhas Bose and others on other questions. If the presidential election was to be made on the basis of such difference in political opinion and programme, the points at issue should be clearly stated and not befogged by putting forward an imaginary difference.[110] Actually by 1939, federation had become a non-issue but was given an exaggerated importance by Bose to capture the imagination of the people at large and emerge as a popular substitute for the Gandhians.

Bose assumed that his presidentship of the Congress in 1938 was a culmination of Left consolidation. In his view, since 1934 the Congress had Left-oriented presidents along with the expansion of kisan and workers movement; it had now reached a stage where it was ready to take the fight Leftwards and the need was for appropriate leadership which he could provide. Such assessment of Bose of Left's position in the Congress and its influence over the rank and file resulted from his inexperience in carrying out a mass movement. He failed to comprehend the actual strength of the Left, both within the rank and file of the Congress and amongst its leadership. His assessment was dogged and opinionated. Therefore, he faced

---

[107] Allegation of Bose did not hold any significance because the senior leaders were also strongly opposed to it. See Rajmohan Gandhi, *Patel: A Life*, 279.

[108] Nehru in his article 'Where Are We?' wrote, 'My own general attitude was that the whole question of federation was out of date now and it was time that the Indian problem was solved by a Constituent Assembly drawing up a Constitution.' See Gopal, SWJN, Vol. 9, 507.

[109] Patel's letter to Nehru dated 24 December 1938. Ibid., 501.

[110] Prasad's Press Statement dated 27 January 1939 in R.P. Papers, NMML.

criticism from the very quarter on whose support he was banking upon for his success as president of the Congress in 1939.[111]

The political immaturity of Subhas Bose could be seen even in the response of the Socialists on whose support he had pinned immense hope. Leaders like Acharya Narendra Dev saw the Tripuri crisis as a game of power politics. In his view, Bose and his associates were not acting in pursuance of definite political principles of work.[112] He criticized Bose for lack of clear-cut strategy and result-oriented perspective. Dev was skeptical of Bose's ability to lead the Congress successfully in 1939 during the uncertain political scenario with the threat of World War looming large on the horizon. He also ridiculed at the vagueness and impracticability of Bose's claim of attaining independence within six months. His assessment of Bose and his political agenda was:

> It is difficult to grasp the theory that underlies the activities of Shree Subhas Chandra Bose. He seems to be living from hand to mouth. He talks of an immediate struggle and does all that lies in his power to make it difficult. He goes about attacking the present leadership of the Congress declaring that it does not want a struggle and accuses it of consciously working for a compromise…. All that he really appears to be concerned with is the struggle for power within the Congress and the national movement. He has helped to disorganize the forces of struggle in Bengal and is out to spread the rot throughout the country.[113]

The socialists were uneasy with Bose's vague socialistic ideology. His acceptance of Bombay Trade Dispute Bill without a murmur in 1938, acceptance of policy of non-interference of Congress in the States Peoples' Movement and his dictatorial tendency did not make him popular among the socialists. Besides, his stubbornness in pursuing his political agenda, even at the cost of breakup of the Congress, further increased their unease. Narendra Dev's reaction to Bose's political shortsightedness was:

---

[111] Statement of Subhas Bose delivered on 25 January 1939, in S.C. Bose, *Crossroads 1938–1940* (Calcutta, 1948), 91–92.

[112] Narendra Dev's Press Statement. See *National Herald*, 5 April 1939.

[113] This statement was made in 1940 in response to the statements made by Subhas Bose during his second Congress Presidential election campaign in which he had charged the Congress leaders with carrying on negotiations in secret with the British government for compromise. For Narendra Dev's statement, see *The Indian Struggle: Next Phase*, published by Congress Socialist Party, Bombay, 1940, as Congress Socialist Tract No. 2 in Sharma, *Selected Works of Acharya Narendra Dev*, Vol. 1, 219.

This is our grievance against Shree Subhas Chandra Bose. We had trusted that he would not try to break the integrity of the Congress. The passionate appeal for unity that he made at the outbreak of the War is still ringing in our ears. He opposed in the past the present leadership but never worked against the Congress itself. A great change has come over him since. He seems to be bent upon splitting the Congress now. It is difficult to say how much of his anti-compromise talk is serious. It may, of course, just be a good stick to beat the Congress High Command with. Shree Subhas Chandra Bose has not always stood out against compromise like this. During his presidentship he was for negotiations with the British Government over the issue of the War.... It is said that such things appeal to the average leftist. He has been fed upon slogans and his political education has been neglected. He is politically immature.... It is a hard fact that today no struggle will have a nationwide character and attract the attention of the world unless Gandhiji associates himself with it. This may provide a sad commentary on the state of our political advancement, nevertheless we cannot afford to ignore it. Today we want a powerful mass movement and unless Gandhiji gives the call the masses and the classes will not be drawn into it in large numbers. So it is no use asking the Congress to start the struggle ignoring Gandhiji or threaten to start an independent struggle on behalf of a section, if the Congress delays the call.[114]

Thus, Narendra Dev aptly summed up the crisis which would arise by aligning with Bose and justified the stand of neutrality the socialists took at Tripuri. By doing so the socialists saved the Left wing from likely disaster, although it temporarily created disunity in the Left camp.[115] The Left within the Congress were dissatisfied with the senior leaders of the Congress but they were not prepared to break either with the Congress or with Gandhi.

The Leftists in the Congress should not aspire to set up an alternative leadership to the present leadership of the 'Right'. They have not the strength to control the destiny of the nation, nor can they hope to attain it in the future. A direct offensive against the 'Right' Congress leaders would result in internal conflict.[116]

---

[114] Ibid.
[115] See Press Statement of Narendra Dev in *National Herald*, dated 5 April 1939.
[116] R.M. Lohia in *Times of India*, 24. November 1939, NMML.

Among the Left leaders, the most difficult position on the Tripuri issue was of Nehru, who was 'in the unfortunate position of a person who does not agree with either of the viewpoints taken.'[117] He did not approve of the way Bose functioned as President of the Congress in 1938. During his tenureship as President, he gave more importance to local and provincial affairs of Bengal. Most of the time, he was staying in Calcutta, showing only functional interest in the AICC office and the organizational side of the Congress. This led to a certain deterioration of discipline within the Congress. Also approval of Trades' Dispute Act of Bombay during his presidentship further alienated Nehru from Bose.[118]

Besides these issues, reducing the issue of presidential election in 1939 to Left–Right conflict and indulging in personal allegations during the election made Nehru unhappy. He was aware of the fact that the Congress had not turned Left because he was twice its president.[119] In his article 'Where Are We?' he accepted that Tripuri crisis was not the result of Right–Left conflict because Gandhiji was willing to accept Narendra Dev as presidential candidate in 1939.[120] In his much-quoted letter to Bose dated 4 February 1939, Nehru expressed his differences with Bose:

There has been a lot of talk of Leftist and Rightist, of Federation etc. and yet so far as I can remember, no vital matter affecting these questions have been discussed by us in the Working Committee during your presidentship. I do not know who you consider a leftist and who a 'rightist'. The way these words were used by you in your statements during the presidential contest seemed to imply that Gandhiji and those who are considered as his groups in the Working Committee are the rightist leaders. Their opponents whoever they might be are the leftists. That seems to me an entirely wrong description. It seems to me that many of the so-called leftists are more right than the so-called rightists. Strong language and capacity to criticize and attack the old Congress leadership is not a test of leftism in politics.... I think the use of the words left and right has been generally wholly wrong and confusing. If instead of these words, we talked about policies it would be far better. What policies do you stand for? Anti-federation, well and good. I think that the great majority of the

---

[117] Nehru's letter to Gandhi, 17 April 1939, Nehru, MSS, Vol. 25, NMML.
[118] Nehru's article 'Where Are We?' in Gopal, SWJN, 516–520.
[119] Ibid.
[120] Ibid., 516.

members of the Working Committee stand for that and it is not fair to hint at their weakness in this respect.[121]

Nehru blamed Bose for giving a personal colour to an issue which arose due to differences over perspective and tactics.

No greater insult could be offered to a person than to suggest that he has secretly betrayed the cause he publicly stands for and even arranged a mutual distribution of ministries in the federation. It was a fantastic statement and it hurt to the quick.[122]

Nehru warned Bose that organization and Nation was more important than a person. 'A great organization has something impersonal about it, although it might be powerfully impressed by a dominant personality. It carries on though person may come or go.'[123]

Furthermore, Nehru did not believe in giving ultimatum to the adversary when one was not fully prepared, on the assumption that the adversary was weak. Therefore, he did not support Bose's 'National Demand' aiming to achieve within six months when the Congress was faction ridden. Bose in turn blamed Nehru for his defeat at Tripuri.

Nobody has done more harm to me personally and to our cause in this crisis than Pandit Nehru. If he had been with us we would have had a majority. Even his neutrality would have probably given us a majority. But he was with the old Guard at Tripuri. His open propaganda against me also has done me more harm than the activities of the twelve stalwarts. What a pity.[124]

Nehru's withdrawal of support for Bose was the result of his lack of faith in Bose's leadership and his ability to carry the organization forward. In his letter to Bose dated 3 April 1939 he wrote:

I was against your standing for elections for two reasons: I thought it probable that you would win the election as against Pattabhi; but I doubted very much whether you could carry the Congress with

---

[121] Nehru's letter to Bose, 4 February 1939, in Jawaharlal Nehru, *A Bunch of Old Letters*, 307.

[122] Nehru's letter to Bose dated 3 April 1939 in Gopal, SWJN, Vol. 9, 538–539.

[123] Ibid.

[124] Bose's letter to Amiya Nath Bose, 17 April 1939 in Bose, *Crossroads*, 113.

you in a clear contest with what is called Gandhism. Even if by any chance you secured a majority in the Congress, this would not represent a strong enough backing in the country without Gandhiji and effective work and even more so preparation for a struggle would be very difficult.... I saw also that you are closely associated with a number of odd individuals who were apparently influencing you considerably. These individuals were, some of them personally desirable but they did not represent to my mind any leftist opinion.... The association of vague leftist slogans with no clear leftist ideology or principles has in recent years been much in evidence in Europe. It has led to Fascist development and staying away of large section of the public.[125]

The above statement of Nehru rightly summed up the difference in the approaches of his and Bose's. In spite of his differences over the modalities of the strategy with the senior leaders like Patel, Rajaji and Prasad, Nehru was elected president of the Congress thrice. The primary reason was that being a true democrat he placed the organization above personal whims and beliefs. He gave priority to confidence building and faith among the senior leaders of the Congress in him because he knew that for a success of political strategy a well structured and united leadership, and organization were essential.[126]

Nehru too harboured Left leanings but he had full faith in the leadership of Gandhi and Congress's strategy of Satyagraha and non-violence. Therefore, he never allowed his personal opinion come into confrontation with the majority opinion of the Congress to the extent that break would become imminent.[127] Through his article 'Where Are We?', Nehru tried to put the Tripuri crisis in the correct perspective. He wrote that his energy was devoted towards bridging the gulf between the old and the young leaders of the Congress because he was convinced that Congress could not do without any of these groups. Young leaders were the sign of growth and dynamism of the movement and 'old leaders were tried men with prestige and influence among the masses and the experience of having guided the struggle for many years. They were not Rightist by any means; politically, they were far more Left and they were confirmed anti-imperialists.'[128]

---

[125] Nehru's letter to Bose, 3 April 1939 in Nehru, *A Bunch of Old Letters*, 346–347.
[126] See Nehru's 'Where Are We?' in Gopal, SWJN, Vol. 9.
[127] Ibid.
[128] Ibid.

Nehru thus functioned within the framework of Gandhian strategy. But Bose began his election campaign by rejecting the Gandhian strategy of collaboration, by making allegations and casting serious aspersions on the Gandhian leaders, their ideology and strategy. His grievances against the 'Right' leaders extended from fictitious to apparently real issues such as issue of federation, coalition ministry in Bengal, giving support to Trade Union and Kisan Sabhas. He verbalized Left ideology but did not give direct support to Kisan Sabha and Trade Union groups or States Peoples' Movement, when he was president in 1938. He did not even offer opposition to Bombay Trades' Dispute Act; instead, he fully complied with the official stand of the Congress. He also rejected constitutionalism but demanded coalition Ministry for Bengal which could be seen as a 'Rightist' stand.[129]

When Bose won election of presidentship in 1939, he projected it as a contest between opposing strategies and programmes of the Congress represented by the Left and the Right. He outlined a scheme at Tripuri Congress for giving British a six-month ultimatum to withdraw or face a Civil disobedience.[130] Exhilarated at his newly won victory, Bose outlined his plan:

> The next Congress meets at Tripuri, we shall be in a position to put our national demand (for Poorna Swaraj) before the British Government and ask for a definite reply within a specified period. With a background of active international tension, it will not be possible for the British government to reject our demand lightly. And if they do reject it or give us unsatisfactory reply, we should start our Satyagraha campaign after giving due notice.... In such a critical situation the British Government cannot permit a major struggle to go on in India. They will have to make peace with India if they are to avoid weakening themselves in Europe.[131]

The 'Right' leaders believed that the time was not yet ripe for an ultimatum because neither the Congress nor the masses were ready for revival

---

[129] See Bose's letter to Nehru dated 24 March 1939 and Nehru's letter to Bose dated 3 April 1939 in Nehru, *A Bunch of Old Letters*, 350–351.

[130] See Bose, *Crossroads*.

[131] Bose's letter to Gandhi dated 21 December 1938. See Patel Papers, File No. Lot 1-33-1 to 4. SPNM, Ahmedabad.

of civil disobedience.[132] Moreover, Congress too was plagued with corruption, indiscipline, bogus memberships, mutual bickerings and rivalries.[133] Therefore, Bose's strategy of giving ultimatum appeared weak not only to the Left in the Congress but also to the Gandhians. Rajaji advised the Congressmen at Tripuri in 1939:

> There are two boats on the river. One is an old but a big boat piloted by Mahatma Gandhi. Another man has a new boat, attractively painted and beflagged. Mahatama Gandhi is a tried boatman who can transport you. If you get into the other boat, which I know is leaky, all will go down and the river Narmada is indeed deep. The new boatman says 'If you don't get into my boat at least tie my boat to yours.' This is also impossible. We cannot tie a leaky boat to a good boat exposing ourselves to the peril of going down.[134]

Rajaji in metaphoric language defined the logic of Gandhian strategy—where the decision, method and responsibility of launching a struggle remained confined within the Congress fold, with Gandhian leaders at its forefront. Any digression from the strategy was not welcomed but if it occurred then the responsibility of 'digression' was to be borne solely by its leader. Bose flouted this logic before declaring his call for 'Civil Disobedience'. He wanted the Congress and Gandhian leaders to take up the responsibility of carrying out the struggle successfully but the reigns of the struggle would be in his hands. The element of unpredictability and high-handedness in Bose's personality further distanced the Gandhian

---

[132] Gandhiji's view was:

> Take Subhas Babu's proposed ultimatum to the British Government. He thinks that the situation is ripe now for throwing a challenge to the Government. I feel that it is impossible to inaugurate and conduct a non-violent campaign today. We have no control on those who believe in violence. Rampur, Ramdurg and Cawnpore are the pointers. Panditji had little non-violent control of the situation in Cawnpore and other cities in UP and the Shia-Sunni trouble is a fresh species of the difficulties we have to face. We have not only no control over the non-Congressmen but little over even the Congressmen. There was a time when the bulk of the country used to listen to us; today even many Congressmen are out of our hands. I cannot think of organizing a Dandi Salt March today. The atmosphere is altogether unpropitious. But Subhas Babu thinks otherwise.

See Tendulkar, *Mahatma*, Vol. V, 94.

[133] Ibid.

[134] Rajaji speaking at Tripuri, while seconding the Pant resolution, strongly rejected any kind of compromise with Bose. See Gandhi, *Patel: A Life*, 280.

leaders from him. Since the strength of the Gandhian strategy was to maintain the relevance and strength of the strategy in the eyes of the masses, unless masses were not fully prepared, no new phase of struggle was to be carried out. But with Bose, neither they nor the Left[135] in the Congress could be sure as to what turn the struggle would take. Nehru too expressed his misgivings: 'I doubt very much whether you could carry the Congress with you in a clear contest with what is called Gandhism.'[136]

Though respecting Bose's genuine nationalist fervor, Patel's opposition to Bose stemmed from the assessment that:

> The present is no atmosphere at present for an ultimatum.... The Congress has no military power. Its only power lies in truth and non-violence. There were dissentions, indiscipline and corruption in the Congress organization.... The present is not the time to launch a Satyagraha fight. If Satyagraha is started there will be anarchy in the country. We are weak and if we give an ultimatum and fail it will be a disgrace to us.[137]

Regarding Tripuri crisis as resulting out of 'Right–Left conflict', Prasad analysed the situation by rejecting such assessment of the problem. In an interview to the Associated Press on 7 February 1939 at Santiniketan he, first, rejected the view that there was any organized party of the Rightists in the Congress like that of the socialists. Nor the so-called 'Rightist' voted during the presidential election as a bloc. Implicitly referring to Left and Bose, Prasad further added that 'a party becomes necessary where someone or some group is anxious or eager to control an organization.' The Gandhians never believed to keep the Congress organization within their control, essentially because their strength lay in the support they got from the Congress and people; there never was any need to form any party like socialists within the Congress.[138] Prasad's advice for Bose was that he should have a Working Committee in which he had full confidence and with which he was in complete agreement, not only on broad principles

---

[135] P.C. Joshi, General Secretary of CPI wrote in April 1939, 'The greatest class struggle today is our national struggle, that the Congress was the main organ of this struggle and that the preservation of its unity was a primary task.' See Patel Papers, File No. Lot 1-33-1 to 4, SPNM.

[136] Nehru's letter to Bose, dated 3 April 1939 in Nehru, *A Bunch of Old Letters*, 346.

[137] See Patel's speech in *Bombay Chronicle*, 11 May 1939.

[138] Prasad's Press interview, dated 7 February 1939 in Choudhary, *Dr. Rajendra Prasad*, Vol. 3, 283.

but also in details of programme and day-to-day administration of the Congress organization.

However, the dilemma of Bose was that the masses listened to Gandhi and Gandhian leaders and without the participation of the latter in the struggle, the response of the masses would be lukewarm. 'A large majority of Congressmen who dislike the High Command did not want to give up Mahatma Gandhi.'[139] The Left too did not want to disassociate itself from Gandhi and the Congress. This reality of Gandhi and Gandhian leaders remaining the true representatives of the masses exposed the inherent futility in Bose's attempt to capture the Congress.[140]

Realizing the folly in his tactics, yet unrelenting Bose requested Gandhi:

> The main problem appears to me as to whether both parties can forget the past and work together. That depends entirely on you. If you can command the confidence of both the parties by taking up a truly non-partisan attitude, then you can save the Congress and restore national unity. I am temperamentally not vindictive. In a way I have boxer's mentality i.e. to shake hand smiling when the boxing bout is over.[141]

Threatening the Gandhians and persuading Gandhi at the same time for supporting his 'ultimatum' to British,[142] Bose did not leave any space for cooperation with them. The stand of the socialists and Nehru explicitly brought out the fact that Tripuri crisis was not a result of ideological conflict but a maneuver for takeover of leadership of the Congress.

---

[139] See *Hindu*, 7 May 1939.

[140] Narendra Dev in his article 'Class Organizations And the Congress' writes, '(whatever our criticism of the Congress) it is the only broad platform of anti-imperialist struggle in India, and it is the only centre today from which such a struggle can be conducted'. Sharma, *Selected Works of Acharya Narendra Dev*, Vol. 1, 142–143.

[141] See Bose's letter to Gandhi, dated 29 March 1939 in Patel Papers, Lot 1-39, 1 to 3, SPNM, Ahmedabad.

[142] Bose's letter to Gandhi, dated 31 March 1939,

> If we come to the parting of the ways, a bitter civil war will commence and whatever be the upshot of it the Congress will be weakened for sometime to come and the benefit will be reaped by the British Government. It is in your hands to save the Congress—People who are bitterly opposed for various reasons to Sardar Patel and his group, still have faith in you.

See R.P. Papers, NMML.

Clarifying the position of the Gandhians on Bose and judiciously summing up their stand, Patel said:

> We were clearly of opinion that it was unnecessary to re-elect Subhas Babu. In our minds there was never any question of left or rightist.... The charges against us are not quite clear.... We are not conscious of having offered any obstruction to any programme kept by the President or his companions before the AICC, the Subject Committee and the Open Session. Most of the resolutions kept before the Subject Committee were drafted by Sri Jawaharlalji. The six months clause in the National Demand resolution was opposed by President's own political allies, the Congress Socialists. Our only responsibility was that we gave our unwilling consent to the resolution which dealt with the political situation arisen out of the Presidential elections. The genesis of the resolution was that the majority of the delegates said that they had not understood the implication of our statement from Bardoli. They also said that they had never suspected that they were voting against Gandhiji's policy and programme when they voted for Subhas Babu.[143]

Bose's re-election as President of the Congress did neither lead to the formation of united Left bloc within the Congress nor did it establish Left ideology as official creed of the Congress. Bose, a poor tactician, did not allow his viewpoint to evolve gradually and capture the minds of the masses. He supported abrupt severance of tried and tested Gandhian strategy and opted for an untested militant and aggressive policy.

Many of the leaders did not like the environment of political uncertainty created by Bose. Nehru's reaction was: 'What is unfortunate is the manner in which this deadlock has come about, for it represents no clear conflict of ideas or policy. It is the outcome of a desire to control the Congress organization, whatever the policy.'[144]

The Bengal supporters of Bose and his brother Sarat Bose tried to give the Gandhian–Bose conflict a regional colour. Nehru complained to Krishna Menon, 'For the moment Subhas has become a kind of a symbol of Bengal and it is quite impossible to argue with or about symbol.'[145]

---

[143] Patel's letter to Sarat Chandra Bose, April 1939, R.P. Patel Papers, File No. Lot 1-39-1 to 3, SPNM, Ahmedabad.

[144] See Nehru's article 'Where Are We?' in Gopal, SWJN, Vol. 9.

[145] Nehru's letter to Krishna Menon 1939 in Nehru, *A Bunch of Old Letters*.

The manner in which the attack was launched on Patel, manhandling of Pant and D.P. Mishra at Tripuri and tearing of Prasad's kurta when he went to meet Bose at Calcutta[146] gave the impression that it was provincialism versus nationalism. But Bose faced major opposition from senior Gandhian leaders of Bengal such as B.C. Roy and Prafulla Chandra Ghosh who wrote to Kriplani, dated 21 January 1939, 'If he wins it will be a very bad thing. So we must have Dr. Pattabhi.'[147] This clearly establishes that the impression of the conflict seen in the context of region versus nation was not true. Maulana Azad regarded it as the conflict between Bose and the Congress. He rejected the view that the differences were either over ideology or attempt of region to dominate over nation. He held:

> It is a pity that Subhas Babu is exactly in the position where he was before Tripuri, and there is no hope that he will improve the situation by acting on the Tripuri resolution. On the one hand he calls the Pant resolution against the constitution as ultra vires, on the other he wants Gandhiji to accept certain conditions. Along with this he does not hesitate in making the extravagant assertion that the Pant resolution would have been lost, had the socialist group not become neutral. However there is no hope of the Congress moving along Subhas Babu. The whole thing will come to dead stop.... I consider the affair of Subhas Babu to be neither a struggle between the right and left nor the question of composite and homogeneous Working Committee. It is only a matter of Subhas and some of his supporters. It matters little in what form the tangle comes to an end.[148]

Thus, despite having radical image, the performance of Bose as President of the Congress in 1938 and later on during Tripuri entanglement, his appeal for support and rejection of Congress strategy of non-violence and Satyagraha projected him as a leader who lacked both ideological and strategic clarity. Therefore, he faced political rejection not only by the Gandhians but also by his socialist and other Left supporters. This debacle of Tripuri was thus a result of the failure of political adventurism, misplaced fervour of nationalism and strategic romanticism.

---

[146] See Rajendra Prasad on Tripuri Crisis in his *Autobiography*.

[147] See P.C. Ghosh's letter to Kriplani dated 21 January 1939 in R.P. Papers, NMML.

[148] Azad to Nehru 17 April 1939 in Nehru, *A Bunch of Old Letters*, 371–372.

FORMATION OF MINISTRY: A PHASE OF TRUCE

Changes have taken place in the political conditions of the country. The person, who wants to cover a particular distance, starts moving, takes a pause of getting tired, but he does not go back. He would take his lunch, have some rest as well as sleep for a while and resume his onward journey as soon as he feels fresh. We fought with the government for 3–4 years. We had a truce and again we fought and now we have ceased war.[149]

In this section, an attempt has been made to examine the acceptance of ministry as part of the anti-imperialist strategy. It is not intended to go into a detailed survey of legislative and administrative policies pursued by the ministries. Attention would, however, be riveted on (a) how far it provided relief to the masses and helped in consolidating the position of the Congress; (b) to what extent the phase of truce was used for recuperation and reinvigoration to restart non-constitutional form of struggle and (c) how far this phase succeeded in restoring self-respect and self-confidence of the people.

The most essential feature of non-constitutional form of struggle was the extent to which the mass discontentment could sustain the extra-legal form of struggle, and how intense it was. For its success mass support was imperative. However, in 1934, there was neither popular enthusiasm nor organizational strength to sustain the extra-legal form of struggle. The Congress was ridden with internal dissensions and did not have adequate reserve of morale and finances to sustain a mass campaign. Rajendra Prasad aptly highlighted the state of affairs.

All Congress offices were closed and practically all Congress property was confiscated and the need of the hour is to channelise all energy towards reorganization of the Congress into an even more powerful and effective organization than what it was when it took up the last campaign of Civil disobedience under Gandhiji's lead.[150]

[149] Patel's Speech at Valsad, 24 December 1934. See *Gujarat Samachar*, 27 December 1934, File No. Lot 1-39-1 to 3, Patel's Speeches 1934 to 1945, SPNM, Ahmedabad.
[150] Rajendra Prasad's Speech at All India Congress Committee, Patna, 20 January 1935. See R.P. Papers, NMML.

The repressive policies of the Government, arrest of 90,000 Congress activists and declaration of Congress as illegal organization further distanced the enthusiasm for reviving extra-legal struggle.[151]

During 1934–1947, a tug of war regarding what strategy should be followed ensued within the Congress. The Left within the Congress was supporting renewal of non-constitutional form of struggle, whereas the 'Right' leadership was for the adoption of constitutional activity as an interregnum for re-launching the struggle subsequently. The Quit India Movement in 1942 was the natural corollary of the basic strategy of the Congress. Patel, Rajaji and Prasad accepted this strategy in words and spirit. Patel in 1935 evaluated the strategy. To quote:

> In these circumstances those who have not fully understood the Gandhiji's principles, find themselves surrounded by a dilemma. But they should understand that the Gandhian Era is an era of tide and ebb. Those who fully understand Gandhiji's principles have realized what tide and ebb means. We know the universal law of nature that the ebb, which succeeds the tide, generates a powerful and deadly energy.[152]

Rajaji too saw this period as that of 'trough'. He was of the view that 'phase of struggle undergoes progressive waves of crests and troughs and Congress would have to carry on many campaigns before we can reach our goal.'[153] Rajendra Prasad also approved of such a strategy. He wrote to Nehru, dated 19 December 1936:

> It is not possible to force the pace or cause any wholesale change. In all big struggles we have come across such situations and however much we may chafe and fume, we have to lie low and work and wait for better times. I see no reason to be disheartened. The spirit of freedom is not crushed nor is there any thing like a spirit of resignation and helpless submission.[154]

The logic behind the ministry formation was to put into action the constructive programme of the Congress, focussing on increasing production

---

[151] Sumit Sarkar, *Modern India 1885–1947* (New Delhi, 1983), 254–311.
[152] Patel's Speech at Ahemdabad dated 25 August 1935. See Chopra, *The Collected Works*, Vol. V, 157.
[153] Rajagopalachari, *Jail Diary*.
[154] Prasad's letter to Nehru dated 19 December 1936 in R.P. Papers, NMML.

of khadi by popularizing *charkha*, removal of untouchability, strengthening and building of village-industries and spread of education. These activities would bring the Congress workers into direct contact with the masses. Therefore, without antagonizing the government and inviting reprisal it would lead to strengthening of anti-imperialism among the people. This could be further strengthened by controlling the government machinery and providing ameliorative measures within the constraints of the colonial government. Therefore, during this phase too the emphasis of the three leaders was to maintain unity within the Congress organization and curb all fissiparous tendencies, both within and outside the Congress.[155]

The electoral success of the Congress in 1937 put considerable pressure for ministry formation in the Congress. Yet to go in for ministry formation was not so easy. For more than two years the subject of office acceptance had roused fierce controversy in the country in general, and in the Congress in particular. The socialists, including Nehru, objected to office acceptance as they feared that once the Congress got involved with the ministries, it might get entangled in petty reformist activities and forget for a while the main issue. They feared that the initiative would pass from the masses and the activities would be largely confined to the stuffy and limited sphere of the Council Chamber.[156] But Nehru was aware of the fact that a considerable force was being built up in the Congress for office acceptance and the decision to oppose it would mean breaking away, which could have led to far reaching consequences. Hence, he felt that,

> The test of any steps taken, such as acceptance of ministry or otherwise depends on how we can propagate our work and what effect it will have on the rank and file of the Congress. We have to see from a long term point of view whether we are taking a false step for a short term and immediate gain.[157]

However, only staunch constitutionalists like Bhulabhai Desai, Satyamurti, Ansari, Prakasam, Jaykar and Sapru were keen on ministry

---

[155] *Times of India*, 16 July 1934, 10. Patel appealed to the members of the CSP to avoid a split in the Congress ranks. He accused them of putting the cart before the horse by raising issues which could be settled after the goal was reached. Once they finish the fight there would be time enough to consider what changes were necessary.

[156] Ibid.

[157] See Nehru's Circular to the Provincial Congress Committees dated 19 February 1937 in Gopal, SWJN, Vol. 8, 49.

formation.[158] The central leadership of the Congress—Gandhi, Patel and Prasad—was aware of the limitations of the parliamentary programme and knew that it alone could not lead the nation to *swarajya*. Moreover, Prasad was of the opinion that a party engaged in a mass revolutionary movement should not accept position of honour, responsibility and profit until it had succeeded in capturing power. The reasons were that such acceptance 'creates personal jealousies among the members, raises hopes among the masses which the party is unable to fulfil and thus a reaction sets in.'[159] Prasad also said at the end of 1935:

> It has been wrongly and unfairly assumed that the Working Committee has been thinking of nothing except offices under the New Constitution. We have as a matter of fact given to the matter no importance. On the other hand, it is others who have been trying to force our hands to come to a decision. The first attempt was made at Jabalpur in April last and we felt it was too early to come to a decision on the question. We have stuck to that decision which was affirmed at Madras.[160]

Nonetheless, once the decision was taken by the AICC in 1937, the Congress with full mast went ahead towards ministry formation and began at once the work of social reform which they had promised in their election manifesto.[161] All Congressmen had accepted the election manifesto as the common plan of action in all provinces. The manifesto had declared that while doing their best to destroy the Act and to resist British imperialism in its attempt to strengthen its hold on India, Congressmen if elected would work for the up-liftment of the masses, the reform of the system of land tenures, the reduction of agriculturalists' rent and the relief of their indebtedness, the improvement of industrial conditions in the towns, insurance against old age, sickness and unemployment, the right to form trade unions, the right to strike, the removal of sex disabilities and of 'untouchability', and the social and economic advancement of the backward classes. In the political field, the first objective was the repeal of all regressive laws

---

[158] Satyamurti wrote to the Prasad, dated 30 August 1939, 'I am clearly and emphatically of the opinion that whatever programme you may take up including the restarting of Civil Disobedience, the parliamentary front ought not to be neglected.' See Satyamurti Papers, NMML.

[159] Rajendra Prasad to Nehru, 26 February 1934, in R.P. Papers, NMML.

[160] Rajendra Prasad to Nehru, 18 December 1935, ibid.

[161] Ibid.

and regulations, the release of political prisoners and the establishment of full civil liberty.[162]

To achieve these reform measures, the Congress leadership was of the opinion that deadlock should not be created immediately. Prasad in his letter dated 14 July 1936 to Patel wrote:

> I consider your idea of resolution of forfeited land or refunding of fine and punitive tax as a programme of immediate deadlock, because I cannot imagine the Governor yielding to it. If we wish to accept office we should have a definite programme e.g. of revolutionising whole educational system, recasting the whole revenue administration and a big push to our constructive programme. I imagine if we have a revolutionary programme the governor will not permit it. If he does we shall have achieved something worthwhile.... In my scheme a deadlock would take some time in coming and in the meantime while we are carrying our own programme through, we shall be doing little bits and odds which will also please the people.[163]

However, there was controversy and at the centre of the controversy was restoration of forfeited land, refunding of fine and punitive tax which Patel favoured and over which Prasad was sceptical because he did not want to raise issues which might cause deadlocks instead of providing swift relief. However, Patel was clear on this issue; he had even promised the kisans of Ras that their lands would come back to them 'by knocking their doors.'[164] In fact in a letter to Ashabhai Patel, a colleague of his from Ras, dated 14 September 1938, Patel wrote:

> The format of the laws relating to the land has appeared in the newspapers. It will be adopted in the same form. It will be introduced in the legislative assembly in a short while, and after that it will become law. Therefore, notices will have to be issued to those land-holders and possession given within fifteen days. In case there is standing crop on the land the collectors will have to decide and money payment will be made accordingly. In any case possession on land will be assured.[165]

---

[162] Ibid.

[163] Patel to Prasad, 14 July 1936, in R.P. Papers, NMML.

[164] Patel to Ashabhai Patel, dated 14 September 1938, in Nandurkar, *Sardar Shree ke Vishista Aur Anokhe Patra*, 259.

[165] Ibid.

The other issue of controversy was Congress–Zamindar Agreement of 1937–1938, which was seen by Kisan Sabha as a compromise with the big landlords and a betrayal of peasant interests.[166] But Congress leaders were interested in providing relief as early as possible and not in raising class question. They believed that it was not necessary to start a capital and labour conflict or a fight between zamindars and kisans. In India, the struggle for national independence was all inclusive; it included and transcended the class war. It had within itself the seeds of every necessary revolution and readjustment.[167]

Moreover, the 'Right' leaders were convinced that ministry could not last long and the day of reckoning was near.[168] Therefore, for swift reforms and legislation, agreement with zamindars was not seen as a retrogressive measure. Even Nehru realized:

On the constructive side, the land and rural debt have to be tackled. These questions are complicated and if an attempt is made to deal with them thoroughly, some delay is inevitable. Such an attempt should of course be made on the lines indicated by Congress resolution, especially the Agrarian resolution of the Faizpur Congress. But it is very necessary that some relief should be given to the peasantry immediately.[169]

Motivated by this zeal for providing immediate amelioration to peasantry, practicability determined the priorities. Rajaji in his Budget Speech said:

We are fully aware that the burden of the land revenue assessment is heavy, but the grant of relief on a scale which would be of material assistance to the individual small ryot would involve such a dislocation of the Budget of the Province that not even a beginning could be made with other ameliorative measures and reforms for the well being of the masses which, in the opinion of the Government, are of great and urgent importance, and which it would not be right thus

[166] Prasad's Correspondence with Sri Krisna Babu, 9 April 1938 in Choudhary, *Dr. Rajendra Prasad*, Vol. II, 32–36.

[167] Copley, *The Political Career of C. Rajagopalachari*, 161.

[168] Patel's Speech at Hubli on the Future of Ministries. See *Times of India*, 27 April 1937, Bombay, SPNM, Ahmedabad.

[169] Nehru to leaders of Congress Party in Provincial Assemblies dated 16 July 1937. See Rajaji Papers, NMML.

for the Government to disable itself from undertaking.... While on the question of the relief of the land revenue burden, I may say, Sir, that my colleagues and I consider that of even greater urgency and value to the agricultural population is the adequate relief of indebtedness and immediate steps will therefore be taken in this direction, which will release the cultivator in our Province from the stranglehold of unredeemable insolvency and despair, and we hope, we make a man of him.[170]

In the twenty seven and a half months of ministerial tenure, Rajaji, within the colonial constraints, was able to give modest relief to Madras province. It seemed modest considering the expectations raised but keeping in mind the temporariness of its tenure and financial limitations, the successes achieved were commendable. His ministry provided temporary subsides to the artisans, non-lapsing fund for taking water to dry villages, built rural roads and dispensaries, remitted land revenue in areas hit by cyclone or drought, halved grazing fee, and negotiated settlement with Hyderabad and Mysore for the use of river waters, thus initiating Tungabhadra scheme. The ministry also initiated thermal plants in Bezwada and Vizag in the Telugu districts. It took power from the hydro system of Pykara and Mettur to eight additional Tamil districts.[171]

The ministry also enacted the first of its kind, Public Health Act. Buttermilk, newspaper, radio sets and Fuller's earth for washing clothes were made available to the prisoners. To reduce expenses, shifting of the government each summer to Ooty was stopped. The most important innovation in finances made by the ministry was introduction of sales tax. Rajaji levied it in 1939. Initially, he imposed it on the sale of petrol and tobacco, later on electricity and finally a general sales tax of half an anna in

---

[170] Rajaji's Speech in the Madras Assembly dated 21 September 1937. See *Madras Legislative Assembly Debates*, Vols. I and II, 120–126. He concluded his budget speech with further reform proposals for the villages. He said that,

> When we think of the pressing needs of the Province in the matter of the supply of clean drinking water for every village, adequate drainage arrangements for all towns and better and more widespread measures for the prevention of disease and the distribution of medical relief, centres of healthy entertainment and culture in all large villages, and the establishment of suitable cottage industries throughout the land, we realize how difficult is the problem of making our limited resources go as far as possible and ensuring that every rupee is spent wisely and to the best advantage.

Ibid.
[171] Gandhi, *The Rajaji Story 1937–1972*.

a rupee, payable on sales by anyone with a turnover of over rupees 10,000 a year were levied. And in implementing the sales tax Rajaji said, 'I do want, I admit and I repeat to shift the burden from the village to the town.'[172]

However, Madras province saw outbursts of agrarian unrest during the period. The most significant agrarian unrest during the period in the Southern province was in Malabar and coastal Andhra. In Malabar, the peasant demands were for abolition of illegal exactions and forced labour, reduction of land revenue, use of certified instruments of weight and measure for the estimation of crop, fixity of tenure and compensation for the improvement effected by tenants.[173] The demands of peasants of coastal Andhra were around the retrieval of land that tenants had been evicted from.[174] Although in coastal Andhra leadership was provided by the District Congress Committee, N.G. Ranga was very active. Referring to Ranga's participation in the agrarian unrest on account of high rent rates, Lord Erskine wrote to Rajaji:

> I do not necessarily hold any brief for the Jamindari system as it exists today and consider that as compared with rents on the large estates in Great Britain, the rentals in some of these areas are extremely high, but the system has survived from the past with gradual mitigation in favour of the cultivator, and until the Madras Committee of Enquiry has reported and the Government has made up its mind as to what action is just and reasonable, I feel that it would be advisable to put a brake upon agitation such as this man Ranga is now engaged in. If it is allowed to go on for long in this strain, the result among the excitable Telugus is not difficult to forecast and we are already seeing signs of it in the West Godavari and Kistna District.[175]

However, the PCC which was led by the socialists who threatened agitation denied that a no-rent campaign was being carried out by them because party leadership did not want to precipitate the situation which in turn might hurt the reform activities carried out by the Congress ministry. This may be the reason why N.G. Ranga, who earlier was very active in agrarian unrest, unexpectedly backed out and accepted the Government's terms:

---

[172] Rajaji's Speech in the Madras Legislative Assembly dated 20 February 1939, 87. See *Madras Legislative Assembly Debates*, Vols. 1–2, 1939.
[173] See Quarterly Survey Reports of the Political and Constitutional Position in British India, no. 6, November 1938 to January 1939, NMML.
[174] Ibid.
[175] Erskine to Rajaji, dated 8 May 1938, Rajaji Papers, File No. 15 to 23, NMML.

The present suspension of satyagraha ... is specially intended to enable the Government to review the special circumstances of the people of Munagala, the conduct of the local authorities during the last three weeks and utter incapacity of most of the riots to pay any more rent arrears. It is also intended to help the Government to get into touch with the local authorities and look into the relevant records in the Collectorate and District Police Station and ascertain through such records whether under the administration of the present zamindar, there is any real likelihood of the re-establishment of peace and tranquility in the estate. I do seriously hope that the ministry will genuinely respond to this gesture of the Ryots Association.[176]

This stand was taken by socialists because they knew that no swift solution could be arrived at. In fact, Munagala dispute continued even after the Congress Ministry resigned. The immense public pressure to review rent demands led to the formation of Prakasam Committee which was set up to examine the tenancy legislation. Prakasam during the Kalipatnam and Munagala Satyagraha had promised the tenants that he would resolve the tenants' grievances and advised the peasants not to get carried away by any ill-considered advice but to abide by the law as his zamindari bill which he was drafting would solve their problems. The Committee recommended a reduction of the rent in zamindaris to the rent received by them in 1802, by reason of their argument that the Permanent Settlement of 1802 had permanently and unalterably fixed the rents received by zamindars, while fixing the *pesh-kush* payable by them to the government. The legal aspect of this argument apart, the implication of carrying this recommendation into effect was destructive of zamindars as a class.[177] But there was stiff opposition to Prakasam Report in Madras. Both Government officials and Congressmen opposed it.[178] Erskine noted that this would mean a very large fall in rental levels.[179]

Patel in a letter to Rajaji, dated 19 July 1939, wrote:

A deputation of Raja of Venkatgiri, Bohbili and Parla Kimdi waited on me here in connection with the Tenancy Legislation

---

[176] N.G. Ranga's address to the Provincial Ryots Association on suspending Satyagraha. See *Hindu*, 19 June 1939, 10.

[177] Rajmohan Gandhi, *The Rajaji Story 1937–1972*, 50–53.

[178] Copley, *The Political Career of C. Rajagopalchari*, 125–129.

[179] Erskine to Linlithgow, 10 November 1938, Linlithgow Papers, MS Eur. F. 125/66, NMML.

which is being drafted under instructions by your Government in accordance with the report of the Prakasam Committee. The report is from their point of view too drastic and is intended to abolish zamindari system indirectly. How far their contention is true, I am not in a position to say, but it is true that they are deeply sore about this matter. On the whole I think they have behaved better than the zamindars of UP and they are in a mood to appease them by doing something which would not involve any compromise with our principles or any concessions which are not justly due to them.[180]

It aptly signifies that the Congress did neither unnecessarily want to get involved in class antagonism, nor did it want to be unfair to any particular class. For providing relief to the peasantry Rajaji's Ministry passed Madras Agriculturalist Relief Act in 1938. It provided relief to the peasantry in that if a person had paid as interest or principal twice the amount that he originally borrowed, the obligation would be taken to have ceased. The second part of the relief was that all interest outstanding on 1 October 1937 would be deemed to be discharged and only the principal would be the amount repayable.[181] The Act gave relief to about 87 per cent of the people.[182] Since the intention of the Gandhian leaders—Patel, Rajaji and Prasad—was not to initiate class struggle at any point of time during the anti-imperialist struggle, moderation was to be the hallmark of the agrarian policy during the ministry period. They

---

[180] Patel to Rajaji dated 10 November 1938. See Rajaji Papers, NMML. Although there was opposition to the Committee's recommendation the general principles of the report were accepted by Madras Legislative Assembly. See Rajaji Papers, Roll No. 3, Microfilm. Patel explained to the landlords that as the general principles of the report had been accepted by the Madras Legislative Assembly, it would be difficult to do anything. Patel to Rajaji, 16 July 1939, ibid. In fact in September 1937, the Congress wanted to pass an amending bill to the Tenancy Act but the Zamindar MLCs made it clear that as a result of indifference on the part of the Congress, the landlords would either reject the bill or make an amendment to it in the Council. Khan Bahadur Mohammad Ismail, MLC, wrote to Rajendra Prasad, 17 October 1937. R.P. Papers, Ms. XI/37 Collection, 1, National Archives of India, Delhi.

[181] Speaking on the proposal on 20 March 1938, Rajaji said:

Ninety percent of our people are concerned here. It is found that nearly 80 percent are in debt. The Bill proposes to make them pay the principal only. They may then begin life again. This new feeling that we propose to give to him is the wealth of the country.

See *Madras Legislative Assembly Debates*, Vol. IV, 20 December 1937, 80–85.
[182] Ibid.

intended to provide relief to the tenant by reducing the remunerations of the zamindars.

The nature of the Madras Estates Land Act Committee Report though moderate in nature was significant, as it produced an 18-volume report and the draft of a bill to safeguard the rights of peasants and tenants. It was restricted to the zamindari areas. It suggested that the ryots were the owners of the land. Permanent Settlement implemented in 1802 had not transferred property rights to the zamindars. The rent paid by tenant to zamindar should accordingly be restored to the rates which prevailed in 1802. The report still left the zamindars as a substantially powerful class but it did create an opportunity for a much more radical assessment of the exploitative system of the land tenure.[183]

The major proposals of the Prakasam Report were accepted by Rajaji because

> I do think that the two cardinal principles which the committee has laid down viz., that the ownership of the land is in the pattadar and that the usurpation by the zamindar of the State's right to enhance the rent should be put an end to because it had not been transferred to the zamindar—these two cardinal principles must be accepted by the House. There is no doubt whatever that the original sanad was wrong. There is no doubt whatsoever that the position must be put an end to.[184]

Rajaji also suggested that the zamindars should surrender their estates to the state without compensation as they had changed their manner of life. He questioned, 'But is the zamindar entitled to the price he asks? Is he entitled to any price, seeing that he held only an office?'[185]

Rajendra Prasad too supported swift passage of ameliorative legislations. No sooner had Congress Ministry's tenure begun, Rajendra Prasad made it clear that though landlords had not cooperated with the Kisan Enquiry Committee, he was still willing to seek their cooperation again. To Honorary Secretary Shah Mohammed Masood, Central Zamindar's Association, Patna, Prasad wrote: 'If the Congress proposals are unsatisfactory the zamindars should be prepared to propose a better solution and I am sure the government will not fail to give it their utmost consideration.'[186]

---

[183] Copley, *The Political Career of C. Rajagopalchari*, 125.

[184] Rajaji's Speech in the Assembly on 26 January 1939. See *Madras Legislative Debates*, Vol. IX, 707.

[185] Ibid., p. 701.

[186] Prasad to Shah Mohammed Massod, dated 12 October 1937. See R.P. Papers, Ms. XI/37 Collection 1, NAI, Delhi.

This did not mean that the Congress 'Right' were attending to the interest of the zamindars only, as Rajendra Prasad noted, that if the zamindars did not find Congress programme acceptable then the concessions made to them would be revoked and legislation would proceed irrespective of negotiations.[187] Such action of Prasad to involve zamindars in negotiations met with criticism not only from Kisan Sabha members but also from Congressmen.[188] But he was willing to take such risks as he was seized with the urgency of pushing the legislation through as swiftly as possible. He wrote to S.K. Sinha:

I do not know when the next constitutional crisis will arise. It may come as suddenly and unexpectedly as the last one. I am therefore anxious that the Ministry should get through as many legislative and administrative measures as possible within the shortest possible time so that when the next crisis comes the country may have before it a record of good work done by the Congress Ministry. I can visualize a conflict between the Ministry and the British Government in connection with the introduction of the Federal Constitution. It is possible that an attempt will be made to introduce it sometime towards the end of the current year and when that comes I do not know what form the conflict may take. It may be a constitutional deadlock or direct action In either case normal work of reform and reconstruction will have to be given; so whatever the ministry can do between now and September next must be done and I feel that unless you are all very expeditious in planning and execution the reforms which you may want to introduce, you will have failed in your attempt and the Congress will stand discredited at the time of conflict, when it will need all the support of the people at large.[189]

Thus in ensuring this goal, agreement with zamindars was essential; otherwise, it could have been interminably delayed by landlords' opposition in the Council. Rajendra Prasad wanted people to feel that 'they have got something out of this understanding'; therefore, he argued with the

---

[187] Prasad to S.K. Sinha, dated 5 December 1937. See Choudhary, *Dr. Rajendra Prasad*, Vol. IV, 137.
[188] See R.P. Papers, Ms. 1-a/38, Collection 1, NAI, Delhi.
[189] Rajendra Prasad to S.K. Sinha dated 4 March 1938. See R.P. Papers, NMML.

Maharaja of Darbhanga to influence prominent zamindars to issue a statement to the following effect:[190]

1. all evictions and illegal exaction should cease,
2. tenants should not be compelled to sell any articles at less than the market price,
3. no payment should be accepted without grant of a receipt in the prescribed form,
4. no forced or underpaid labour should be allowed.[191]

Prasad further emphasized that any complaints against *amlas* or landlords' agents would be looked into by the zamindars concerned and action would be taken wherever found valid. In return, the ministry would issue a statement urging that rents be paid,[192] and if within six months rent was not realized, legislative and other forms of action would be taken. Since the agreement had the sanction of the Provincial Congress Committee, all subordinate District Congress Committees would support it or face disciplinary action and it would be up to the Congress to ensure that an atmosphere of peace was maintained and rents paid.[193]

However, Kisan Sabha was creating difficulties in rent collection.[194] Prasad complained to Patel that:

> My feeling is that the Province is in a most unfortunate situation. Everything that we have been trying to do some how or the other miscarries. The first big thing which the Ministry and I on the behalf

[190] Rajendra Prasad to Maharaja of Darbhanga, 20 April 1938, R.P. Papers, Ms. 1-a/38 Collection 1, NAI, Delhi.

[191] Ibid.

[192] Ibid., dated 25 June 1938.

[193] Ibid.

[194] Kisan Sabha attacked ministry's attempt to give concession to zamindars. Sahajanand Saraswati said,

> [i]t is not the mere absence of the legal provisions for helping the Kisans which has caused their miseries, degradation and ruin in the end. In fact a lot of such provisions are already there to save them to a considerable extent from the clutches of, and the troubles from, the zamindars and yet the lot of the kisans has ever remained unaltered because there has been no vigilant and prompt machinery to enforce them strictly with its eyes towards the maximum benefits accruing thereby to the kisans.

See Sahajanad Saraswati, *Congress Zamindar Agreement in Bihar* in File No. 800(53), Home Special Department, MSA, Bombay.

of the Provincial Congress Committee attempted was the question of tenancy legislation. I thought and I still claim that I had secured concessions and relief which no other province has so far succeeded in getting for the tenants. I got this with the consent of the land-lords and the necessary legislation was passed quickly within a year of the Congress Ministry taking office. More than 200 officers are at present engaged in giving effect to the provisions of the new law. Out of some 15 lakhs of cases which have been filed for relief, about two lakhs have already been disposed off. When the whole thing is completed it will give a permanent reduction in the income of the Zamindars to the extent of something like two crores annually and the corresponding saving to the tenants from what they have been paying up to now. In one of the new laws passed the tenants have been given the right to get back all land sold by landlords in execu-tion of decrees for arrears of rent since 1929 on payment of only half of the amount for which the land was put up for sale. That is to say on payment of 50% of the amount decreed for the arrears and the costs and even this 50% is not to be paid in one instalment, but in five yearly instalments, the first instalment being paid before the land is restored.

Till last year a landlord was entitled to put up the entire holding of a tenant for sale in execution of his rent decree, however small the amount decreed and however big the holding. Now only that portion can be sold which is sufficient to cover the decreed amount and even that portion cannot be which means that landlord has to purchase it for the price fixed by a court if no purchaser is available. Unfortunately, however from the very beginning the attitude that was adopted by Kisan Sabha workers was that nothing had been done for the benefit of the tenants, that the ministry had not fulfilled the promise made in the election manifesto and that it was in league with the landlords. The result has been that instead of satisfaction and relief given, an atmosphere of discontent is being created every-day. There is a general non-payment of rents and landlords complain that in spite of their having agreed to legislation which was very detrimental to their interests, they are not getting even the rents to which they are entitled.[195]

---

[195] Prasad to Patel, dated 22 July 1939, R.P. Papers, NMML.

The Bihar Assembly passed the Tenancy Amendment Bill with slight alteration on 3 August 1938. Both Houses passed the Restoration of Bakasht Lands Bill early in August 1938. In his speech on 27 October 1938, Prasad claimed that the Bill fulfilled the Congress Election Manifesto of 1937. The main features of the Bill were: (a) rents should be readjusted and reduced; (b) arrears of rent of previous years should be abolished; (c) arrears of rent should be recovered like civil debts and not by ejection; (d) debts should be liquidated or reduced; (e) agricultural income should be taxed; (f) tenants should be given fixed tenure with heritable rights; (g) a living wage should be assured to agricultural labourers.[196] This arrangement provided by the Bihar legislation cancelled all enhancements in rent made since 1911, and consequent reduction was to be about 25 per cent or interest at 12½ per cent were realizable on arrears of rent; damages were abolished and rate of interest was reduced by half. The system of fixing rent by appraisement of the standing crop was abolished, and rent in kind was made commutable into cash rent. Land which had been sold (*bakasht*) in execution of decrees for arrears between 1929 and 1937 was to be restored to the original tenants, if they paid half the amount for which the land was put up for sale. Powers of the landlords in realizing his dues were considerably reduced. He could no longer arrest or imprison tenant for default, nor could he sell his moveable property without his consent. The entire holding of the tenant could not be sold in execution of a decree, unless he was declared by a competent court to be a habitual defaulter. In addition, a Money Lenders Act was also passed which prevented tenants' entire holding being sold in execution of money-lenders' decree and fixed a minimum rate of interest at 9 per cent for secured and 12 per cent for unsecured debts.[197]

Also zamindars' income was made liable to taxation. Security of tenure of occupancy was also provided; any tenant who had cultivated land for 12 years was considered a settled tenant with an occupancy right which was heritable, transferable, without payment of fee to the landlord. Under the new law, an occupancy tenant could not be ejected from his holding for non-payment of rent or for any other reason except that he had rendered his land unfit for cultivation.[198]

---

[196] See Quarterly Survey of Political Constitutional Position in British India dated 27 October 1938, Survey No. 5, 1 August to 31 October 1938, Microfilm, NMML.

[197] Ibid.

[198] Ibid.

Right from the outset Patel had been saying:

We know that we are not going to achieve much by going in the Councils and Assembly. We want to send our men there with a view to remove the obstacles that are coming in our way. We don't want to give a false promise and hopes to the peasants that after entering the Councils we will be able to reduce their taxes. By all means we will do everything to make the masses happy. Above all this, there are parties organised within the Congress who form the greatest stumbling blocks in the Ministries' work. They criticize the Ministries day in and day out and place enormous obstacles in their way of doing good to the masses. A sympathetic and friendly criticism is welcome. But hostile ones are likely to make the ministries capable of doing no good. Ultimately, the responsibility is of the electorates and they are the final judges. The moment you feel the ministries are acting against your interest and are no more useful recall them from office.[199]

The other important move was made in Orissa. In 1938, a bill was passed which reduced all rents in the zamindari areas of the province to the rates of land revenue payable for similar lands in the nearest ryotwari areas plus two annas in the rupee as compensation to the zamindars. However, till the lifetime of the Congress ministry the bill did not blossom into an act, it was reserved by the Governor for consideration by the governor-general under Section 299 of the Act of 1935, which dealt with rights in land and assent was ultimately withheld.[200]

Apart from these, the Peasants Enquiry Committee of the Maharashtra Pradesh Congress Committee[201] recommended that:

---

[199] Patel's Speech at Surat, 6 January 1936. See File No. 800(98) Home Special Department, MSA, Bombay.

[200] Coupland, *The Constitutional Problem in India*, 11–17.

[201] Extract from the Bombay Presidency Weekly Letter No. 44 dated 6 November 1937 reports:

The peasantry problem continues to receive attention from Congress workers. A peasant Conference at Prantej in Ahmedabad was held on 20 October 1937, similar conferences were held at Kandan in East Khandesh District on 22 October, at Manmed in Nasik on 22 October, at Bhokar in East Khandesh District under Congress MLAs. At these meetings resolutions in favour of a reduction of land assessment, a moratorium for debts, establishment of Panchayats in village with a population of over 500 were passed.

See File No. 922(2), Home Special Department, MSA, Bombay.

Primitive methods of cultivation, paucity of manure, chaotic mar-keting of raw produce, absence of credit facilities, sub-division and fragmentations of holdings etc. are beyond dispute at the root of the poverty of peasantry. But the three biggest drains of cultivators' income are interest charges, rent and revenue. The cumulative effect of all this has been to make cultivation of land a positively uneco-nomic proposition. Ownership of land is being concentrated in the hands of non-agricultural classes and the upper strata of peasantry. 72% of land is owned by 29% of land owners. This has given rise to the problems of tenancy. Rents need to be scaled down in view of fall in income. Occupancy rights should be conferred on tenants who have cultivated the land continuously for twelve years. The system of Khoti should be completely abolished within a period of twenty years. Historically there is no element of rent in our land tax. The assessment is heavy. Manner and method of collection is rigid and inelastic. Complete overhauling of the land tax is needed to provide for (a) lower exemption limit (Rs. 250 net income), (b) principal of graduated rise in tax to large land holders, (c) assessment by an advisory committee like the Standing Finance Committee, (d) non-official district Commission to assist in anna valuation.[202]

However, Bombay Ministry gave exemption from grazing fees. In vari-ous political conferences at Dindori, Wani, Sholapur and Pandharpur, the general demands and resolutions made were regarding reduction of land assessment.[203]

Thus, no attempt was made to upset the existing land tenure system. The basis of the Permanent Settlement was not questioned in Bihar nor was there any interference with proprietary rights outside the Permanent Settlement areas.[204] But within the limits of the existing system, the agrar-ian policy of the Congress made a considerable advancement. In the first place it dealt vigorously with tenancy rights and rents, a question which had long been acute in almost all provinces and had created there an alarm-ing amount of agrarian unrest.[205]

[202] See File No. 800(53) P III, Home Special Department, MSA, Bombay.

[203] See File No. 922(1), Home Special Department, MSA, Bombay. Also see *Times of India*, 16 August 1937.

[204] Coupland, *The Constitutional Problem in India*, 11–17.

[205] Extract from the Weekly Confidential Report of the District Magistrate, Karia, dated 16 September 1937 in File No. 922 (1), Home Special Department, MSA, Bombay.

In the United Province, the tenancy reforms' main objective was to provide for further security of tenure, for the fixation of rents by government agency and for the abolition of a number of vexatious restrictions on tenants. The more important measures were as follows: firstly, the tenant rights differed in Agra from those of Oudh. Therefore, a good deal more than half of the tenants' land in Agra was held with a hereditary occupancy right acquired by 12 years of possession only; while in Oudh only a small area was thus protected and most tenants could count only on a statutory tenure of seven years. The United Province Act of 1921 had given these statutory tenants in Oudh a life tenure with a remainder to the heirs for five years. By the Act III of 1926, similar rights were bestowed on the non-occupancy tenants in Agra and the further growth of occupancy rights was stopped. The new Act of 1936 pursued this method of safeguarding the position of the tenants to its logical conclusion. It gave all statutory tenants in Oudh as well as in Agra full hereditary rights in their holdings.[206] The second reformative measure was as follows: formerly, landlords could prevent the growth of occupancy or statutory rights by cultivating land for 12 years after which it was classed as *sir* and treated as land in which tenants could acquire no rights whatever. This process had been stopped in 1901 but partly renewed in 1921. The new Act cancelled the renewals except in the case of the smaller landlords who needed land for their own cultivation. Thirdly, by the Acts of 1921 and 1926 landlords could acquire tenants' land for many purposes including large farms subject to order of a court. The provision was being used to prevent the acquisition of hereditary right or to oppress tenants and was now limited to the acquisition of more than five acres for a house, garden or grove and the scale of compensation was increased. Thus, the new Act also gave the tenant the right to construct on his holding a residential house or any other building serving an agricultural purpose without the permission of the landlord. He was also given an unrestricted right to plant trees on his holding. The rents of hereditary tenants were to be determined periodically by special officers and rent having once been fixed, the tenant was entitled to hold at the same rate for 10 years. In fixing rents, it was to be ensured that the rent did not exceed one-fifth of the value of the produce and the cost of production was to be taken into consideration. The new Act further gave the right both to the landlords and tenants of Oudh and Agra to claim that rents paid in kind should be commuted into cash. A tenant was no longer

---

[206] G. Srivastava, *When Congress Ruled: A Close Range Survey of the Congress Administration During the Twenty Eight Months (1937–1939) in the United Province*, Lucknow, 1940, 22–70.

to be liable to arrest or imprisonment for failure to pay his rent. If execution of a decree of ejectment for arrears was ordered, it could extend only to an area the rent of which did not exceed 1/6th of the arrears decreed. It also provided that all receipts for rent must be on a printed form sold by government, and the landlord was liable to fine or even imprisonment for habitual neglect in giving receipts. The new Act also made the tenure of grove holders heritable.[207]

The relief of peasant indebtness was linked with tenancy reform in the election manifesto, and in Bihar, Bombay, the Central Provinces, Madras, the North-West Frontier Provinces and Orissa, a series of Debtors Relief Acts were passed which provided in a more or less uniform manner for the registration of moneylenders and the regulation of their business, for the cancellation or reduction of interest on debts incurred before a certain date, and for the limitation of future charges to fix rates of simple interest ranging from 6.25 per cent in Madras and North-East Frontier Province to 9 per cent in Bihar. Thus, it can be certainly said that the Congress Government dominated by the so-called 'Right-wingers' did a great deal to improve and secure the interest of millions of agricultural and indebted peasants.

The Congress Ministries especially in Bombay returned the lands and other immovable properties forfeited and sold in consequence of the Civil Disobedience Movement back to the *satyagrahi*s by repurchasing them at the cost of the government and restoring them to the original holders or their heirs free of occupancy price.[208]

Throughout during the ministerial tenure, moderation was the hallmark of the policies pursued by the 'Right' leaders, whether it was towards agriculture or labour. To the *talukdar*s, Patel said, 'The Congress is not an enemy of talukdars but the Congress will not tolerate the deprivation of the rights of farmers in order that talukdar may live comfortably'.[209] And to the peasants, he said that they could secure relief only if they had a powerful organization. He pointed out the futility of high sounding socialist programme when they were unable to secure simple relief. So, he advised peasants who had faith in government to go to government officers and place their grievances before them. Because the only other remedy was to resist unjust demands for unlawful dues but he would not advise them to

---

[207] Ibid.

[208] Sitaramayya, *History of Indian National Congress 1935–1947*, 66.

[209] Patels's address to talukdars of United Province, dated 1 December 1937. Patel Papers, Lot 1-39, SPNM, Ahmedabad.

take that course when they were ill-organized and the Congress had suspended the Civil Disobedience Movement.[210]

To combat the labour problem, various labour enquiry committees such as Cawnpore Labour Enquiry Committee or Bihar Labour Enquiry Committee were constituted which drafted a comprehensive programme of reform. In its resolution of 1937, the All India Congress Committee laid down such reforms like:

1. Introduction of legislation facilitating the collection of statistics
2. Extension of Factories Act to unregulated establishments
3. Stricter enforcement of the Factories Act in the case of seasonal factories
4. Introduction of legislation providing for maternity leave for a period of not less than eight weeks in provinces where it does not exist
5. Inquiry into the question of adequacy of wages in organized industries
6. Labour exchanges
7. Leave with pay during sickness
8. Minimum wage fixing machinery
9. Machinery for the settlement of disputes
10. Recognition by the State and employers of trade unions which accept the policy of using peaceful and legitimate means
11. Housing for labour
12. Scaling down of debts
13. Holiday with pay
14. Employment insurance
15. Conditions for state aid to industries in regard to treatment of labour.[211]

As with the agrarian question similarly with the labour issue, the Congress did not want to launch a capital–labour conflict. From the beginning, the Congress 'Right' leaders had made it clear that they were accepting office not to bring about socialist revolution but to carry out some reform measures which would infuse the masses with revolutionary fervour. The masses, it was seen, were tired of struggle and their revolutionary fervour had started sagging; measures were needed to motivate them

---

[210] Patel's address to Jetalpur Peasants Conference. See *Bombay Chronicle*, dated 1 February 1936.

[211] Sitaramayya, *History of Indian National Congress 1935–1947*, 60–66.

with extra zeal and enthusiasm to start the movement afresh.[212] Speaking at Ahmedabad on 3 January 1935, Patel said:

> We have not given up the fight for freedom. We have merely changed the mode of fight. It is no use now going to jail or conducting no-tax campaign. We have to fight our own weakness without coming into conflict with Government so that we may acquire the strength to fight when it is resumed.[213]

He further said, 'The new Constitution is a stone in the way determined to throw it aside. We do not want to make false promises because we believe the reforms are a mere eyewash.'[214]

Therefore, the Congress 'Right' wanted to stem the overzealous and ambitious socialists and the Left who perceived Ministerial tenure as licence for launching anti-feudal and anti-capitalist movements. Patel cautioned the socialists to avoid a split in the Congress ranks; he accused them of putting the cart before the horse by raising issues which could be settled after the goal was reached. 'Once they finish the fight there would be time enough to consider what changes were necessary.'[215]

However, the Ministry period saw unleashing of labour militancy especially in Bombay and UP Presidencies. It was seen by the Congress Ministry simply as a law and order problem as, according to them, instead of resorting to strike, labour–capital conflict could be resolved by arbitration,[216] thus not digressing from the non-violent strategy.

On the outbreak of strike in Ahmedabad Mills, Patel reported that:

> I have closely gone into the circumstances connected with the sudden stoppage in the individual mills were [sic] not spontaneous in

[212] See Survey Report of AICC 1936–1939, Patel Papers, File No. 13, Lot 1-39, SPNM, Ahmedabad.

[213] Patel's Speech at Ahmedabad, dated 3 January 1935, ibid.

[214] Ibid.

[215] *Times of India*, 16 July 1934, 10.

[216] Patel Papers, File No. 13, Lot 1-39-1to 3, SPNM, Ahmedabad. Speaking at Ahmedabad in 1939 Patel suggested to the mill-owners that 'I hope and trust that the mill-owners of Ahmedabad will not adopt the suicidal course of evading the principle of arbitration which has been accepted for the last fifteen years and which has brought peace and prosperity to the city and by which they have been able to amass considerable wealth. I do not believe that the combined wisdom of mill-owners of Ahmedabad will not be able to overcome the apparent differences. If they will abide by the principle of arbitration all difficulties are bound to be solved amicably.' Ibid.

the sense of having their origin in any immediate grievances. It is true that improper cuts were made in several mills, but that happened months ago. A number of mills where strikes have occurred, have not made cuts at all. It is clear that the strike was engineered for purpose not related to the immediate grievances of the workers. It was in any case totally wrong to try to force members of the Labour Association and other unwilling workers to join the strike in an attempt to make it a general stoppage.

The Labour Association has a unique reputation and a position of outstanding importance in this country. It is well known as the best organised union in the country with a large and regular membership. This membership is pledged to the principle of Arbitration and it is not open to join a strike in contravention of the procedure of Arbitration.

It is well known to those who are responsible for instigating the strike that it was not possible to bring about the general stoppage of the industry without perpetrating violence on thousands of workers who are members of the Association. The fact that the Red Flag Union had neither membership nor any organization may also be taken as a sure indication that it could not promote its object of extending the strike with recourse to methods of coercion. There is overwhelming evidence of intimidation and coercion of workers to compel them to stay away from work.

While the present trouble has ended, the danger to the future peace of the city has by no means disappeared and attention may now be turned to the avoidance of similar developments again. To this end the public, the Mill Owners Association and the Labour Association will do well to combine and evolve measures for the effective maintenance of non-violence and elimination of such future risks. It is necessary to point out that as long as a section of mill owners and a section of the working class are outside the control of the two Associations and as long as the public of the city does not become alive to the gravity of the position that is created and the seriousness of the risks that lie ahead, one cannot feel assured that a worse situation will not recur in a worse form.

I am glad to be able to say that both the Associations have decided to strengthen their respective organizations by extending their membership to the entire industry and taking steps to achieve that object. The principle and machinery of Arbitration which have been accepted and tried by Employers and Workers in the city, under the guidance of Mahatama Gandhi during the last two decades, are weakened by delays and breaches. The best augury of future peace of the industry is that both Associations after giving serious considerations to the causes of the recent trouble have agreed to revise the Arbitration procedure and put it on a firm basis so as to obviate the defects which were steadily undermining the value and efficiency of the system.

To expedite the settlement of day to day grievances of the workers the Associations have taken a very useful step of supplementing the Arbitration machinery by the appointment of a sub-arbitrator for summary disposal of minor complaints. They have also agreed to evolve a sanction for proper observance and execution of the agreements arrived at by the two Associations and the decisions of the Arbitration Board and Sub-Arbitration.

The strike will have served a very useful purpose if it has awakened the public of Ahmedabad and the working class to the dangers, to the peace and progress of the city, which are inherent in the advice and activities of those who have no faith in non-violence and receive inspiration and direction from outside. Misled by them the workers have already lost lakhs of rupees in the strike.

My advice to them is that while on the one hand they should achieve complete solidarity to obtain their legitimate rights, they should on the other hand spurn the advice of those whose methods and activities cannot but injure deeply the interests of the working class as well as of the industry.[217]

Moreover, the 'Right' leadership of the Congress was astute enough to comprehend the weakness inherent in the radicalism of the Leftists. Even some of the Left ideologues had also realized the futility of proposing a radical programme which the masses could not comprehend. Achyut Patwardhan speaking at the meeting of Labour Sub-Committee convened by Bombay Provincial Congress on 6 December 1931 at Ahmedabad stated that the leaders of the workers were members of the Congress before the Merrut Conspiracy Case and that the object of the meeting was to show that there was no difference between the Congress and the Red Flag. Later in 1939, he expressed the opinion that the Congress and the Red Flag should work jointly for the masses to relieve them of their distress. He refuted the statement that the Congress Ministry was not doing anything for the masses and asserted that the ministries were doing everything that

---

[217] Ibid.

was possible in the circumstances.[218] Moreover, Patel did not want ministries to get embroiled into labour–capital conflict. To Prasad he wrote, dated 20 June 1939:

> The question assuming that the labourer's cause is the just and that there is a strong combination of powerful interests, how is the Working Committee to help them except by expressing sympathy in general terms and lending moral support and by condemning the action of the company and its supporters! If we were to take any further responsibility financial or otherwise, we will ultimately be lending ourselves into great difficulties, because this precedent, if created would be quoted against us by all the labour organizations in the numerous strikes that may take place hereafter.[219]

However, to curb the labour unrest, premiers of provinces responded differently. Some were so firm like Munshi and Rajaji that their actions were criticized by Congress leaders,[220] and some were hesitant like Pant, whose irresolution was not liked by the British.[221]

To control rise in labour unrest, especially in Ahmedabad Mills, Bombay Ministry was resorting to Criminal Law Amendment Act, which was condemned by many Congress leaders in the past. Munshi defended himself and his ministry stating that the Congress Government was determined to maintain law and order. He vigorously defended the steps taken towards that end including the application of Section 144. According to Munshi,

> It was done entirely in the interest of preserving peace and government hope to do so in spite of the political vandalism masquerading as trade unionism, with the object of placing Government in a false position—we do not propose to rush where angles fear to tread.[222]

[218] Achyut Patwardhan's Speech at Bombay in 1939. See File No. 922(2), 1937, Home Special Department, MSA, Bombay.

[219] Patel to Prasad, dated 20 June 1939, R.P. Papers, NMML.

[220] See File No. 934/137, Home Special Department, MSA, Bombay.

[221] The Governor Haig acknowledged that Pant reacted differently as compared to his other colleagues. See Haig to Linlithgow, 10 January 1938, Linlithgow MSS, Eur. F.125/1000, NMML.

[222] See *Bombay Weekly*, 29 Janaury 1939, in File No. 922(2) Home Special Department, MSA, Bombay.

On the other hand, Rajagopalachari was resorting to strict administrative action against those whom he viewed as seditionists because in his view now that the Congress was in office, no agitation should be allowed which demanded doing away with the government. Government officers, who were now cooperating with the ministry, should not be criticized. Certain Congress programmes should now be postponed.[223]

To curb Left-wing tendencies, Rajagopalachari Government employed CID surveillance and confiscated the 'seditious' literature, so much so that Patel rebuked Rajaji for employing CID: 'You seem to have superfluous staff in this Department. Why don't you employ them in the prohibition, they would be usefully employed.'[224]

However, the Left wing consistently made attempts to attack the 'conservatism' inherent in the Ministry, during its tenure. *Yugantar*, the Leftist paper, reported in its issue of 6 August 1937 that:

The Bombay government has retained all restrictions imposed on Communists and their institutions and have issued a communiqué which does credit only to a dictator. It is clear that the Bombay Government have girded up their loins to kill socialism. We however want to suggest that it is the capitalists, Sawakars and zamindars that spread class-hatred and not the socialists. The Congress should therefore try to dig out the very root of class hatred that is capitalism.[225]

Indulal Yajnik complained that the new Bombay Ministry 'is undoubtedly the weakest in the entire six Congress provinces. He complained as to why Press Amnesty was given to two Marathi Papers only?

Is it by accident or by design that the 'Advocate of India', Press—which prints two Gujarati dailies and one weekly, has been excluded from the scope of the order? Let them not throw out a few crumbs at some favourite papers but pass forthwith comprehensive orders withdrawing all repressive decrees against all newspapers and printing press under the Press Act.[226]

---

[223] *Hindu*, 5 September 1937.
[224] Patel to Rajaji, dated 21 December 1938, Rajaji Papers, NMML.
[225] *Yugantar*, 6 August 1937, File No. 934/1937, Home Special Department, MSA, Bombay.
[226] *Bombay Sentinel*, 23 July 1934.

The government's explanation on the question of removing ban on certain prescribed books and publications was:

As the Government proposes to cancel where possible orders in respect of books hitherto banned ... the government desires to make it clear that while giving the greatest freedom of thought and expression they will not be prepared to lift the ban on books which directly or indirectly incite communal bitterness or disseminate ideas involving organized or unorganized violence.[227]

The 'Right' believed in civil liberty as the cornerstone of democracy. However, they insisted on civil liberty bounden by a sense of responsibility.

Civil Liberty must have the full scope in Congress regime.... No responsible government can allow license or unlimited liberty to the people. If a criminal liberty of few persons should be restrained in exercise of the civil liberty of lakhs of law-abiding citizens and if the Congress ministries fail to impose restrictions on those few then they will be failing on duty.[228]

K.M. Munshi who was under severe attack from Left wingers and also from some of the Congress leaders like Nehru for his 'repressive' measures against the Leftists during the Ministry period, stated that:

Congress stands for the liberty of the individual because it has an unshaken faith in democracy and non-violence.... Liberty for us is not a matter of material benefit. It is not a matter to be weighed in the scales of a materialistic interpretation of history.... Civil liberty is really the foundation of democratic government. Democracy implies a faith which society can evolve gradually and by mutual discussion and persuasion rather than by breaking each other's heads. But Civil Liberty presupposes that there must be an atmosphere of non-violence in which one can discuss each other's opinion freely without physical violence or the coercion of the individual or mass violence. That is a fundamental limitation of the principle of civil liberty.

---

[227] See File No. 194, Home Special Department, MSA, Bombay.
[228] Patel on Civil Liberty, *Bombay Chronicle*, 31 December 1934.

One cannot have a civil liberty in any atmosphere surcharged with violence and excitement such as a breach of the peace.[229]

However, in the Congress provinces, there was a release of large numbers of political prisoners and the removal of the ban on political organizations. The refund of securities from presses was also a common feature. The bans on films and literature were lifted in all suitable cases. Restrictive orders on labour leaders were cancelled. Congress ministries also took considerable steps towards implementing prohibition on a substantial scale.[230]

The development of the depressed classes had been one of the chief items of the Congress programme since 1920 and once the Congress formed ministries it was pursued more vigorously. Gandhi was opposed to the depressed classes' separate representation in the legislature. Since he regarded them as part of the Hindu community, he had pinned his hopes for their advancement not on division and antagonism between them and caste Hindus, but on awakening in the latter a sense of social justice and duty. With this in mind, he had drafted a new scheme the 'Poona Pact', whereby the principle of separate electorates would only be applied in a primary stage of the elections. The depressed class voters would just elect a panel of candidates and from this the members of the legislature would be elected by the general electorate. Thus, in Bihar, 14 out of the 15 and in Madras 26 out of 30 Harijan representatives elected were Congressmen. In Bombay, Dr Ambedkar's 13 out of 15 representatives elected belonged to Ambedkar's party. It should also be noted that the Madras and Bihar ministries each included a 'scheduled caste' member.[231]

---

[229] File No. 934/137, Home Special Department, MSA, Bombay.

[230] Sitaramayya, *History of Indian National Congress 1935–1947*. Congress leaders like Patel launched campaign to make their programme for prohibition successful. Patel used prohibition programme as measure to spread social awakening among the depressed classes, among whom drinking was a way of life. *Time of India*, 23 November 1937, reports:

> Drinking, slavery of a kind, which is believed to prevail among the Dubla community was condemned by Mr. Vallabhbhai Patel at a villagers' meeting in Varad (Bardoli Taluka) organized to do propaganda for prohibition. 'The Congress, he said, would never keep or treat anybody as slave under its Raj'. He assured the gathering that the present Congress Government were sure to introduce legislation for rooting out the evil, but advised the Dublas to make independent attempts before Government moved in the matter. Mr. Patel hoped that the entire Taluka of Bardoli would be free from the drink evil, before the Haripura Session of the Congress.

[231] See File No. 934/137 Home Special Department, MSA, Bombay. Also see Coupland, *The Constitutional Problem in India*, 143–149.

The major hurdle in improving the condition of the Harijans was the stigma of untouchability and this was taken up as one of the primary issues for improving the social status of Harijans. The Madras ministry passed several laws to remove the ban on Harijans from entering a temple: for example, the Malabar Temple Entry Act 1938, the Removal of Civil Disabilities Act and the Madras Entry Identity Ordinance and Madras Temple Authorization and Indemnity Act.[232]

Steps were also taken to provide free education to the depressed classes. In Bombay, almost all the separate schools for Harijans were converted into ordinary schools and the number of Harijans admitted to ordinary schools steadily increased. This process had been hastened in some provinces by drastic government measures.[233] In Bihar, Orissa and Madras, schools were given official recognition on the condition that they would take in Harijan pupils and provide them the same facilities enjoyed by the children of higher castes. The provincial governments had also granted special concessions like scholarships, exemptions from fees and free textbooks to the Harijan children. These methods were further maintained and in some cases expanded under the Congress regime.[234]

Reform measures were also taken up in the field of education. Attempts were made by the Congress ministries to link education with the constructive programme of Gandhi so that instead of creating a live bank of information, a new force of skilled artisans could be created to solve the problem of unemployment. 'Basic education' system was thus conceived. At Wardha, in October 1937, a National Education Conference was held which passed a resolution endorsing the proposals made by Mahatma Gandhi:

[t]hat the process of education throughout this period (of seven years schooling) should centre around some form of manual and productive work, and that all the other abilities to be developed or training to be given should as far as possible be integrally related to the central handicraft chosen with due regard to the environment of the child.[235]

---

[232] See File No. 934/137, Home Special Department, ibid. Also see Dove, *Forfeited Future* (Delhi, 1987).

[233] File No. 934/137, Home Special Department, ibid.

[234] Ibid.

[235] Coupland, *The Constitutional Problem in India*, 146. Also see Sitaramayya, *History of Indian National Congress 1935–1947*, Vol. I, 51–71.

Basic education was to be imparted through the vernacular medium, linked with manual productive work. Schools along these lines were set up in the Congress provinces with government help. Basic education boards were set up in Bihar. Basic Training Colleges were opened in Allahabad and Patna. Refresher course centres were also established to train district and municipal board teachers in the task of converting their schools into basic schools.

Eventually, such reformative measures by the Congress ministries bore political fruit and the Congress membership increased from half a million in 1936 to 3.1 million in 1937 and 4.5 million in 1938. It also provided impetus to labour and kisan organizations, whose movement during the ministry period forged ahead with new zeal and spirit. Coming into existence of Congress ministry also invoked massive anti-imperialistic and anti-feudal movements in the Indian states.[236]

Despite giving rise to such positive development, the ministries failed to curtail criticism, since during its tenure it failed to scale the heights of radicalism demanded by the Left critics. A number of allegations were lodged against the ministries. First was that though being a party which was totally committed to *poorna swaraj* and bitterly critical of 1935 Constitution, the Congress ministry was working within its framework, with powers limited by official reservations and safeguards as well as restricted by financial resources, and having to implement decisions through a civil service and police with which its relations had so long been extremely hostile.[237]

Secondly, in the provinces, squabbles for power were taking shape. Central Provinces, Orissa and Bihar were all ridden with internal conflicts and power game. On the emergence of various rival groups in provincial Congress ministries, Prasad wrote to Nehru regarding the ensuing election to the District Boards in Bihar that:

> [t]he election to the District Boards, which are going on in this province are a perfect eye opener to me. It seems everybody is anxious for a seat and as there are many more candidates than seats for them and many have to be disappointed there is open rebellion, insidious propaganda and formation of rival groups and parties in almost every district.[238]

---

[236] Sumit Sarkar, *Modern India*, 351.

[237] Ibid., 349–370.

[238] Prasad to Nehru dated 19 April 1939. R.P. Papers, NMML.

Not only Prasad but also Patel was perturbed at the growing disaffection among the influential Provincial Congress leaders for higher offices in the Ministry. To Prasad, Patel wrote:

> There is no doubt that ambition for personal position, scrambling for position of power have resulted in lowering the standard of our public life after the acceptance of office. Men holding high position in the Congress in the past have set very bad example and they have been encouraged by the Press. This has been noticed in about all provinces.[239]

Nehru too regarded the record of Congress ministries as static, if not counter-revolutionary.[240] They were alleged to have become friends of the Capitalists, defenders of rich peasants and patrons of hand spinners and weavers. Instead of accommodating the radical upsurge within the Congress, the Congress ministries were not only alienating the radicals but were also taking regressive measures towards them specifically in Bombay and Madras. Nehru issued a circular to the leaders of the Congress party in provincial assemblies directing them to release all political prisoners, interns and detenus and also to return the securities taken from newspapers and presses.[241] But K.M. Munshi, home minister of Bombay, was seen to have ignored this directive. Instead, he seemed to be keen on detaining the Communists and Left-wing leaders, so much so that he asked the higher authorities to put the CID of Bengal in touch with his CID to deal with Communists in and around Bombay. This led to Nehru's protest in the Working Committee that Congress ministries were more concerned about the effect their actions would have upon the British Government than in carrying out the programme on whose basis they accepted the offices.[242] In Madras too, Rajagopalachari was carrying out repressive measures against the Communists. He ordered the police to shadow and arrest Congress

---

[239] Patel to Prasad 9 July 1938, R.P. Papers, NMML.

[240] To Govind Vallabh Pant, Nehru wrote:

> If I may put it in technical language the Congress Ministries are tending to become counter-revolutionary. This is of course not a conscious development but when a choice has to be made the inclination is in this direction. Apart from this the general attitude is static.

See Nehru to Pant, 25 November 1937, in Nehru, *A Bunch of old letters*, 256–257.

[241] Nehru's circular to leaders of Congress Parties in Provincial Assemblies, 16 July 1937 in Gopal, *SWJN*, Vol. 8, 280.

[242] See AICC, File No. 42/1936, NMML.

Socialists. He invoked the Criminal Law Amendment Act, which the
Congress had vehemently denounced.[243]

As far as the coordination among the ministries went, the state of affairs
was such that it forced Prasad to write on 22 July 1939:

> It is true that there is not as much cohesion and cooperation amongst
> the ministries as one would wish there should be. It often happens
> that one minister does not know what is happening in the depart-
> ment of another minister even on important matters. I have been
> trying from the very beginning to impress upon them the desirability
> of frequent meetings amongst themselves at which even informally
> they could talk matters over and keep one another informed of all
> important actions taken in their respective departments. But I am
> sorry that there has not been as much success in this as I would have
> liked to have.[244]

Further, absence of central responsibility created difficulties in coor-
dinating the measures carried out in the different Congress provinces.
Uncertainties prevailed over the jurisdiction mainly related to the legislative matters. In UP tenancy, legislation did not receive the assent of the
Governor-General so long as the ministers were in power and for well over
a year after the war had broken out, while the Orissa measures were rejected
by him. The Debt Relief Act of Madras was challenged before the Federal
Court but was upheld, while a certain section of the Prohibition Act was
declared ultra vires. In Bombay, the provisions relating to foreign liquors
were abrogated by the High Court as falling outside the jurisdiction of provincial legislature. Likewise, there were difficulties raised as to whether law
relating to interest on debts and promotes as negotiable instruments which
fell in two different categories in the allocation of subjects provincial and
central could be dealt with by the Provincial legislatures in schemes of debt
relief, whether exemptions given to the loans due to banks could or could
not be granted by them because banks were a central subject.[245] However,
to see that the provincial legislatures worked unobtrusively, the Working
Committee had to step in either through its sub-committees or directly
undertake the task of coordination.[246]

[243] Gopal, *SWJN*, 230.
[244] Prasad to Patel, 22 July 1939, R.P. Papers, NMML.
[245] P. Sitaramayya, *History of Indian National Congress 1935–1947*.
[246] In July 1936, the Working Committee appointed the Congress Parliamentary
Board Executive consisting of Patel as President and Prasad and Pant as Secretaries and one

As to the impact of the social reforms undertaken by the Congress ministries, in the field of education, basic education was a success.[247] However, it never became a viable alternative to conventional schools and colleges, and the link with cottage crafts was felt by many as unrealistic. On the labour front, the Congress did take up certain reform measures to uplift the social and economic condition of labour and such measures did stimulate labour organization, the manifestation of which was seen in increased labour activities and movements. But still the bulk of trade union movement remained under the leadership of the Left and steps were taken to curb the communists' involvement with the labour through measures such as the Bombay Trades Disputes Act. With regard to agrarian reform, a great deal was achieved but the Congress ministries were attacked for not taking steps towards abolition of zamindari and for not incorporating the Kisan Sabha in the Congress.[248] Although the Socialists and the Left elements in the Congress were not pleased by the steps taken by the ministries they did not raise the issue of differences to such a pitch that it left no other alternative but to break away from the Congress. This was basically the reason why both Nehru and Bose did not pursue the issue of scrapping the Bombay Trades Disputes Act.

Undoubtedly, the dominant streak in most of the policies of the Congress ministries was moderation. The Congress 'Right' had not gone in for ministryship to bring about a structural change by unleashing anti-landlord, anti-feudal and anti-capitalist movements. The general policy of the Congress was to forge a united front on the basis of the concept of class collaboration in order to launch a powerful anti-imperialist movement. The rest could follow once the primary objective was attained.[249] S. Ramnathan, Minister of Propaganda in Rajaji's Ministry, articulated the general stance of the Congress.

In India it was not necessary to start a capital and labour conflict or a kisan and zamindar conflict because the struggle for independence

---

representative from each major province. Its function was to transform the Congress organization into an electoral organization and to revitalize it to this end. It was also constituted to maintain coordination among the ministries, to review the steps ministries were to take and to mediate and maintain harmony in case of crisis. See *Leader*, 4 July 1936 and 9 July 1936.

[247] See Nehru's article 'Where Are We?' in Gopal, SWJN, Vol. 9, 505.

[248] Sarkar, *Modern India*.

[249] See Copley, *The Constitutional Problem in India*, 161.

was all inclusive. It included and transcended class war. It had within itself the seeds of every necessary revolution and readjustment.[250]

The ministry formation was a phase of truce and consolidation. The very fact that out of this period of flux, Congress was to raise a 1942 is evidence enough to prove that it was a period of truce in the ongoing struggle for anti-imperialism. The assessment of the Congress ministries dubbed as being reactionary on the ground that they did not initiate radical measures such as abolition of zamindari misses the basic orientation of the strategy. This is one reason why the criticism of the Left elements remained feeble.

The Congress ministries were hemmed in by various constraints and the major constraint was not to follow any step which might lead to alienation of any section of the society which could jeopardize the prospect of collaboration among all classes against anti-imperialist struggle. Therefore, the objective with which the Congress went in for office acceptance was to provide some respite to the tired masses by carrying out ameliorative measures in the agrarian and administrative field. It was also meant to show up the difference between an alien government which worked by excluding the opinion of the people and a nationalist regime which was receptive to the people's demands. It is seen that the reform measures, even if limited in nature, gave the people hope and they began to regard the new Congress government as their own.[251] Even Nehru, who had doubts over the efficacy of Congress accepting office, admitted that the country was pulsating with a new life and a new vision. Politically and constitutionally, the new Act and the establishment of Congress governments in the provinces made no vital differences to the British structure of government. But the psychological change was enormous and an electric current seemed to run through the countryside. There was a sense of immense relief as of the lifting of a weight which had been oppressing the people. There was a release of long-suppressed mass energy which was evident everywhere. The fear of the police and secret service vanished for a while at least and even the poorest peasant could feel a sense of self-respect and self-reliance. For the first time, he felt that he could not be ignored; Government was no longer an unknown and intangible monster, separated from him by innumerable layers of officials, whom he could not easily approach and much less influence and who were bent on extracting as much out of him as possible.[252]

---

[250] Ibid.
[251] B.R. Tomlinson, *The Indian National Congress and the Raj*, 86.
[252] Nehru, *The Discovery of India* (Bombay, 1961), 369–370.

In his article, 'Where Are We?' published in the *National Herald* on 28 February 1939 and 1 to 6 March 1939, Nehru accepted that:

> It is true that they had done good work, their record of achievement was impressive, the ministries were working terribly hard and yet had to put up with all manner of attacks and criticisms often based on ignorance. Theirs was a thankless job.[253]

---

[253] Nehru, 'Where Are We?' in Gopal, Vol. 9, 502.

6

The Congress 'Right': The Princes and the States Peoples' Movement

Let no one run away with the idea that the Working Committee or any member of the Working Committee is anxious to placate the Princes.... Therefore what actuates us is not any overflowing love for the Princes or anything in the nature of extra unjustified regard for their interests; but it is in the interest of the people of the States and the desire to make their conditions somewhat better than they are which actuates the Working Committee in the policy which it follows and which it now places before you for your acceptance.... I ask you to have that attitude in mind in regard to this question. It is undoubtedly true that if we can have a perfectly democratic constitution in the States conditions will be infinitely superior to what they are at present. There can be no question about that. As the statement itself says we have the same desire to achieve that objective as anybody else, either in this House or outside this House. But we have to recognize facts. We have to recognize our limitations—If recognizing these, we have to act cautiously or as some might call moderately all that I can plead is that you should give us credit for the best intentions in favour of the States.

——Rajendra Prasad[1]

I was telling the people that the problem was as to how to snatch power from the ruler. From the times immemorial those kings who did not know how to rule were deposed by the people. I told the same theory. Congress has decided that it wants to keep friendly relations with the rulers, but if there is misrule in the States, Congress cannot be a silent witness to it, because British Indian people and native states people are one and indivisible.

——Sarardar Patel[2]

---

[1] Prasad reacting to the suggestions made by the socialists at Madras, 18 October 1935. See File No. 6-1934-35, in lot I-32, 1 to 5, Patel Papers, SPNM, Ahmedabad.
[2] Patel's Speech at Ahmedabad dated 21 November 1938, Chopra, *The Collected Works*, Vol. 7, 218.

The Congress 'Right' were mass leaders and they stood unequivocally for the rights of the masses as against the Princes whom the British regarded natural representatives of their respective states. But for Patel, Prasad and Rajaji, the notion of any group being the 'natural representative' was antithetical in a democracy and more so in case of the Princes.[3]

The social background to which the three leaders belonged had inherent distrust and dislike for feudal autocracy. Prasad speaking at the AICC Conference in Madras in 1935, categorically stated that no one in the Congress should be under the illusion that any member of the Working Committee was anxious to placate the Princes.[4] Sardar Patel, too, re-emphasized in 1935 that it was hardly necessary to assure the people of the states that the Congress and its members would never be guilty of sacrificing their interests in order to buy the support of the Princes.[5] The 'Right' leaders had the clarity based on experience of the ground reality that complete Independence for India could not be secured by following singularly sectoral politics; single-minded participation in Indian States' affairs could affect the central focality of the national struggle for freedom.[6]

The attempt of the Congress 'Right' was, however, to establish linkages with the States Peoples' Movement and encourage pro-democracy and anti-colonial ideology, so that when independence became a reality, unity of both parts of India could smoothly take place.[7] The leaders of the 'Right' hue came from a social background which made them experience the grassroots realities of deprivation and suffering both at public and personal levels. This increased their sensitivity to easily understand the issues involved in political mobilization and sponsorship of political causes at the level of the masses. Therefore, they were more pragmatic in their approach rather than given entirely to formal and idealistic strategies. Such experiential advantages the Leftist in the Congress like Nehru could

---

[3] Prasad to Rajaji, dated 25 November 1939 and 26 November 1939, Patel Papers, File No. IX Lot 38 (Congress Affairs between 1932-38-39), SPNM, Ahmedabad.

[4] Prasad's Speech at AICC, Madras in October 1935. See AICC, File No. G-27 NMML and Sardar Patel Correspondence, File No. Lot I-32 1 to 5, File No. 13-1935-45, Ahmedabad.

[5] Sardar's Speech at Madras 18 October 1935, ibid.

[6] Ibid.

[7] Patel in his Speech at Ahmedabad on 21 November 1938 said, 'Congress has decided that it wants to keep friendly relations with the rulers but if there is misrule in the States, Congress cannot be a silent witness to it, because British Indian people and native States' people are one and indivisible'. See *Gujarat Samachar*, 22 November 1938, Patel Papers, SPNM, Ahmedabad.

not have, and therefore, possibly they could not accurately anticipate the likely response of the people of the Princely States.[8] Nehru along with the socialists in 1935 personally favoured Congress's direct involvement in the States Peoples' Movement.[9]

The 'Right' leaders, however, differed from the Left in their approach. They were conscious of the fact of weak response of the States' people to the call for political mobilization for want of civil liberty, civic institutions and uninhibited power of the feudal autocrats of the states. Therefore, Patel forthrightly advised both the Congress and the Left in the Congress at Madras in 1935 that the Indian National Congress recognized that the people in the Indian States had an inherent right to *swaraj* no less than the people of British India. The Congress had accordingly declared itself in favour of establishment of a representative responsible government in the states and had not only appealed to the Princes to establish such governments in their states and to guarantee fundamental rights of citizenship like freedom of person, speech, association and the press to their people but had also pledged to the states' people its sympathy and support in their legitimate and peaceful struggle for the attainment of full responsible government. By that declaration and by that pledge the Congress stood all through. 'The Princes will be well advised to establish at the earliest possible moment full responsible government within their states carrying a guarantee of full rights of citizenship to their people', Patel exhorted.[10] He further reiterated his personal position and position of his colleagues and the Congress to the nation in general and Left leaders like Nehru in particular.[11] He stated:

> It should be understood however that the responsibility and the burden of carrying on that struggle within the States must necessarily fall on the States' people themselves. The Congress can exercise moral and friendly influence upon the States and this it is bound to do wherever possible. The Congress has no other power under existing circumstances although the people of India whether under the British, the Princes or any other power are geographically and historically one and indivisible. In the heat of controversy the limitation

[8] Nehru to Gandhi, 14 November 1937 in Gopal, SWJN, Vol. 8, 367–368.

[9] Ibid.

[10] Patel's Speech at Madras 18 October 1935, File No. 13, Congress Affairs 1935–1942, Lot I-32, 1 to 5-1934-35, SPNM, Ahmedabad.

[11] Ibid.

of the Congress is often forgotten. Indeed any other policy will defeat
the common purpose.[12]

The 'Right' leaders also understood the emotional attachment and sense
of loyalty the natives had for their rulers. Therefore keeping in mind the
difficulty in mobilizing the masses of the Princely States, the leaders of the
'Right' faction were extra cautious while dealing with them, as they did
not want to get embroiled with 'the local vagaries and idiosyncrasies of a
variety of States, 562 in number, a task beyond the pale of practical politics of the Congress'.[13] And they also did not want to precipitate a conflict
in the states prematurely, which would give opportunity to the British to
play their divisive role to the hilt.[14] Accepting both the aforementioned
scenario, Patel confessed in October 1935 that there were many practical
difficulties in carrying them on. Besides, there were cases in which the
states' subjects themselves did not desire their interference.[15] Therefore,
the Congressmen should realize their limitations and weakness and should
refrain from making promises which they might not be able to fulfil.[16]
He impressed upon the Congressmen and the socialist leaders like Yusuf
Meherally, Kamladevi Chattopadhya and the rest at Madras:

> When Congress gathers strength in British India its strength would
> be reflected in the Indian States also. They knew what the position
> was in 1931 during the Truce period then the Princes thought it
> better after all to make friends with the Congress. Congress worker
> could certainly exercise friendly and moral pressure for the ameliora-
> tion of the States' people. But today the Congress office was under a
> ban. Why? Was it not because the Congress organization was weak
> and not because of any change of policy? Today they would be doing
> a disservice to the Congress organization if they forced on them the

---

[12] Ibid.

[13] Sitaramayya, *History of Indian National Congress*, Vol. II, 79.

[14] Patel therefore in his Speech on 28 December 1938 at the Bombay Provincial Congress
Committee emphasized on how the primary fight of the Congress was against the colonial
power. He said the Congress was not the enemy of Princes. The Congress fight was against the
Paramount Power who he alleged were trying to use the States to consolidate their own posi-
tion. The Congress and the States' subjects wanted to protect the Princes from the Paramount
Power as much as they wanted to protect themselves. See *Times of India*, 29 December 1938,
NMML.

[15] Patel's Speech at Madras, 18 October 1935, File No. 13 in lot I-32, 1 to 5, Patel
Papers, SPNM, Ahmedabad.

[16] Ibid.

resolution when they stated plainly that they could not shoulder the responsibility.[17]

Patel well understood that an organization of such a vast magnitude like Congress which had national stature was bound to have groups of people who might differ from the official position and who did have a right to influence it.[18] But according to the 'Right'-wing leaders this was not the time to encourage discussion on small issues and sacrifice the achievements gathered by the Congress till now.[19] On 15 July 1935, Patel in an interview appealed to the Congress socialists that 'our boat is now in the mid ocean and if we do not close up our ranks we will sink.'[20] Keeping this fact in mind, therefore, the strategy of the 'Right' not to get directly embroiled in the Princely States was a sagacious move.[21] Yet Patel reprimanded the Socialists for not involving themselves in the States Peoples' Movement and instead blaming the Congress. He said at Madras in 1935 when Yusuf Meherally's resolution got defeated and Patel's succeeded that there had been persistent attempt to drive the Congress and the Congress executives to fight battles in the Indian States by certain people who would not themselves start the struggle or do the work.[22]

The 'Right' leaders were aware that the political stability of the Princes was fragile, being dependent on the paramount power, as it was obvious in the case of Rajkot, where all decisions of the Thakore Saheb were superseded by Sir Patrick Cadell, the British Resident.[23] The Right-wing leaders did not want an irreversible confrontationist relationship with the Princes in order to check them from being strong allies of the British. The 'Right' also did not want to open front on all quarters at the same time. Therefore, they demanded introduction of reforms in Princely States so that pressure might be maintained on the Princes and the spirit of reform kept alive among the subjects. The magnitude of pressure was designed to be just right so as not to alienate the Princes and drive them totally into the British

---

[17] Ibid.

[18] Ibid.

[19] Ibid.

[20] Ibid.

[21] Ibid.

[22] Ibid. Speaking at Rajkot on 28 December 1938, Patel asserted that the Thakore Saheb of Rajkot himself had no power to appoint even a minister. It was the agents of the Paramount Power who acting in the name of the Thakore Saheb tried to beat down the people and sought to teach them their duty to their Rajas. See *Times of India*, 29 December 1938.

[23] Patel's Speech at Madras 18 October 1935, File No. 13 in Lot 1-32-1 to 5, Patel Papers, SPNM, Ahmedabad.

camp. Therefore, along with the demand for reforms, Patel insisted on keeping the doors open for negotiation. He stated at Madras in 1935 that all Princes were Indians, some of them might be good, others bad, some others indifferent and some of them might be devils.[24] He accepted the fact that Princes were not the representatives of their people but 'After all so long we call in terms of agreements and progress by negotiations we cannot refuse to negotiate with any party in this country at variance with our views and forego the chance however slight of winning it over to our side.'[25]

Clarifying the position of the senior leaders on the strategy adopted by the Congress as its official policy vis-à-vis the States Peoples' Movement, Patel observed that:

> Both Gandhiji and myself thought that we should not carry agitations in the States too far because the Princes too were not free, and even if they were willing it was not in their power to fully concede to our demands depending as they were on the sweet will of the residents who in fact represented the will of the foreign power.[26]

The 'Right' realized that attaining substantial change in the Princely States was a dim possibility as long as the British were there. For them the Princely States were the essential pawn, the other being the League to be used as counter-pressure against the Congress. The only way left to the 'Right' leaders was to appeal to the Princes and hope that 'You must bear in mind that you will be benefited if India is benefited.'[27]

Patel tended to hold a radical view on solving the problems of the people of the Princely States. In his speech at Ahmedabad, dated 21 November 1938 he admitted that the movement had been popular enough for him not to ignore it.

> I was telling the people that the problem was as to how to snatch power from the ruler. From the times immemorial those kings who did not know how to rule were deposed by the people. I told the same theory. Congress has decided that it wants to keep friendly relations with the rulers, but if there is misrule in the States, Congress

[24] Ibid.
[25] Patel's Speech at Bangalore 25 February 1949. See Nandurkar, *Sardar Patel: In Tune with the Million-II*, 190–191.
[26] Ibid.
[27] Rajendra Prasad's Speech to the Deccan States People, May 1935. See *Fortnightly Report for the Deccan States and Kolhapur*, Home Political Proceedings, NAI, New Delhi.

cannot be a silent witness to it, because British Indian people and native states people are one and indivisible.[28]

Prasad, however, held a different view on the methodology of intervention. At the Lucknow Congress, he highlighted the difficulties in launching an anti-imperialist struggle similar to the one in British India. He said:

> Until the two Indias joined there would remain a difference in their (the States) development. The chief cause of their backwardness was that the British Government would not let them excel the British standard of administration…. We believe that if we can make British India totally democratic its influence on Indian States would be an effective step. At the moment we do not wish to add to our problems and therefore do not wish to raise false hopes in the minds of the Indian States' subjects.[29]

Yet having inherent abhorrence for the feudal decadence prevailing in the native states with the encouragement and abetment of the British, Prasad in 1935 at Madras warned that the strategic cautiousness of the senior leaders of the Congress should not be misread as love for the Princes. He said:

> Let no one run away with the idea that the Working Committee or any member of the Working Committee is anxious to placate the Princes…. Therefore what actuates us is not any overflowing love for the Princes or anything in the nature of extra unjustified regard for their interests; but it is in the interest of the people of the States and the desire to make their conditions somewhat better than they are which actuates the Working Committee in the policy which it follows and which it now places before you for your acceptance…. I ask you to have that attitude in mind in regard to this question. It is undoubtedly true that if we can have a perfectly democratic constitution in the States conditions will be infinitely superior to what they are at present. There can be no question about that. As the statement itself says we have the same desire to achieve that objective as anybody else, either in this House or outside this House. But we have to recognize facts. We have to recognize our limitations—If recognizing

---

[28] Patel's Speech at Ahmedabad dated 21 November 1938, Chopra, *The Collected Works*, Vol. 7, 218.

[29] *Bombay Chronicle*, dated 14 April 1936.

these, we have to act cautiously or as some might call moderately all
that I can plead is that you should give us credit for the best intentions in favour of the States.[30]

The strategy of the 'Right' in the case of the Princely States was to let the
gradual evolution of political mobilization grow from below. Interference
from outside was to be desisted from in order for the internal movement to
become a force to reckon with so that it was not prematurely suppressed.
It was also envisaged that this would lead to the emergence of the local
leaders better equipped to understand local aspirations and realities. The
States' people were also required to learn how to face sacrifices entailed
in the actual experience of carrying out the movement in order to make
them ready for their ultimate participation on the larger national canvass.
The Haripura resolution of 1938 adopted by the Congress contained the
fundamental principles on which the approach of the Gandhian leaders to
Princely States was based.

In the scheme of things, direct action against the Princes was not to
be resorted to. This was, however, not because of any fondness for the
Princes; it was primarily dictated by the consideration for the growth of
self-strengthening urge of the people of the Princely States at large. They
believed in gradual evolution of a political organization from below to
take roots in the States. The policy of 'non-interference' and support from
outside was adopted to allow the nascent murmur of protest in the states
to evolve independently till it became a full battle cry without raising the
suspicion of the Princes, as the Moderate Congress leaders had earlier done
during the early phase of the anti-colonial movement in British India. The
reason behind the adoption of Haripura resolution in 1938 was that the
Gandhian leaders wanted to buy time to consolidate not only their organization in British India but also to give time to the local people of the States
to study and understand how the Congress was waging struggle in British
India, the sacrifices it was making and then review their own position in
the Princely States. Patel said:

The Haripura resolution had given the correct lead to the States'
people. By throwing them on their own strength the Congress has
spurred the States' people to organize themselves, to develop political
consciousness and cultivate the virtue of self-reliance. Haripura had

---

[30] Prasad reacting to the suggestions made by the socialists at Madras, 18 October 1935.
See File No. 6-1934-35, in Lot I-32, 1 to 5, Patel Papers, SPNM, Ahmedabad.

opened the way for their onward march and judging from recent happenings in several Indian States it was clear that the Congress had acted wisely.[31]

Explaining further he said:

People of Princely States could not escape the influence of what was happening in the adjoining British territory. He was glad that people of Baroda had become conscious of their rights that was obviously largely due to the fact that they saw evidence of such consciousness in the British territory all around them. The villages of Baroda must have watched with interest the brave fight put up by their brave brethren across the border in Borsad, Matar and Ahmedabad and the historic Dandi March.[32]

The States' people also had no early experience of representative institutions either and thus they might be easily led astray by the interested parties as in the case of Rajkot where bogey of Hindu domination was raised if democracy was introduced. In Baroda, domination of Gujarati speaking over Marathi was highlighted. In Kathiawada, dominance of Vania Caste was raised. Patel at Baroda said:

We see before our eyes what is happening in various states. The Congress at Haripura asked the people of the Indian states to rely on their own strength and we see today the fruits of such advice wherever it has been acted upon. If you march with hope and faith and courage and steadiness your future is bright, the day will soon come when responsible government will be born out of your own strength.[33]

The impact of Haripura Session of the Congress in 1938 led to the popularity of *Praja Mandals* or People's Associations. Many protest movements in Mysore, Travancore, Kashmir, Hyderabad, Jaipur, Baroda, Rajkot and in many small principalities particularly in Gujarat emerged during this period. In these states, especially, in Mysore, Jaipur, Baroda and

---

[31] Patel's Speech at a public meeting at Bhadran on 28 October 1938. See *Hindustan Times*, 29 October 1938, NMML.
[32] Ibid.
[33] Ibid.

Rajkot, there were spontaneous and enthusiastic mass demonstrations.[34] Mentioning the rise of new spirit in British India and its impact on the States, Patel said:

> In British India we have started the historic experiment of responsible government and provincial autonomy—patriotic Ministers have taken the place of the autocratic administrations of olden days—a new spirit has come over the people. The new spirit cannot but be felt by the States' People. Mysore, Travancore, Kashmir, Rajkot and Dhenkanal and the like are all examples. People there are making history and demanding self-government. No good can come without Self-Government.[35]

The movements were popular enough, not to be ignored. The popularity of the Congress in the election too might have given confidence to the Congress leaders to independently participate in the States Peoples' Movement. Moreover, the repression of the masses by the autocrats, had reached such a level of cruelty that the leaders such as Patel and Prasad felt that if they did not intervene and if minimum demands were not met by the Princely States with goodwill, the States might have to give in after a fierce struggle which would cause heavy loss of prestige and finances to the states and would strain forever the good relations between the state and the people.[36]

Patel's attention was drawn specifically to the problems of the kisans of the Princely States of Baroda and Rajkot. Encouraged by the enthusiasm of the States' subjects, Patel warned, while addressing the Rajkot States People's Conference, in September 1938:

> We are not desirous of dethroning the ruler. We wish to limit his authority. That State cannot survive whose Raja wastes an enormous amount of money on dances etc while the peasants die of starvation.... If you are determined, no one can stop your progress not even if all the rulers get together.[37]

---

[34] See Patel's Speech at Bhadran, on 28 October 1938, ibid.

[35] Ibid.

[36] Patel to Dewan Saheb of Rajkot dated 7 September 1938. See File no. 1-45-2 Rajkot in Lot-I-45 1 to 5, Patel Papers, SPNM, Ahmedabad.

[37] Ibid.

While following the consistent policy of avoiding direct confrontation with the Princes, they conveyed the befitting message to the Princes that 'If there is awakening among the people, can a ruler so rule upon them?'[38] The 'Right' leaders were using both polite and harsh language, while encouraging the people of the states to organize and create a political space for the movement as the Congress was doing in British India. Patel said:

It is inherent right of the people of the state to demand such responsible government as they desire and to secure its functioning by all Constitutional means and to secure its functioning by falling on their bended knees before the ruler. But if such a cause does not materialize, they must after proper training and strength resort to direct action and once determined they must fight to the finish by all possible sacrifices.[39]

At Ahmedabad on 21 September 1938, Patel said that he had been telling the people that the problem was how to snatch power from the ruler. Drawing analogy with the Congress he said, 'A priest only performs marriage ceremony but does not run the house of those where he performs the ceremony. But when kings do not know how to rule, they were deposed by the people.'[40]

According to Patel:

There is going to be one solution and that is that the reins of the Government shall be handed over to the people. It is not Cadell or Gibson's job to decide how to rule and how to frame rules and implement them. They have no right to do so.[41]

The 'Right' leaders regarded as their foremost duty to create awareness among the States' people towards goodness of democracy in contrast to the feudal decadence, which was protected and promoted by the British. He warned:

---

[38] Patel addressing Rajkot States' Peoples' Conference, dated 8 September 1938. See Patel Papers, Lot I-39-1 to 3 Patel's Speeches, 1935–1945, SPNM, Ahmedabad.
[39] Ibid.
[40] *Gujarat Samachar*, 22 November 1938, File No. I-39-1 to 3. Ibid.
[41] Ibid.

Loyalty to the State cannot be manufactured. The people can be satisfied only when their legitimate demand for responsible Government is conceded. The demand being unanimous neither the State nor the Paramount Power has any legal or moral justification for its denial, much less for the present policy to suppress such a demand.[42]

Addressing the peasants of the Baroda State on 28 October 1938 at Bhadran, Patel reiterated his advice to the kisans for taking action and not wallowing in the spirit of defeat because:

If they sacrificed their fundamental rights in this matter the day would soon come when they would be completely crushed. The time for speeches and resolutions has gone, the time for action has come. It is no use expecting self-government to come from above. It will not be conferred as a boon by the rulers. It must be acquired by the people by virtue of their inherent strength.[43]

The 'Right' leaders emphasized the full flowering of representative institutions before actualizing the scheme of federation. In his presidential address to the 15th session of the Baroda States Subjects Conference on 28 October 1938, Patel said that 'unless and until popular legislatures were established in the States and administration was carried out with the full consent and approval of the people representatives, it was futile to talk of federation.'[44]

For the 'Right' leaders, neither the federation nor internal party bickering or growing militancy of kisan and labour movements were the restraining force vis-à-vis States Peoples' Movement.

Haripura resolution had created a false impression among the socialists that Congress was keen to negotiate on the Federal scheme with the British and the Princes. It also gave false complacency to the Princes and the British that as now the Congress was not directly participating in any pro-democracy movement in the Princely States, they had freedom to deal with the political movements within the borders of their States the way they wanted.[45] On the contrary, the Gandhian leaders were never oblivious of the doings of the Princes and the British, and the response of the people of these States. The climax was reached with the eruption

[42] Patel's Speech at Baroda, dated 6 December 1938. Ibid.
[43] Patel's Speech at Bhadran, 28 October 1938. See *Hindustan Times*, 29 October 1938, NMML.
[44] Ibid.
[45] Rajendra Prasad, *Autobiography*, 409–416.

of violence in the Princely States. This led to the concretization of revised stand of these leaders on the Haripura resolution. They made it clear that non-intervention did not mean licence to the Princes to resort to repression of any kind in countering the movement for responsible government. Events in Travancore, Mysore, Hyderabad, Rajkot, Baroda, Kashmir and Orissa were clear warning to them that the movement for freedom and self-government which originated in British India had also spread to Indian States. The leaders clarified that the Congress could not be the unwilling witness to unhappy events in Indian States even though not bracketing the Indian Princes with the alien British government. Their initial aloofness was on account of the fact that the Princes after all happened to be Indians and the struggle of the States' people was endogenous. This, however, did not imply a charter of licence to the Princes to go ahead with medieval methods of administration uninfluenced by democratic ideas.[46]

Dispelling the rumours that the Congress 'Right' were keen to implement Federal Scheme as they were soft on Princes, Patel made it clear to the Princes and the British government that without popular government in the States it was useless to talk about federation:

British India is keen to establish Federation but to acquiesce in a Federation where Princes enjoy immeasurable power would be to imperil the little freedom the subjects of British India had secured and at the same time it would doom the subjects of Indian States to eternal bondage. If the people of the States were to pull their full weight with the people of British India in Federal affairs, not only should the representatives of the States to the Federal legislature be sent through some process of election to the Centre but within the States also there must be constitutional machinery to ensure the administration of the States on lines approved by the people. Popular representation in the Federal sphere to be genuine must presume popular government inside the states. The only future to which the Indian Princes can look forward is that of constitutional rulers.[47]

Nehru and Bose, although they differed from the 'Right' on States People's issue and wanted more active role for the Congress, also realized that for the time being direct involvement would be injurious to Congress's

---

[46] Patel's Speech at Baroda State Subjects' Conference. See *Hindustan Times*, dated 30 October 1938, NMML.

[47] Ibid.

main goal. Realizing the danger involved in direct participation in the States People's Movement in 1938, Nehru accepted the practical approach of the 'Right'.

> The burden of struggle in the States must inevitably be on the States' people. The stress on this fact may be too great but the fact remains that the Congress cannot do much today in the States and it would be deluding the States' people to make them think otherwise.[48]

Bose too realized that 'we are running the risk of being sidetracked from our main fight if we drop the issue of Swaraj and begin fighting the British and the Princes over States' problems exclusively.'[49]

Therefore the 'Right' leadership focused more on arousing the masses and sensitizing the Princes in the Princely States so that they could comprehend the writings on the wall.[50] Thus, when Independence became a reality, the 'Right-Wing' leaders did not adopt any 'soft-glove' policy towards the Princes. Gandhi himself articulated the approach to be adopted towards the Princes in 1947. He categorically stated:

> Time was when I myself used to be severe with the States People telling them not to force their burden on the Congress, for we were fighting against a third power and the States People also were giving us help in our fight. I had wanted them to consolidate that strength. But now with British gone we cannot let the Princes do as they please.... They were content to be vassals of a foreign government, the British government, for so many years, but now that the millions of India are going to have the reins of power in their hands, the rulers refuse to be subservient to the people's government. We do not want to be enemies of the Princes ... we shall not imprison them. If they want to stay on in the country, they must understand that their subjects are with us. If they do not want to stay in the country they may go and settle down in Paris or elsewhere. But if they want to remain in India they must remain as servants of the people. They must understand the implications of the democratic government. They must concede that all men are created equal. They must not don the mantle of

---

[48] Nehru to Malappa (Editor, *The New Indian States Journal*, Bombay), 1938, File No. G. 27, AICC, NMML.

[49] Bose to Nehru 10 February 1939. Nehru), *A Bunch of Old Letters*, 323.

[50] Prasad's Speech on July 1935, File No. G 27, AICC, NMML.

superiority. They must recognize the paramountcy of the people as they recognize the paramountcy of the British government.[51]

The 'Right' leaders were clear on what should be the place of princes in independent India. Patel endorsing the view of Gandhi, while addressing the Delhi citizens during the Liberty Celebrations on 11 August 1947, said that 'with the exit of foreign power, the princes would have to adjust themselves to the democratic order. The days of those rulers who do not command the confidence of their subjects are numbered.'[52]

The primary concern of the Right-wing leaders was to achieve independence for a united India and not for a truncated India, divided into many small principalities. They knew that it could be achieved only in two ways: either by conflict or by negotiation. The World War had bled India white to save England from ruin, and devastation and communalism had not only bifurcated India but created situation of blood, loot and arson. Therefore, the strategy adopted by Patel with full support of his senior colleagues like Rajaji and Prasad was that of negotiation which meant that the rulers had to be given some concessions for parting with their power.[53] The granting of Privy Purse to the rulers was adopted under this belief. In a letter to Nehru, dated 9 August 1949, advising him not to react sharply on Privy Purse issue, keeping in mind the cost involved in relation to the purpose achieved, Patel wrote:

I do not think that having taken from them everything else that mattered, we should show any niggardly attitude in these matters.... Few people have an idea of the numerous ways in which they had squandered away the revenue of the state. There were in fact, in a large number of cases, no limits to these Privy Purse and if they had continued to rule a few years more they would have squandered away a considerable amount of the country's wealth. There were a few honourable exceptions but you could count them on the tip of your fingers. Thus the capacity for mischief on the part of the Rulers in this respect was far greater than one could imagine. Even now the

[51] Gandhi's Speech at New Delhi on 14 June 1947. See Choudhary, *Dr. Rajendra Prasad*, Vol. 7, 05.

[52] Patel's Speech at New Delhi on 11 August 1947. Nandurkar, *Sardar Pael: In Tune with the Millions-II*, 6.

[53] Patel to Sitarammayya, 21 June 1948. Nandurkar, *Sardar's Letters: Mostly Unknown-II*, 61.

amount of harm that would be caused to the country by going back
on our solemn promises would be very substantial.[54]

Rajaji too observed:

It cannot be overlooked that unity of all the territories within
boundaries of India and re-establishment of Paramountcy have been
achieved on the strength of assurances given by the Government of
India. We have to see that those assurances are honoured.[55]

The policy of 'non-interference' in the States Peoples' Movement, of the
'Right-wing' leaders, thus should not be seen as a policy of appeasement
towards the Princely States. Nor should it be regarded as an appropriate
ground for branding them as 'Rightist', as both Nehru and Bose ultimately
accepted the difficulty in Congress's direct participation in the political
struggle taking place in the Princely States, exactly on the lines of the
so-called 'Rightists'.

Outlining the contours of the nature of present and future relationship
with the Princely and feudal forces, Patel observed:

Today we have consolidated the country. But if we had not succeeded in winning over the Princes and induced them to play their
part the situation would have been difficult for them as well as the
people.... In India, there were many small states. They remained in
the same condition in which they existed hundreds of years ago. The
States of the type that were there before the foreigners came have, of
course, ceased to exist. But the States of the type which the foreigners created and preserved for their own ends remained without any
reform or progress. With some of them we had to enter into a struggle to secure human rights and our very existence. But very soon we
felt that the Princes themselves were not free and that so long as the
foreign power remained in India we would not be able to put matters
right. Putting their faith in the existence of these numerous States,
many people thought that as soon as India became free it would
break into pieces. But it must be said to the credit of Rulers that they
realized their patriotic duty and instead of balkanization of India,
we had integration and unification. The process of integration is

[54] Patel's letter to Nehru, 9 August 1949, ibid., 294–296.
[55] Rajaji's letter to Nehru, 12 August 1949, ibid., 78.

on.... The Princes have done their duty magnificently, but there are others who are hesitant, suspicious or turbulent. We shall strive to persuade them, but those who are out to do mischief have to be dealt with differently.... They must learn a lesson from the fate that has overtaken those who did not fall into line in the march of democracy or in the process of integration. Even the biggest among this section had to give in.. The times have changed and no human being can wish to live on the sweat of others' labour. There is ample scope in the world for talent and ability. If you keep pace with the times, you can also remain in the vanguard, but if you go on as you have been going on for the last few centuries, even the position at the rear will not be available to you.... Many felt that once paramountcy was over they would become independent. Some of them had dreams of becoming His Majesty. This was entirely wrong and has proved to be so. Paramountcy can never be destroyed. It must always reside in the central authority because it belongs to the people. Whoever challenges it must perish.[56]

---

[56] See *Hindustan Times*, dated 25 January 1949 and 26 January 1949.

Conclusion

IRRELEVANCE OF THE NOMENCLATURE

Historical facts do not support the prevalent stereotype that our national leaders within the Indian National Congress such as Sardar Patel, Rajagopalachari and Rajendra Prasad among others were followers of the ideology of the Right, and Jawaharlal Nehru, Subhas Chandra Bose, members of the Congress Socialist Party and the like stood for Left ideology. To begin with, there is a fallacy of nomenclature in the very use of the terms 'Right' and 'Left' abstracted as they are from the Western context and applied to the Indian historical realities. This, however, does not mean the absence of ideological groups with 'Right' or 'Left' leanings in the political realm of India. They did exist but the genre had specific cultural and ideological identity which gave it a unique character and particularity, thus making it nation specific.

Patel, Rajaji and Prasad, being mass leaders in their own independent capacity, not only influenced the thinking of a large number of people but were also at the helm of affairs of the Congress during the period. The Left intending to take over the reigns of the Congress found them a formidable force to contend within pursuit of their objectives. They, therefore, used the nomenclature 'Right' for such leaders in order to discredit and dislodge them from the position of power and influence. They tried to project them as 'obscurantist' and 'conservative'. They held that the 'Right's concept of social, political and economic regeneration was more metaphysical than material and progressive. This was a ploy the Left used to make the senior leaders accept that the days of their kind of politics and leadership were over. The underlying motive was to make them defensive so that they took a rear seat and cleared the way for the new young leadership who were apparently more radical and revolutionary.

In his letter to Nehru dated 1 July 1936, Prasad highlighted the attempt of the Left to control the Congress:

> There is a regular continuous campaign against us, treating us as persons whose time is over, who represent and stand for ideas that are worn out and that have no present value, who are only obstructing the progress of the country and who deserve to be cast out of the position which they undeservedly hold.... Apart from all personal

considerations we have also strongly felt that the ideals and policy for which we have stood all these sixteen or seventeen years and which we believe to be the only right one for the country are being most assiduously undermined.[1]

Patel too complained to Gandhi that the Left leaders in the Congress were paying only lip service to his advice, that they respected him as a saint but looked upon them as worn-out leaders who should be listened to but not followed. The Left decried in public that their way had proved its inefficacy and impracticability.[2]

The term 'Right' has a specific connotation. It has its specific European lineage. It appeared as a negative force advocating conservatism, encouraging reactionary forces and delimiting progress, freedom and individualism. It was synonymous with anti-people, anti-democracy, anti-intellectualism and anti-socialism. The Left leaders never engaged themselves into serious analysis of the policies and programmes of Sardar Patel, Rajagopalachari and Rajendra Prasad before branding them as 'Right'. The determining criteria in the Indian context, if at all, should have been whether they were pro-imperialist, pro-feudal, anti-progress, anti-people and pro-exclusion. But the Left did not go into these aspects. They, in fact, never engaged themselves into serious analysis of the policies and programmes of these leaders before branding them as 'Right'. In the tradition of Dadabhai Naoroji, Pherozeshah Mehta, Gopal Krishna Gpkhale and others, Patel, Rajaji and Prasad believed in a liberal democratic welfare state, anti-colonialism, class adjustment with a pro-poor orientation in the scheme for nation-building. Like the Moderate leaders, they also believed in cultural pluralism, religious tolerance and coexistence. They insisted on secular citizenship and placed it above religious, ethnic, caste and class identities. The Left never called the Moderate leaders of the Congress as 'Right', despite the fact that they too respected private property and never advocated socialism. This explains the genesis of this otherwise irrelevant ideological divide which appears to have been prompted more by the internal attempt to control the reigns of power within the Congress. It appears to have prompted the Left to highlight the apparent ideological divide during this period to achieve this end.

The ambition of the Left to control the organization along with their conceptual rigidity and doctrinaire orientation made them indulge in semantic militancy articulating high-sounding programme. However, they

---

[1] Prasad's letter to Nehru, dated 1 July 1936. See R.P. Papers, NMML.
[2] Patel to Gandhi, 24 February 1946. See Nandurkar, *Sardar's Letters*, Vol. IV, 161.

were not oblivious of the weakness in their own independent strength. For instance, Jayprakash Narayan threatened the senior leaders of the Congress in 1934 with a programme of going to the villages not with a spinning wheel but with a 'militant economic programme'.[3] But he also accepted in the same breath that the socialists had no desire to split the Congress on this issue. He said:

> Our position is not that the Congress must accept our programme or we shall leave it. We merely place our views before the Congress and the country and through the most proper and legitimate methods expect to bring the Congress to our point of view. This can in no way be construed to mean causing or contemplating a split.[4]

Being in minority within the Congress with hardly any mass base, the strategy the Left adopted was to 'to have the full protection of the Congress, the advantage of its prestige, and yet to attack it and criticize it from outside.'[5] The Left hoped that by projecting them as anti-people, anti-kisan, anti-youth and anti-labour they would be able to cut the social base of these leaders and thus they would be in a position to take over the control of the Congress, the only mass party. However, their marginal status in the organization, poor response of the masses to them and fear of facing oblivion outside the Congress fold forced them to remain within the Congress.

The politics of the time rather than objective criteria largely determined the currency of the nomenclature which further exposed its inherent vacuity and irrelevance. Apart from the nuances of style which could vary, Patel, Rajaji, Prasad and Bose shared the vision of a future Indian social and economic reconstruction in common. The views of these leaders on most crucial issues were more convergent than divergent in quality and content. Significantly, the approach of the 'Right' was circumscribed by the multiclass, anti-imperialist struggle which necessitated class accommodation. Most of the criteria used by the Left for branding the Gandhian leaders as 'Right' thus appeared meaningless as the 'Right' leaders themselves subscribed to the same, differing only on the issue of their implementation which was circumscribed by the need of the ongoing anti-imperialist struggle. Class collaboration and not class war was the need of the hour which the Gandhian leaders could well understand and respond to. Patel

---

[3] *Bombay Chronicle*, 19 July 1934.
[4] Ibid.
[5] Gopal, SWJN, Vol. IX, 503.

reminded the socialists that the Congress goal had been defined at the Karachi Congress and it was accepted, and socialism was accommodated when the struggle was in full swing. Yet the programme was not as effective as it had been visualized.[6] He said:

> You have yourself observed, how much less we could put into practices. And now at this moment, when the entire country has become breathless by making wearisome efforts for the programme, which has proved to be a dismal failure, you are seeking a hundred per cent acceptance of socialism.[7]

Patel criticized the socialists that they want 'spicy and confrontation-oriented programme'.[8] But he further said:

> All these clearly show that what you are advocating is far from practicable. I do not believe that there is any wisdom in raising bookish quarrels, lest breaches occur in our already weakened strength and we miss the main point of our struggle against the foreign power.[9]

As the evidences show it was a one-sided struggle for control of the Congress by the Left. The sole concern of the Left was to convert the Congress into a socialist organization. The fear of the 'Right' leaders was that the militant language and confrontationist stance of the Left might lead to the disarray of the Congress and disintegration of the anti-imperialist struggle.

The 'Right' were skeptical over this attitude of the Left in the Congress. Patel in 1937 pointed out the futility of a high-sounding socialistic programme when they were unable to secure even simple relief.[10] Further enumerating his understanding of the ground reality and feasibility of socialistic programme, Patel said:

> We should welcome the new ideas as well as new parties, if they are helpful in leading us nearer towards freedom. If they prove hindrance

---

[6] Patel's Speech at Benaras Vidyapeeth on 1 August 1934. See *Gujarat Samachar*, 7 August 1934 in Patel Papers, File No. Lot 38-Congress Affairs between 1932 to 1938 and 1939, SPNM, Ahmedabad.

[7] Ibid.

[8] Ibid.

[9] Ibid.

[10] *Times of India*, Bombay, 1 February 1937, 14.

to our goal of achieving freedom, we should not hesitate to leave them.[11]

I have no quarrel with socialism or the Congress Socialist Party as such, but I cannot too strongly deprecate the habit of youth to make a fetish of alluring catch-words and theories mechanically adopted from their reading without regard to the peculiar conditions prevailing in the West. I am neither a scholar nor a theorist, but I know enough of theories in general to be able to say that they are not full proof. Some of the theories that are the subjects of so much controversy here are still under experiment in the West. The technique of socialism had under our very eyes been exploited in the service of Fascism. As a man of common sense, therefore, whilst keeping my eyes and ears open to all fresh developments and new ideas, I prefer to keep my judgment unfettered and examining every step on its merits. I yield to none in my love for the masses. I am a peasant born and bred and I will not suffer any person to set limits to measures to ameliorate the condition of the peasants till they are fully restored to their own. I want to go forward at double quick pace but I am afraid the so-called 'forward policy' of the socialists or for that matter, of that any party [sic], come forward with a really forward programme and demonstrate their capacity to enforce it here and now and they will command my services.[12]

The Left's strong language and high-sounding symbols borrowed from the Western socialist literature had little impact on the villages of India, in comparison to the impact Patel, Rajaji and Prasad wielded over rural India. This showed that the 'Right' group represented contextual politics, whereas the Left primarily remained confined within the framework of what Patel called textual politics. The Left could not chalk out an independent path in spite of their claim that the lower rung of the Congress was drawn towards socialism and were thus in a position where they could not afford to ignore the support of these leaders. For every political move whether electing Leftist President of the Congress in 1936, 1937 and 1938, or electing Left-oriented leaders to the official committees of the Congress or being active in the affairs of the Congress in various capacities or getting socialism incorporated in the Congress programme, they sought

[11] See *Gujarat Mamachar*, 18 July 1934.
[12] *Times of India*, 6 August 1934.

the help of these three leaders.[13] Prasad in a long letter dated 19 December 1936 showed the willingness of the senior leaders to cooperate with them in the interest of a united front against colonialism. Rajendra Prasad explained their position and lamented at the uncharitable criticism of the socialists:

I believe unless a radical change comes to be made in the programme and methods of our work it will still be possible for all of us to work together. You are undoubtedly dissatisfied with the present condition of things. Not one amongst here is satisfied with them. But the difficulties are inherent in the situation and it seems to us that it is not possible to force the pace of cause for any wholesale change. In spite of known differences of opinion and outlooks, we hoped it would be possible to evolve a common line of action and to work jointly, keeping in the background the differences and concentrating on the point of agreement. We have been trying our best to accommodate ourselves but unfortunately we find that it has not been possible to secure an adjustment that can enable the two different elements to work harmoniously or speak with one voice. We feel that preaching and emphasizing of socialism particularly at this stage by the President and other socialist members of the Working Committee while Congress has not adopted it is prejudicial to the best interest of the country and to the success of the national struggle for freedom which we all hold to be the first and paramount concern of the country.[14]

Patel, Rajaji and Prasad understood the situation and knew that to make the struggle successful against British imperialism, unity of all views was essential. Socialists such as Narendra Dev were aware of this fact. He said:

The Congress today wields enormous influence both at home and abroad and though we may differ from official policies and acts, it would be the height of folly to think of breaking it up. The Congress

[13] Elections of Nehru and Bose to Congress Presidentship was not possible without the support of Patel, Rajaji and Prasad. Nor the passing of the Congress programme with socialistic bent like the Karachi Declaration of Fundamental Rights, the Agrarian Resolutions of the Lucknow and Faizpur Congress, the Election Manifesto of the Indian National Congress, the Wardha Resolution of February 1937 and the Faizpur Resolution on War could be achieved without the consent of these three leaders.

[14] Prasad to Nehru dated 19 December 1936 in R.P. Papers, NMML.

symbolizes Indian unity and democracy. It is the only solid anchor of our hopes and aspirations in an otherwise troubled state of affairs.[15]

The most important fact which the 'Right' leaders were aware of and some of the socialists like Narenda Dev and Left sympathizers like Nehru too realized was that during an anti-imperialist struggle to enter into an ideological debate of 'Left' and 'Right' was irrelevant because as Patel said:

> As Pt. Jawaharlal stresses, and rightly too, our present purpose is to free India from foreign subjection and thus destroy imperialistic exploitation root and branch. When we have attained this it will be time to enforce our theories and plans. For the present there should not be divided counsel but perfect co-operation between all forces that are to be found in the vast national organization of ours.[16]

Narendra Dev too spoke on similar lines. Speaking at the Subject Committee meeting of Tripuri Congress on 9 March 1939, he said that if there was disunity in the Congress neither the 'Right' nor the 'Left' could hope to survive. He appealed to Patel, Prasad, Rajaji and other members of the old Working Committee to give in on minor issues, because they could afford to be generous. Whether they were in the Working Committee or out of it, they were the undisputed leaders of the country. Defining the Right, he said that they were not those who were prepared to align with British Imperialism, and if anybody could think that a member of the old Working Committee could be called a Rightist in that sense, there could be no hope of freedom for this country. They were not Right, they were anti-imperialist to the core and revolutionaries. The question of Right and Left could only arise when a 'social' revolution was on the agenda and not a 'national' revolution.[17] Narendra Dev also warned the more militant Leftists, both within and outside Congress, that:

> [R]eactionary forces are trying to form a powerful combination in alliance with British Imperialism to crush the forces of progress and freedom. They are making the Congress and the national leadership their target. It is foolish to imagine that they are only opposed to the

[15] See Narenda Dev, *The Indian Struggle: Next Phase*, published by Congress Socialist Party, Bombay, 1940 in Sharma, *Selected Works of Acharya Narendra Dev*, Vol. I, 148, 220.

[16] See *Times of India*, Bombay, 28 November 1936.

[17] Speech of Narendra Dev at Tripuri on 9 March 1939. See Sharma, *Selected Works of Acharya Narendra Dev*, Vol. I, 148.

present high command and would gladly join the Congress under a new dispensation. These factors impose a special obligation on us to see that nothing is done that may tend to weaken or disintegrate the Congress.[18]

Reading into the imperativeness of the situation, Narendra Dev emphasized:

If we wish to move the entire Congress towards a struggle, we cannot carry on a crusade against its leaders, suggesting that they want to avoid a struggle at all costs and accusing them of wanting to compromise with British Imperialism in disregard of the principles of the Congress. This is just the way to sabotage a struggle. When the country is asked not to trust even the explicit declarations of the Working Committee, we cannot expect people to take the necessary preparations for struggle seriously. Nothing on the part of the members of the Working Committee entitles us to insinuate that they are men of dishonor. Such propaganda defeats its own purpose.[19]

The 'Right' accepted the fact that in any national organization like Indian National Congress which was carrying out mass movement, groups with different ideological beliefs were bound to co-exist but since their main goal was similar, there was always a space for cooperation. However vociferous the socialists' outcry over the leadership of the Congress being reformist might have been, the steel frame of the anti-imperialist movement and the Congress were the Gandhians, who were neither anti-people, nor anti-progress, nor pro-rich, nor anti-democracy, nor anti-intellectual. The so-called 'Right' were basically liberal democrats who emerged in India as a protest against the exploitation and domination of the colonial rule.

Patel stated that on some vital matters, his views were different from Nehru, as he did not believe in inevitability of class war. But he detested imperialism and admitted existence of destructive inequality between the capitalist class and the famishing poor, but the answer to it was not in the annihilation of one class for the progress of another.[20] Patel further elaborated that it was possible to purge capitalism of its hideousness. And he too

---

[18] Ibid., 221.
[19] Ibid.
[20] *Times of India*, Bombay, dated 28 November 1936.

was peasant enough to know where the 'shoe pinches the most'; therefore, he subscribed to the doctrine that 'all land and all wealth belonged to all'.[21] But nothing could be done, according to him, if people were not ready, as it could only be achieved through the power of the people. Patel said that power of non-violence and non-cooperation had been seen by the nation and when people 'learn the art of withdrawing their cooperation from the forces of evil it will perish for want of nourishment'.[22] However, Patel laid stress on the priorities of the nation at that time, before arguing over theories and future plans. According to him, 'to enforce our theories and plan, it is essential first to free India from foreign subjection and destroy imperialist exploitation'.[23]

Rajendra Prasad in the Subject Committee in May 1936 drew a vivid distinction between academic revolutionaries who derived inspiration from the foreign literature and local patriotism that depended more upon a close and personal study of local conditions. He concluded that while the Gandhian leaders represented the patriots rooted in ground realities, the socialists and the Leftists were engaged in the bookish understanding of revolution, cushioned in comfortable armchairs. Prasad appealed to save the country from the disastrous result of a blind application to Indian politics of foreign theories and maxims as derived from abstract studies of revolutionary literature of the world.[24]

These three Gandhian leaders were actively engaged in steering the anti-imperialist struggle against the foreign domination. The situation demanded a united front, the participation of the entire populace in this national project. The adoption of non-violence as the underlying ethos of the struggle reinforced the mass character of the movement. Caution, co-operation, underplaying of class interests in the interest of united opposition to foreign rule—these considerations weighed heavily in the minds of these leaders. Moreover, they were pitted against wily foreign power that lost no opportunity in inflaming divisiveness among the various groups and communities in the country.

The Congress emerged as a mammoth mosaic of diverse views and hues. The democratic character of the Congress witnessed prolonged argumentations amongst different views and groups, at times, of course, dictated by the urge for supremacy within the Congress fold. This became much pronounced with the advent of the Left and Left-wing politics in

[21] Ibid.
[22] Ibid.
[23] *Times of India*, 6 April 1934.
[24] *Bombay Chronicle*, May 7 1936.

the 1930s. The demarcation of nationalist leadership in terms of Left and 'Right' was primarily the product of this specific contextual setting, and historians have to be extra-vigilant against the easy proclivity to speak in the language of the 'actors'. The politics of the past might not be allowed to colour historiographic interpretations without situating the context of these categorizations.

Bibliography

PRIMARY SOURCES

Institutional Records

All India Congress Committee Papers, Nehru Memorial Museum and Library (NMML), New Delhi.

Quarterly Survey of Political Constitutional Position in British India (on microfilm), NMML, New Delhi.

Records of the Home Department, Political Branch, 1934–48, National Archives of India (NAI), New Delhi.

Home Special Department, MSA, Bombay.

Private Collections

Bhulabhai Desai Papers (on microfilm)
G. Natesan Papers
Govind Vallabh Pant Papers
Hary Haig Papers (on microfilm)
J.B. Kripalani Papers
Jawaharlal Nehru Papers
Jayprakash Narayan Papers
K.M. Munshi Papers
Linlithgow Papers
Lord Erskine Papers (on microfilm)
Lord Zetland Papers
M.A. Ansari Papers (on microfilm)
Patel Papers
Rajagopalachari Papers
Rajendra Prasad Papers
Satyamurti Papers
Sudhir Ghosh Papers (on microfilm)
Swami Sahajanand Saraswati Papers
Templewood Collection (on microfilm)
(All available at the NMML, New Delhi)
M.R. Jayakar Papers, National Archives of India (NAI), New Delhi
Purshottam Das Tandon Papers, NAI, New Delhi
Sardar Patel Papers, Sardar Patel Memorial Museum, Ahmedabad.
T.B. Sapru Papers, NAI, New Delhi.

Newspapers and Journals

Bombay Chronicle, Bombay
Bombay Sentinel, Bombay

Bombay Weekly, Bombay
Gujarat Samachar, Bombay
Hindustan Standard, Calcutta
Hindustan Times, Bombay
The Amrita Bazar Patrika, Calcutta
The Free Press Journal, Bombay
The Hindu, Madras
The Leader, Allahabad
The National Herald, Lucknow
The Pioneer, Lucknow
The Statesman, Calcutta
The Times of India, Bombay

Oral History Transcripts

(Available at the Oral History Division, NMML, New Delhi)
Acharya Kripalani
Amiya Chakravarty
Ashok Mehta
C.C. Desai
Iqbal Singh
Jayprakash Narayan
Kamlashankar Pandya
Minoo Masani
Mohammad Yunus
Ram Narain Choudhary
S.K. Patil

Speeches and Writings

Adhikari, G. *Communist Party and India's Path to National Regeneration and Socialism*. New
    Delhi, 1964.
Azad, Maulana. *India Wins Freedom*. New Delhi, 1989.
Bose, Sisir Kumar and Sugata, ed. *Netaji's Collected Works*, Vol. 9. Delhi, 1995.
Bose, Subhas Chandra. *Through Congress Eyes*. Allahabad, 1938.
Bright, J.S., ed. *Important Speeches and Writings of Bose*. Lahore, 1946.
Chopra, P.N. (ed.), *The Collected Works of Sardar Vallabhbhai Patel*. Delhi, 1994.
Choudhary, Valmiki, ed. *Dr. Rajendra Prasad: Correspondence and Select Documents*,
    Vols. 1–10. Delhi, 1984.
Collected Works of Mahatma Gandhi. Ahmedabad, 1971.
Dalton, Hugh. *High Tide and After Memoirs, 1945–1960*. London, 1963.
Das, Durga, ed. *Sardar Patel's Correspondence, 1945–1950*. Ahmedabad, 1971–1974.
Desai, Bhulabhai. *Speeches, 1934–1938*. Madras, 1938.
Deva, Acharya Narendra. *Socialism and the National Revolution*. Bombay, 1946.
Fischer, Louis. *The Life of Mahatma Gandhi*. New York, 1983.
Gandhi, M.K. *Jawaharlal Nehru: The Jewel of India*. Bombay, 1960.
————. *Letters to Sardar Vallabhbhai Patel*. Ahemdabad, 1957.

Golwarkar, M.S. *We or Our Nationhood Defined.* Nagpur, 1947.

Gopalan, A.K. *In the Cause of the People.* New Delhi, 1978.

Gopal, S. (ed.), *Selected Works of Jawaharlal Nehru.* New Delhi, 1972.

Grover, M. and Appadori, A. *Speeches and Documents on the Indian Constitution, 1927–1947.* Vol. 1. London, 1957.

International Encyclopedia of Social Sciences, Vol. V. New York, 1968.

Jagdisan, T.N. (ed.), *Letters of V.S. Srinivas Shatri.* Madras, 1944.

Lenin, V. *Selected Works.* Vol. II. Moscow, 1970.

Linlithgow. *Speeches and Statements, 1936–1943.* Delhi, 1945.

Kripalani, Sucheta. *An Unfinished Autobiography.* Edited by K.N. Vaswani. Ahemdabad, 1978.

Mansergh, Nicholas. *Transfer of Power, 1942–1947,* Vol. II. Delhi, 1977.

Masani, Minoo. *Bliss Was it in That Dawn: A Political Memoir up to Independence.* New Delhi, 1977.

———. *Our India.* New Delhi, 1953.

Mishra, D.P. *The Nehru Epoch: From Democracy to Monocracy.* Delhi, 1978.

Mookerjee, Shyama Prasad. *Leaves from a Diary.* Calcutta, 1993.

Munshi, K.M. *The End of an Era.* Bombay, 1957.

———. *The Indian Deadlock.* Allahabad, 1945.

Nandurkar, G.M., ed. *Sardar's Letters—Mostly Unknown-I and II* (Birth Centenary Volumes IV—1945–1946 and V—1947–1948). Ahmedabad, 1977–1978.

———. *Sardar Shree Ke Vishishta Aur Anokhe Patra, 1918–1948.* Ahmedabad, 1981.

———. *Sardar's Letters—Mostly Unknown* (Post-Centenary Volume I-1947–1948 and Volume II-1949). Ahmedabad, 1980–1981.

———. *Sardar Patel: In Tune with the Millions-I and II* (Birth Centenary Vols. II and III). Ahmedabad, 1975–1976.

Namboodiripad, E.M.S. *History of Indian Freedom Struggle.* Trivandarm, 1986.

Narayan, J.P., *Towards Struggle.* Bombay, 1946.

Nariman, K.F. *Whither Congress.* Bombay, 1933.

Nehru, Jawaharlal. *Glimpses of World History.* Allahabad, 1934.

———. *A Bunch of Old Letters.* Bombay, 1958.

———. *Discovery of India.* Bombay, 1961.

———. *An Autobiography.* New Delhi, 1962.

Pant, G.B. *Words That Proved: Speeches.* Lucknow, 1954.

Patel, Vallabhbhai, *Sardar Patel Ke Bhashan, 1918–47* (in Hindi). Ahmedabad, 1950.

Prasad, Rajendra. *India Divided.* Bombay, 1946.

———. *At the Feet of Mahatma Gandhi.* Bombay, 1955.

———. *Atmakatha* (in Hindi). New Delhi, 1965.

Rajagopalachari, C. *Chats Behind Bars.* Madras, 1931.

———. *Indian Prohibition Manual,* 1936.

———. *Defence of India.* Madras, 1942.

———. *The Way Out.* Oxford, 1944.

———. *Reconciliation.* Bombay, 1945.

———. *Speeches.* Bombay, 1948.

———. *University Address.* Bombay, 1949.

———. *Governor General's Speeches, 1948–50.* New Delhi, 1950.

———. *Hinduism: Doctrine and Way of Life.* Bhartiya. Madras, 1959.

———. *Satyam Eva Jayate,* Vols. I–IV. Madras, 1961.

———. *Gandhiji's Teachings and Philosophy.* 1967.

Ranga, N.G. *Peasants and Congress*. Madras, 1939.
————. *Outlines of National Revolutionary Path*. Bombay, 1945.
————. *Revolutionary Peasants*. Delhi, 1949.
Sampurnanand. *Memoirs and Reflections*. London, 1962.
Selected Speeches of Subhas Chandra Bose. New Delhi, 1962
Shankar, V., ed. *Select Correspondence*. Ahemdabad, 1977.
Sharma, Hari Dev, ed. *Selected Works of Acharya Narendra Deva*, Vols. I and II. New Delhi, 1998.
Tilak, B.G. *The Orion or Researches into the Antiquity of the Vedas*, eighth edition. Poona, 1999.
Wavell, Viscount. *The Viceroy's Journal*. Edited by Penderel Moon. New Delhi, 1977.
Zaidi, A.M., ed. *The Story of Congress Pilgrimage: Official Reports of Congress General Secretaries, 1916–1955*, Vols. 3 and 4. Delhi, 1990.
Zaidi, A.M. and Zaidi, S.G., ed. *Encyclopedia of the Indian National Congress*, Vol. II. New Delhi, 1981.

Other Published Records

Documents from India House Library, London. Sardar Patel Memorial Museum, Ahemdabad.
Indian National Congress Resolutions on Economic Policy, Programme and Allied Matters 1924–1969, New Delhi, 1969.
Madras Legislative Assembly Debates, 1936–39, 1950–52.
Towards Freedom: Documents on The Movement for Independence in India, 1943–1944, ed., Partha Sarthi Gupta, Delhi, 1997.
Transfer of Power Volume Series, NMML.

SECONDARY SOURCES

Books

Ali, Sadiq. *The Congress Ideology and Programme*. New Delhi, 1958.
Andrews, C.F. *Mahatma Gandhi's Ideas*. London, 1929.
Azad, Abul Kalam. *India Wins Freedom*. New Delhi, 1959.
Baker, C.E.U. *Changing Political Leadership in an Indian Province: The Central Provinces and Berar, 1919–1939*. New Delhi, 1980.
Bakshi, S.R. *Indian Freedom Fighters' Struggle for Independence*. New Delhi, 1992.
Barrier, N.G. *Banned Controversial and Poltical Control in British India, 1907–1947*. Delhi, 1976.
————. *Roots of Communal Politics*. Delhi, 1976.
Becker, H. and Barnes, E. (ed.), *Social Thought from Lore to Science, 2 Vols.* New York, 1961 (third edition).
Bell, Daniel (ed.), *The Radical Right: The New American Right Expanded and Updated.* New York, 1964.
Bhattacharjee, Ajit. *Jai Prakash: A Political Biography*. Delhi, 1975.
Birla, G.D. *In the Shadow of Mahatma*. Calcutta, 1952.
————. *Bapu: A Unique Association*, Vol. 3. Bombay, 1977.

Bolitho, Hector. *Jinnah: Creator of Pakistan.* London, 1954.

Bondurant, Joan V. *Conquest of Violence.* Princeton, 1958.

Bose, N.K. *My Days with Gandhi.* Calcutta 1953.

Botton, Glorney. *The Tragedy of Mahatma Gandhi.* London, 1934.

Brecher, Michael. *Nehru: A Political Biography.* London, 1959.

Brown, Judith. *Gandhi's Rise to Power: Indian Politics, 1915–1922.* Cambridge, 1972.

———. *Modern India: Origins of an Asian Democracy.* New Delhi, 1984.

———. *Gandhi: Prisoner of Hope.* New Delhi, 1990.

Campbell-Johnson, Alan. *Misson with Mountbatten.* London, 1972.

Caveesher, S.S. *India's Fight for Freedom: A Critical Study of the Indian National Movement Since the Advent of Mahatma Gandhi in the Field of Indian Politics.* Lahore, 1936.

Chandra, Bipan. *Modern India.* Delhi, 1971.

———. *Nationalism and Colonialism in Modern India.* New Delhi, 1981.

———. *Communalism in Modern India.* Delhi, 1984.

———. *P.C. Joshi: A Political Journey.* Delhi, 2007.

Chandra, Bipan et al. *India's Struggle for Freedom.* New Delhi, 1987.

Char, K.T. Narsimha. *C. Rajaji, His Life and Times.* New Delhi, 1978.

Chatterjee, Partha. *Nationalist Thought and the Colonial World.* Delhi, 1986.

Chattopadhyay, Kamladevi. *At the Crossroads.* Bombay,1947.

Chaudhuri, Sandhya. *Gandhi and the Partition of India.* New Delhi, 1984.

Chintamani, C.Y. *Indian Politics Since the Mutiny.* London, 1940.

Chopra, P.N., ed. *Quit India Movement: British Secret Documents.* New Delhi 1986.

Chowdhuri, S.R. *Leftist Movement in India, 1917–1947.* Calcutta, 1976.

Cobban, Alfred. *Aspects of the French Revolution.* New York, 1968.

Copley, A.R.H. *The Political Career of C. Rajagopalachari, 1937–54: A Moralist in Politics.* Madras, 1978.

Coser, Lewis. *The Foundations of Social Conflict.* London, 1956.

Coupland, R. *The Cripps Mission.* London, 1942.

———. *The Constitutional Problem in India: Part II, Indian Politics, 1936–40.* Madras, 1944.

Dalton, H. *High Tide and After.* London, 1962.

Damodaran, Vinita. *Broken Promises, Popular Protest: Indian Nationalism and the Congress Party in India, 1935–1946.* Delhi, 1992.

Das, Manmath Nath. *Partition and Independence of India.* New Delhi, 1982.

Das, M.N. *Partition and Independence of India: Inside Story of the Mountbatten Days.* New Delhi, 1982.

Das, Suranjan. *Communal Riots in Bengal, 1905–1947.* Delhi, 1991.

Dasgupta, Biplab. *The Naxalite Movement.* New Delhi, 1974.

Datta, K.K. *History of the Freedom Movement in Bihar,* Vols. 1–3. Patna, 1957.

———. *Rajendra Prasad.* New Delhi, 1970.

Davies, Peter. *The Extreme Right in France, 1789 to the Present.* New York, 2002.

Desai, A.R., ed. *Peasant Struggles in India.* Bombay, 1979.

Dhanagare, D.N. *Agrarian Movements and Gandhian Politics.* Agra, 1975.

Dhawan, G.N. *The Political Philosophy of Mahatma Gandhi.* Bombay, 1946.

Dobbin, Christine. *Urban Leadership in Western India, 1840–1885.* London, 1972.

Dove, M.R. *Forfeited Future: The Conflict over Congress Ministries in British India 1933–1937.* Delhi, 1987.

Drummond, I.M. *British Economic Policy and the Empire, 1919–1939.* London 1972.

Dutt, B.C. *Mutiny of the Innocents.* Bombay, 1971.

Dutt, R.P. *India Today.* London, 1979.

Eatwell, Roger and Wright, Anthony, eds. *Contemporary Political Ideologies.* London, 1999.

Evans, Hubert. *Looking Back on India.* London, 1988.

Farooqui, M. *India's Freedom Struggle and the Communist Party of India.* New Delhi, 1974.

Fine, Sidney. *Lasseze Faire and the General Welfare State.* Michigan, 1955.

French, Patrick. *Liberty or Death, India's Journey to Independence and Division.* London. 1997.

Gallaghar, John. *Locality, Province and Nation: Essays on Indian Politics, 1870–1940.* Cambridge, 1973.

Gandhi, Rajmohan. *A Warrior from the South: The Rajaji Story I*, Bharatam. Madras, 1978.

——— *The Rajaji Story, 1937–1972.* Bombay, 1984.

——— *Patel: A Life.* Ahmedabad, 1990.

Gellner, Ernest. *Post Modernism, Reason and Religion.* London 1992.

Gentile, Emilo. *The Origins of Fascist Ideology 1918–1925: The First Complete Study of the Origins of Italian Fascism.* New York, 2005.

Ghosh, Sudhir. *Gandhi's Emissary.* London, 1967.

Gledevon, John. *The Viceroy at Bay: Lord Linlighgow in India, 1936–1943.* London, 1971.

Gopal, S. *Jawaharlal Nehru: A Biography, 1889–1947.* New Delhi, 1975.

Gopalan., A.K. *In the Cause of the People.* London, 1959.

Guha, Ranajit, ed. *Subaltern Studies III: Writings on South Asian History and Society.* New Delhi, 1984.

Gupta, A.K., ed. *Myth and Reality: The Struggle for Freedom in India, 1945–1947.* New Delhi, 1987.

Gupta, Partha Sarthi. *Imperialism and the British Labour Movement, 1914–1964.* London, 1975.

Hamid, Shahid. *Disasterous Twilight: A Personal Record of the Partition of India.* London, 1986.

Hasan, Mushirul, ed., *India's Partion—Process, Strategy and Mobilisation.* Delhi, 1993.

Haithcox, J.P. *Communism and Nationalism in India.* Princeton, 1971.

Halifax, Birkenhead. *The Life of Lord Halifax.* London, 1965.

Handa, R.L. *History of Freedom Movement in Princely States.* New Delhi, 1968.

Hodson, H.V. *The Great Divide: Britain, India, Pakistan.* London, 1969.

Hughes, H. Stuart. *Consciousness and Society: The Reorientation of European Social Thought 1890–1930.* New York, 1958.

Hunt, R. and Harrison, J. *The District Officer in India, 1930–1947.* London, 1980.

Hutchins, Francis. *Spontaneous Revolution: The Quit India Movement.* New Delhi, 1971.

Jalal, Ayesha. *The Sole Spokesman: Jinnah, the Muslim League and the Demand for Pakistan.* Cambridge, 1985.

Jayakar, M.R. *The Story of My Life.* London, 1959.

Jay, Martin. *The Dialectical Imagination: A History of the Frankfurt School and the Institute of Social Research, 1923–50.* London, 1973.

Josh, Bhagwan. *Communist Movement in Punjab.* Delhi, 1979.

Karnik,V.B. *Strikes in India.* Bombay, 1967.

Jeffrey, Robin. *People, Princes and Paramount Power.* Delhi, 1978.

Kaushik, P.D. *The Congress Ideology and Programme (1920–1947).* Bombay, 1964.

Khosla, G.D. *Stern Reckoning: A Survey of the Events Leading Upto and Following the Partition of India.* Delhi, 1989.

Kochan, Lionel. *The Struggle for Germany.* Edinburgh, 1963.

Kochanek, S.A. *The Congress Party of India: The Dynamics of One Party Democracy.* Princeton, 1968.

Kriplani, J.B. *Gandhi—His Life and Thought.* New Delhi, 1970.

Kumar, Ravinder, ed. *Essays in Gandhian Politics.* Oxford, 1971.

Kwajima, Sho. *Muslims, Nationalism, and the Partition: 1946 Provincial Elections in India.* Delhi, 1998.

Laclau, E., ed. *The Making of Political Identities.* London, 1994.

Laqueur, Walter. *Fascism: Past, Present, Future.* New York, 1997.

Lipset, S.M. *Political Man: The Social Bases of Politics.* New York, 1963.

Low, D.A., ed. *Soundings in Modern South Asian History.* London, 1968.

Low, D.A. *Lion Rampant: Essays in the Study of British Imperialism.* London, 1973.

Mahajan, Sucheta. *Independence and Partition: The Erosion of Colonial Power in India.* New Delhi, 2000.

Majumdar, R.C. *History of the Freedom Movement*, Vols. 1–3. Calcutta, 1963.

Malkani, K.R. *The Sindh Story.* New Delhi, 1984.

Martin, J. *The Dialectical Imagination.* London, 1974.

Mason, Philip. *The Men Who Ruled India.* London, 1985.

Masselos, J., ed. *India: Creating a Modern Nation.* New Delhi, 1990.

Mehrotra, S.R. *Towards India's Freedom and Partition.* New Delhi, 1979.

Malraux, Andre. *Man's Hope.* 1937.

Markovits, Claude. *Indian Business and Nationalist Politics From 1931 to 1939: The Political Attitude of the Indigenous Capitalist Class in Relation to the Rise of the Congress Party.* D.Phil diss., University of Cambridge, 1978.

Mathur, J.S. and Mathur, A.S. *Economic Thought of Mahatma Gandhi.* Allahabad, 1962.

Mehta, Ashok. *Economic Consequences of Sardar Patel.* Hyderbad, 1949.

Mehta, Ashok and Nai, Kusum. *The Simla Triangle.* Bombay, 1945.

Menon, V.P., *The Transfer of Power in India*, Calcutta, 1957.

Menon, Visalakshi. *From Movement to Government: Congress in Uttar Pradesh.* New Delhi, 2003.

Micaud, Charles A., *The French Right and Nazi Germany, 1933–39: A Study of Public Opinion.* New York, 1972.

Mitra, N.N., ed. *Indian Annual Register: An Annual Digest of Public Affairs in India.* Calcutta, 1934–1946.

Moore, Barrington, Jr. *Social Origins of Dictatorship and Democracy.* Boston, 1976.

Moore, R.J. *Crisis of Indian Unity, 1917–1940.* London, 1974.

———. *Churchill, Cripps, and India, 1939–1945.* Oxford, 1979.

———. *Escape from Empire: The Atlee Government and the Indian Problem.* Oxford, 1983.

Morris, I.I. *Nationalism and the Right Wing in Japan: A Study of Post-War Trend.* London, 1960.

Mukherjee, Aditya. *Imperialism, Nationalism and Making of the Indian Capitalist Class, 1927–1947.* New Delhi, 2002.

Mukherjee, Mridula. *Peasants in India's Non-violent Revolution. Practice and Theory.* New Delhi, 2004.

Mukherjee, S.N. *The Movement for National Freedom in India.* London, 1966.

Murthi, R.K. *Sardar Patel: The Man and His contemporaries.* New Delhi, 1976.

Namboodiripad, E.M.S. *The Mahatma and the Ism.* Calcutta, 1958.

———. *A History of India's Freedom Struggle.* Trivendram, 1986.

———. *How I became a Communist.* Trivendram, 1976.

Nanda and Joshi, V.C., ed. *Studies in Modern Indian History*, Vol. 1. New Delhi, 1972.

Nanda, B.R., ed. *Socialism in India.* Delhi, 1972.

———. *Mahatma Gandhi.* Oxford, 1958.

Nolte, Ernst. *The Three Faces of Fascism:Action Francaise, Italian Fascism, National Socialism.* London, 1965.

Orwell, S. and I. Angus, ed. *The Collected Essays, Journalism and Letters of George Orwell: Vol. II, My Country Right or Left, 1940–1943.* London, 1968.

Pandey, B.N. (ed.), *The Indian National Movement, 1885–1947: Select Document.* Delhi, 1979.

———. *A Centenary History of the Indian National Congress,* Vol. 3. New Delhi, 1985.

Pandey, Gyanendra. *The Ascendency of the Congress in Uttar Pradesh: A Study in Imperfect Mobilization, 1926–1934.* Delhi, 1978.

Panikkar, K.N., ed. *National and Left Movements in India.* Delhi, 1980.

Parikh, N.D. *Sardar Vallabhbhai,* Vols 1 and 2. Ahmedabad, 1956 (reprint 1971).

Patil, V.T. *Nehru and the Freedom Movement.* New Delhi, 1977.

Philips, C.H. and Wainwright, M.D., ed. *The Partition of India: Politics and Perspectives, 1935–1947.* London, 1970.

Prabhakar, Vishnu. *Sardar Vallabhbhai Patel.* New Delhi, 1977.

Prasad, Bimal. *Gandhi, Nehru and J.P.: Studies in Leadership.* Delhi, 1985.

Prashad, Ganesh. *Nehru: A Study in Colonial Literature.* New Delhi, 1976.

Raina, K.N. and Ratnam, ed. *Tej Bahadur Sapru: Profiles and Tributes.* Allahabad, 1971.

Rao, Amiya and Rao, B.G. *Six Thousand Days.* New Delhi, 1974.

Rao, Shiva. *India's Freedom Movement.* New Delhi, 1972.

Revri, C. *Indian Trade Union Movement.* Delhi, 1972.

Rogger, Hans and Weber, Eugen, ed. *The European Right: A Historical Profile.* London, 1965.

Roy, Dilip. *The Subhas I knew.* Bombay, 1946.

Roy, Rajat. *Urban Roots of Indian Nationalism: Pressure Groups and Conflict of Interests in Calcutta City Politics, 1875–1939.* Delhi, 1979.

Rusch, T.A. *The Role of the Congress Socialist Party in the Indian National Congress,* (unpublished thesis). NMML, New Delhi, 1955.

Saiyid, M.H. *The Sound of Fury: A Political Study of Mohammed Ali Jinnah.* New Delhi, 1981.

Sarkar, Sumit. *Modern India, 1885–1947.* New Delhi, 1983.

Sen, Mohit. *Revolution in India: Path and Problems.* New Delhi, 1977.

Sen, Shila. *Muslim Politics in Bengal, 1937–1947.* New Delhi, 1976.

Setalwad, M.C. *Bhulabhai Desai.* New Delhi, 1968.

Shankar, V. *My Reminiscences of Sardar Patel.* Delhi, 1974.

Shankardass, Rani Dhavan. *Vallabhbhai Patel: Power and Organization in Indian Politics.* New Delhi, 1988.

Singh, Anita Inder. *The Origins of Partition of India, 1936–1947.* New Delhi, 1987.

Singh, Neerja, ed. *Gandhi–Patel: Letters and Speeches: Differences within Consensus.* New Delhi, 2009.

———. *Nehru–Patel: Agreement within Differences, Select Documents and Correspondences 1933–1950.* New Delhi, 2010.

Singh, Yogendra. *Modernization of Indian Tradition.* New Delhi, 1973.

———. *Social Change in India: Crisis and Resilience.* New Delhi, 1993.

Sinha, L.P. *Left Wing in India, 1919–1947.* Muzaffarpur, 1965.

Sisson, Richard and Wolpert, Stanley, ed. *Congress and Indian Nationalism: The Pre-independence Phase.* Oxford, 1988.

Sitaramayya, P. *The History of Indian National Congress 1935–1947,* Vols. I and II. Bombay, 1947 (reprint 1969).

Som, R., *Differences Within Consensus: The Left and the Right in the Congress, 1929–1939.* New Delhi, 1985.

Srivastava, Gopinath. *When Congress Ruled: A Close Range Survey of the Congress Administration During the Twenty-Eight Months (1937–1939) in the United Provinces.* Lucknow, 1940.

Sundarayya, P. *Telengana People's Struggle and Its Lessons.* Calcutta, 1972.

Suntharalingam, R. *Indian Nationalism: An Historical Analysis.* Delhi, 1983.

Tahmankar, D.V. *Sardar Patel.* London, 1970.

Tamlon, J.L. *The Origins of Totalitarian Democracy.* London, 1952.

Tarachand. *History of the Freedom Movement of India,* Vols. 3–4. New Delhi, 1972.

Taylor, D.D. *Indian Politics and the Elections of 1937* (unpublished thesis). London, 1972.

Tendulkar, D.G. *Mahatma: Life of Mohandas Karamchand Gandhi.* Bombay, 1952.

Thomas, K.P. *Dr. B.C. Roy.* Calcutta, 1955.

Thompson, David. *France: Empire and Rrepublics, 1850–1940: Historical Documents.* New York, 1968.

Tomlinson, B.R. *The Indian National Congress and the Raj, 1929–1942.* London, 1976.

Trevelyan, H. *The India We Left.* London, 1972.

Vaidehi, Krishnamoorthy. *Alladi—Freedom Movement in India, 1858–1947.* Hyderabad, 1977.

Venguswamy, N.S. *Congress in Office.* Bombay, 1940.

Wasi, S.W. *President Prasad: A Biography.* Calcutta, 1962.

Weber, Eugen. *Varities of Fascism:Doctrines of Revolution in the Twentieth Century.* New York, 1964.

Werthein, W.F. *Evolution and Revolution: The Rising Waves of Emancipation.* Harmondsworth, 1974.

Wolpert,Stanley. *Jinnah of Pakistan.* New York, 1984.

Zeldin, Theodore. *France 1848–1945: Ambition and Love.* Oxford, 1979.

———. *France 1848–1945: Politics and Anger.* Oxford, 1979.

———. *France 1848–1945: Intellect and Pride.* Oxford, 1980.

Articles

Argov, Daniel. 'The Conflict Between Gandhi and Nehru in 1928 over the Issue of Dominion Status vs. Independence'. *Asian and African Studies* 10, no. 1 (1974–1975).

Baker, Christopher. 'The Congress at the 1937 Elections in Madras'. *Modern Asian Studies,* no. 10 (1976).

Bhambri, C.P. 'Nehru and Socialist Movement in India, 1920–47'. *Indian Journal of Political Science* (April–June 1969).

Broomfield, J.H. 'The Regional Elites: A Theory of Modern Indian History'. *Indian Economic Social Historical Review* 3, no. 3 (September 1966).

Davidson. 'Antonio Gramsci: Towards an Intellectual Biography'. *International Library of Social and Political Thought* (1977).

Gordon, Leonard A. 'Brothers against the Raj: Subhas and Sarat Chandra Bose, 1936–1947'. *Oracle* 1, no. 3 (July 1979).

———. 'Subhas Bose and the Indian Left'. *Mainstream* 15, nos. 1–16 (1976).

Haithcox, J.P. 'Left Wing Unity and the Indian Nationalist Movement'. *Modern Asian Studies,* 111 (1969).

Hauser, W. 'The Indian National Congress and Land Policy in the 20th Century'. *Indian Economic Social Historical Review,* no. 1 (1963–1964).

Kumar, Ravinder. 'Class, Community or Nation? Gandhi's Quest for a Popular Consensus inIndia'. *Modern Asian Studies,* no. 3 (October 1969).

Morris-Jones, W.H. 'From Monopoly to Competition in Indian Politics'. *Asian Review* 1, no. 1 (1967).

——. 'The Indian Congress Party: A Dilemma of Dominance'. *Modern Asian Studies* 1, no. 1 (1964).

Pandey, Gyanendra. 'The Shastris of Kashi and Lahore: The Making of Congress Leaders'. *Asian Studies* (1976): 77–86.

Reeves, Peter. 'Landlord and Party Politics in the United Provinces 1934–37'. In *Soundings in Modern South Asian History*, edited by D.A. Low. London, 1968.

Rothermund, D. 'Constitutional Reform vs. National Agitation in India, 1900–50'. *Journal of Asian Studies*, no. XXI, (1961–1962).

Sundaram, R. 'Many Faceted Rajaji', *Bhavan's Journal* 22, no. 11 (December 1975).

Tomlinson, B.R. 'India and the British Empire, 1935–47', *IESHR,* 13, no. 3 (July–September 1976).

Index

About the Author

Neerja Singh is Associate Professor, Department of History, Satyawati College, University of Delhi. She did her PhD from Jawaharlal Nehru University, New Delhi, under the supervision of Professor Bipan Chandra. Recipient of UGC National Research Award, the author is a renowned academic and has published two books namely, *Gandhi-Patel: Letters and Speeches: Differences within Consensus* and *Nehru-Patel: Agreement within Differences*. She has participated in many national and international seminars and presented papers.